*To my colleague Jeanine,*

*It is a pleasure...*
*a lot of love and tea*
*my book. Best...,*

*Phil Pressel*

*December 2004*

# THEY ARE STILL ALIVE

A Family's Survival in France
During World War II

*PHILIP PRESSEL*

**DORRANCE PUBLISHING CO., INC.**
**PITTSBURGH, PENNSYLVANIA 15222**

# CONTENTS

My mother, Maman, was a heroine who supported our little family financially during World War II and the Holocaust by working as a seamstress. With her courage and chutzpah, she managed to take care of our basic needs. She stood on lines to obtain rationed food and carried sacks of coal on her back. While she helped us stay strong spiritually and physically, she also carried deep worries about the fate of her brother, sisters, and parents. Without my mother and good luck, we would not have survived.

My courageous father, Papa, kept his wits about him through all the hard times. He, too, was a hero who made valiant efforts to prevent us from suffering the horrors of the war. He stood by my mother and shielded me from harm. He, like my mother, was burdened by not knowing the fate of his parents, sister and brother. He was terrified of being arrested by the *Gestapo* if he went outdoors, and the stress took its toll. He died too young. I wish I could have known him during my adult years and that he could have known my family.

During the war, when all the children of Lyon were evacuated because of the bombings, I was separated from my parents. They said good-bye to their only child, perhaps forever.

I also want to dedicate this book to all of our relatives who died during the war. There is a wonderful inscription on a wall in the old Ghetto of Venice, Italy that honors the victims of the Holocaust. It reads:

## *"Our memories are their only grave."*

**Samuel and Helen Pressel**, my father's parents: My grandmother Helen was deported from Mechelin, Belgium on or about October 27, 1942 and died in Auschwitz. My grandfather Samuel died in 1941 at German hands in Belgium and is buried in a cemetery in Putte, Holland, as there were no Jewish cemeteries in Antwerp.

**Charlotte and Naphtali Hamel**, my father's sister and her husband: Deported from Drancy, France in 1942 and both gassed in Auschwitz.

**Norbert and Hilda Schwerner and their daughter Margot**, my mother's brother and family: They were deported from Mechelin, Belgium. Hilda and Margot were sent to the gas chambers upon their arrival at Auschwitz in October 1942. Norbert was selected to work and was then gassed on December 1, 1942.

**Nachman Landenberg**, my mother's brother-in-law (my Aunt Ella's husband): Deported to Auschwitz in 1942.

**Maurice and Rebecca (Suskin) Fischer, and their son Siegfried**, my Uncle Louis Suskin's sister and family: Deported to Auschwitz in 1942. Their daughter, Raymonde was adopted after the war by Louis and Sonia (my mother's sister), who raised her in the United States.

*The following relatives are unaccounted for, and this book is dedicated to them as well.*

**Harry Schwerner**, my mother's cousin.

**Isidore Kincler**, my mother's uncle.

**Salla Kincler**, my mother's cousin.

**Hirsch Schwerner**, my mother's uncle.

**Hartwich Goldschmidt and family**, my mother's uncle.

**Bella Goldschmidt**, my mother's aunt.

**Evan Goldschmidt and family**, my mother's uncle.

**Miriam Goldschmidt and family**, my mother's aunt.

# ACKNOWLEDGEMENTS

I give my wholehearted thanks to my wife Patricia Pressel. I thank her for the support she has given me during all our years together. She is part of everything that relates to my life: my health, my work, my sports activities, and my children. I thank her for her wonderful editing skills, encouragement, suggestions, ideas, and recommendations in writing this book. She was there to comfort me while writing these sad wartime memories. Most of all I thank her for being there whenever I need her.

I thank my cousin Jeanine Klein for giving me the letters my father wrote to her father, Elie Schwerner. I am also grateful to Helen Fogel, and her sister Carol Samet, for giving me the letters my father wrote to their mother, Suzi Pantzer. These letters were the inspiration behind this memoir.

I also thank my good friend Dan Schaffer for his editorial comments, grammatical, and spelling corrections. I appreciate his objective reviews, his encouragement, and his knowledge of the Holocaust and European history.

I thank Jeanette Friedman. She helped with Jewish history and made my words flow and smoothed out the rough edges.

Lastly, I thank Jeremy Hollins, a charming young graduate student at the University of San Diego. He made significant literary suggestions and corrections in a most objective way.

Philip Pressel
San Diego
August, 2004

# INTRODUCTION

As I am writing the final chapters of this book, it is raining ash outside and the air stinks from the October 2003 San Diego wildfires. Days earlier, my wife and I were evacuated from our home and told to take with us our most valuable possessions. I felt like I had come full circle, reliving the days of my early childhood during World War II.

Life being what it is, I understood even more intensely why I want my descendants to understand what my parents and I went through during those days, running from the Holocaust. As one who bears witness to the past, I do not want the world to forget what happens when hate is allowed to rankle and fester over centuries.

Although many Holocaust survivors have written their stories, we must remember that each story is unique. While all our stories are similar, together our experiences document the reality of the apocalypse we call The Holocaust. I also want my family to understand what made me the way I am, why I have my peculiarities and beliefs.

My parents and I are survivors. Though we were not deported to concentration camps, for five long years we experienced the horrors of living in dreadful conditions, fearing for our lives. Too many times we narrowly escaped capture. Skills and luck made sure we survived.

So that I would not forget, as an adult I took notes of things that happened to my family and I as they floated through my memory. I also documented information on our family and some of the wartime events I was told about over the years by my mother. Maman, a 98-year-old delightful lady, continues to be a blessing. Our ever-increasing desperate status during the war and eventual survival were captured in poignant letters my father wrote to his family in America and England during the war. You will find many of them in the appendix.

For most of the war, my parents and I lived in terrible circumstances. When Lyon was constantly bombed in 1944, an edict ordered all children to be evacuated from the city, and so for many months I lived in Vourles, a suburb, with a kind Catholic family. Neither they nor I knew I was Jewish.

I was young enough, when the war began, for my parents to protect me by not telling me I was Jewish. That way, I could not inadvertently divulge the dangerous secret to anyone. I was heartbroken to be alone in Vourles and had a constant lump of loneliness in my throat. My parents realized full well that they might never see me again. I was also terrified of the local dangers, unanticipated by my parents. I was supposed to be in the quiet, safe countryside. But the *Maquis*, the French underground, was stationed in Vourles, so there were constant skirmishes and incursions by German soldiers. I witnessed bombings, airplane dogfights, and saw people die.

I have always found it difficult to think about—much less talk about—what happened. The process of reading other survivors' memoirs and of putting my thoughts down on paper has allowed me to express my emotions about it for the first time, finally feeling more at ease with my childhood and myself.

In September 1992 I received a thick manila envelope from my cousin, Jeanine Klein, containing dozens of letters my father had written to her father, Elie Schwerner, in New York. The letters' contents flooded my heart with memories and feelings. Jeanine found the 50-year-old undamaged letters in her mother's desk when her estate was dissolved. Some were typewritten and others were written by hand. They described our situation, repeatedly asking for help in obtaining visas to the United States. As I read them, I could see how the letters became more and more desperate as my father described worsening events. When I translated them from the French, memories of my father, mother and the war became quite vivid. Helen, a cousin in London, also gave me letters my father wrote to her mother, Suzi Pantzer, his niece.

I was 7 ½ years old in 1944, when my father sent out the first news anyone had heard from us in two-and-a-half years. That letter, when I read it for the first time in 1992, had tremendous impact on me and others who read it. I believe it is the centerpiece of the letter collection. My son David has turned reading it into a family tradition by incorporating it into the annual Passover Seder for his family and friends.

**24 Quai Fulchiron**

**Lyon, France**

September 28, 1944

Mr. E. Schwerner
539 Ocean Parkway
Brooklyn, NY

Dear Uncle Elie,

*"They are still alive!"*

Yes, we are still alive and we can finally breathe in freedom. We are living in Lyon since the end of 1942. The city was liberated on September 3. We feel like the survivors of a cataclysm. The joy of feeling free is profound, but we have seen too much suffering, and we worry a great deal about all those dear to us whose fate is unknown, for this joy to be complete.

It is almost a miracle that we were able to survive safe and sound from this torture. For the past two years, human life counted for nothing. Perhaps later we will have the opportunity to tell you in more detail all that we went through. On November 11, 1942, we saw the arrival of the masses of German troops in Marseille, and we had to wait until the month of August, 1944 in Lyon, to see the withdrawal of this army, in endless file in front of our house, while being routed and pursued by the allied armies coming up from the south of France. What a relief! We waited for so long, and so fervently hoped for deliverance. Our son was evacuated under mandatory order to the countryside since last May in order to be sheltered from the bombings. We rejoined him on the 28th of August to be together no matter what would happen. The village where we found ourselves was already in the hands of the French resistance and all around the French Army of the Interior were attacking the German troops. Also, in the distance we could see the Allied planes diving and strafing the German convoys and releasing their bombs on the enemy trucks. The village was caught in crossfire and for several days we lived in an agonizing situation. Anyway the essential thing for the moment is that we can announce to you that we three are safe and sound and happy that we were able to save our little Philippe - who is now 7 years old and who never lost hope and who had confidence in everything that we had to do to shelter him from harm.

We have not heard from Belgium for about 6 months. At that time my in-laws as well as Ella were still there and we hope that they are safe and sound. My mother, unfortunately, was deported in 1942 and I have not heard about her fate; my sister and her husband were also taken in 1942 to "a destination unknown." Will I ever see them again?

Hoping that we soon receive detailed news from you, we sent you our best wishes and kisses,

Your,
Jos, Mir and Philippe

My dear all,

We have returned to life; let us hope that our dear parents are also safe and sound, as well as brother, sister, sister-in-law, brother-in-law, mentioning only the immediate family. You cannot realize the good fortune of all those who did not have to live in Europe for the last two years. As far as the future is concerned, we cannot make any plans, but I want to return to Belgium as fast as possible.

Write to us quickly if possible, it has been so long since we have heard any news from the family that every letter give us a great deal of pleasure.

A thousand kisses to divide among you all

Your,
Mir


I would like to see you all again. I send you lots of kisses for both cheeks.

Philippe

# ROOTS

My father Joseph Pressel was a Polish citizen and remained so all his life. He never became a Belgian citizen, because that cost money he could not afford. Even though I was born in Belgium, I was considered a Polish citizen until my American naturalization in 1955.

My father attended public school in Belgium and Holland. Although he never attended university in Europe—because neither he nor his parents could afford the tuition—Joseph was an intellectual and a proficient linguist. He was a self-taught writer, translator, and fluent in five languages: French, Flemish, German, English and Spanish. He spoke French and Flemish in Belgium and learned German from his mother. Later in his life he also learned to speak and write Esperanto and Hebrew.

One of my father's interests was studying Dutch stenography, called *Groote* after its inventor. He became very proficient at it, and was able to take dictation at 125 words per minute, an invaluable asset for most of his professional life. My father died in 1952 at the young age of 51, when I was just 15 years old. When he was alive, I couldn't glean much information from him about his family and youth. I was simply not mature enough to ask him about details, and he, like many other survivors, was prone to silence.

He was a soft spoken and gentle man, who enjoyed conversations with others. He was a good listener. Besides his interest in his family, he loved to participate in discussions on almost any subject: music, chess, sports and world affairs. In Antwerp, in his teens, he belonged to a sports and social organization called *Maccabi*, and for the rest of his life lived by the *Maccabi* motto: *"Mens Sana in Corpore Sano"* ("A healthy mind in a healthy body.") *Maccabi* had approximately 1,000 members and was the primary social outlet for young Jews in Antwerp. Located in a distant part of southern Antwerp, the young members walked great distances to the club on *Blockstraat* several times a week. Everything he did there was on a volunteer basis, and by the time he reached his early 20s, my father had become the athletic director and the coach for gymnastics and track and field.

*Maccabi* was where many couples met, including my parents and my Aunt Sonia and Uncle Louis. *Maccabi* is also where my father met his best friend, Haskel Balken. My father's Zionist roots were set and nurtured at *Maccabi*. He loved the Zionist ideas of Theodore Herzl, who believed in the establishment of the secular State of Israel as a safe haven for Jews. My father was proud of being Jewish and of Judaism's emphasis on education, but he was not a religious person—though his parents did keep a kosher home.

My father attended Zionist meetings where, because of his skills in shorthand, he was able to transcribe speeches of well-known people. Some of the speeches were from men like Chaim Weizman, one of the leaders of the international Zionist movement and later, the first president of Israel. Also, Dr. Nachum Goldmann, founder and president of the World Jewish Congress and a major activist in New York, and Vladimir Jabotinsky, a Russian journalist who became a major Zionist and founder of the Irgun, an underground liberation organization in Israel.

My father took down entire speeches then typed them in French and other languages he knew. At one point he had a large collection of these important speeches, but unfortunately they were all lost during the war— when he had to abandon them in Belgium as we ran for our lives. They would have provided major historical perspective as treasured historical documents. Since my father had attended numerous anti-Nazi meetings and placed on the Gestapo black list, we had to flee at the onset of the occupation of Belgium, taking only the essentials we could carry

Before the war, it looked like my father might have had the beginnings of a promising career. The Ford Motor Company hired him in 1930. Then, from December 1932 until August 1939, he worked at translating and transcribing documents in Brussels for the Floridienne Company, an oil consortium and candle manufacturer, with offices in Belgium, France, England, Holland, and Italy.

My father's sister, Charlotte, the eldest of the siblings, married Naphtali Hamel, a young man in the wholesale clothing business. Charlotte and Naphtali first lived in Cologne, Germany, and then moved to Belgium. When the war broke out they took refuge in Nice, France because it was unoccupied. My parents stayed in touch with them and when we went to Marseille, early in the war, my parents warned them to leave Nice before it became dangerous. They refused to face reality and were seduced by the charm of the area. They told my parents, "It is so beautiful here; we will be alright."

Eventually, they were arrested, sent to Drancy, France and deported to Auschwitz, where they died in 1942. Before the war, Susi, their only child, had married Joe Pantzer, an Englishman, and immigrated to London. She is the Suzi Pantzer who received the letters from my father and whose daughter, Helen, recently returned them to me.

My father's brother, Jules, the youngest of the siblings, became a medical technician in the merchant marines, on cargo ships plying the seas from Antwerp to the Belgian Congo. During the war, he served on convoys to many northern European ports, including Murmansk, Russia. He survived the war and remained in Antwerp. I saw him after the war and remember him as a quiet, nice person. He would usually wear long greenish, gabardine raincoats and always had a cigarette dangling from his lips. He was a loner—you might even say a hermit—though he did correspond with us periodically. Because his wife forsook him during the war, he was bitter about women, divorced her and never re-married. After he retired, he lost a leg to disease and died in Antwerp in 1984.

My paternal great grandfather, Joseph Pressel, was born in Krakow in then-Austria/Poland. He was a religious man who taught Jewish culture, Hebrew prayers and the laws of *Kashrut*. Joseph's wife (name unknown) gave birth to my grandfather Samuel Pressel. Samuel married Helen Peiper in Krakow. Eventually, the family immigrated to Antwerp, Belgium to escape pogroms and service in the Austrian army. Great grandfather Joseph died in Antwerp on May 19, 1932, when he was run over by a streetcar. He is buried in Putte, Holland.

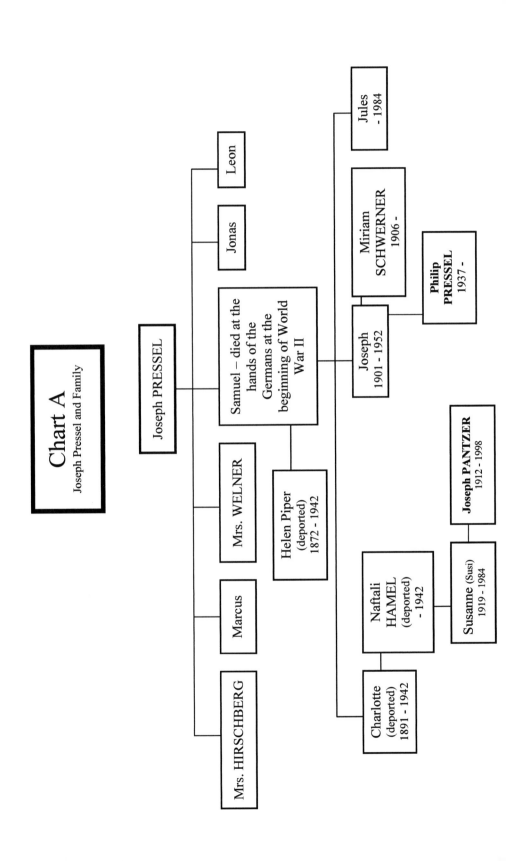

# Chart A
Joseph Pressel and Family

Joseph PRESSEL

Mrs. HIRSCHBERG

Marcus

Mrs. WELNER

Samuel – died at the hands of the Germans at the beginning of World War II

Jonas

Leon

Helen Piper (deported) 1872 - 1942

Joseph 1901 - 1952

Miriam SCHWERNER 1906 -

Jules - 1984

Philip PRESSEL 1937 -

Charlotte (deported) 1891 - 1942

Naftali HAMEL (deported) - 1942

Susanne (Susi) 1919 - 1984

Joseph PANTZER 1912 - 1998

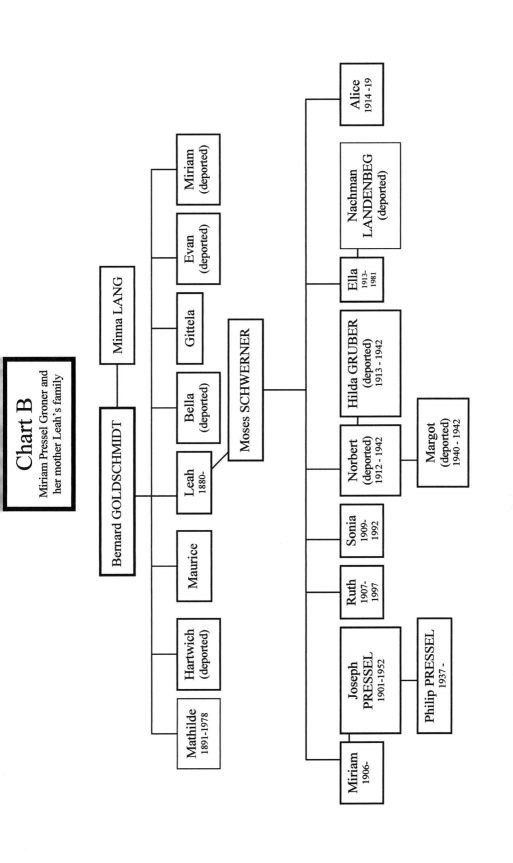

# Chart B
Miriam Pressel Groner and her mother Leah's family

Bernard GOLDSCHMIDT — Minna LANG

Mathilde 1891-1978

Hartwich (deported)

Maurice

Leah 1880- — Moses SCHWERNER

Bella (deported)

Gittela

Evan (deported)

Miriam (deported)

Miriam 1906- — Joseph PRESSEL 1901-1952

Ruth 1907-1997

Sonia 1909-1992

Norbert (deported) 1912 - 1942 — Hilda GRUBER (deported) 1913 - 1942

Ella 1913-1981 — Nachman LANDENBEG (deported)

Alice 1914 -19

Margot (deported) 1940 - 1942

Philip PRESSEL 1937 -

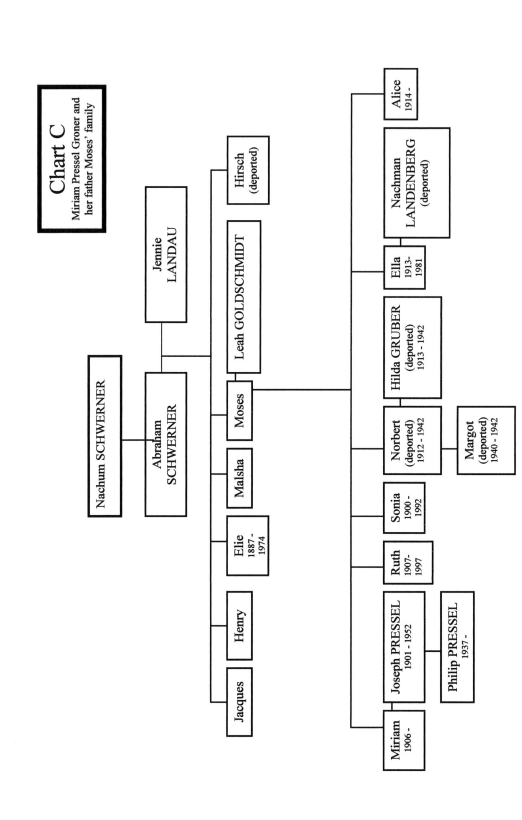

# Chart C
Miriam Pressel Groner and
her father Moses' family

**Jules, Joseph, Charlotte Pressel, 1912**

**Jules, Helen, Samuel, Joseph Pressel, 1925**

**Joseph Pressel (fourth from the left), Maccabi coach, 1924**

**Joseph Pressel seated second from left, at
Maccabi Athletic Club Directors meeting**

My paternal grandmother, Helen, went back to Krakow to be with her mother while giving birth to her first son, Joseph, my father, in 1901. (To the best of my knowledge, none of my family members on either my father or mother's side had middle names). Samuel was a self-employed diamond merchant. In that business, anti-semitism was almost unheard of because most of the dealers were Jewish. Samuel was not a very good businessman, so the family wasn't affluent—they lived in a simple apartment in Antwerp.

My mother's family was from Austria/Poland, a region where the Jews were called Galitzianers. Her paternal grandfather, Abraham Schwerner, who was in the hair processing business, came to Fulda, Germany from Austria/Poland around 1910 to avoid the military draft, like many other Polish and Russian Jews. These drafts could last for thirty years or more, during which the Jews would be subjected to anti-semitic violence on a regular basis. My mother's uncles also left Poland for Germany and they all eventually moved to Belgium.

My mother's parents, Moses Schwerner and Leah Goldschmidt, were Orthodox Jews who lived in Fulda, Germany where my grandfather Moses studied for the rabbinate under Rabbi Kahn. He eventually gave that up to join his father, Abraham, in the family hair processing business. Moses was about 5' 7" tall, and had dark eyes. From his youth he always wore a full dark beard and mustache with long, curled waxed tips. He always wore a hat or a *yarmulke* (skullcap/*kippah*).

My maternal grandmother Leah was about 5' 3" tall, with a medium figure and a head full of dark hair cut to just above the shoulders. Until the war, she always wore a *sheitel,* a wig religious married women wore. She stopped wearing it when World War II started and never wore it again. Leah had a soft tender face, dark brown eyes, and was a warm and charming woman. She had been brought up in Lubek, Germany, then moved to Fulda with her three brothers; Hartwich, Maurice and Evan, and her four sisters; Mathilde, Bella, Gittela and Miryam. In Fulda, Bella and Gittela made wigs for another company and Moses met Leah through her sisters.

My mother was born in 1906 in Fulda. My mother was the oldest of six children. Her siblings were Ruth, Sonia, Norbert—the only son—Ella and Alice. My mother's given name was Miryam, with the old German spelling. This is how my father referred to her in his letters and until the end of the war. They both used Miriam from then on, although occasionally my father would revert to the old spelling. He called her Mir, and that is usually how she signed letters. She was named after her maternal great-grandmother Miryam Landau. After my mother and two of her sisters were born, prior to World War I, Moses moved the family to Antwerp, Belgium.

Years before World War I, Moses and his four brothers, Jacques, Henry, Elie and Hirsch, and their sister, Malsha, greatly expanded and relocated the family human hair processing business from Germany to Antwerp by buying space in a building on Rue Millistraat. The company concentrated on preparing human hair and shipping it to European wig manufacturers. The processing included washing, bleaching, dyeing, and curling human hair. The company was important to religious Jewish married women, since Orthodox women must cover their heads with wigs in the presence of men other than their husbands.

The business offices were on the ground floor, and the factory was located in the back section; there were living quarters on the second and third floors. In 1917, during the First World War, the company purchased a large plot of land in Broocham, a suburb of Antwerp. The plot included the factory, which had been a brewery, offices, two summer cottages and beautiful gardens. The gardens contained fruit trees, hot houses, grape vines, a walnut tree, currant bushes, and melons. In order to make the half-hour commute from Broocham to the house on Lange Leemstraat in Antwerp, Grandfather Moses purchased a Mercedes-Benz convertible.

After World War I, the *Schwerner Freres Cie.* (Schwerner Brothers Co.) was the only remaining center in Europe that processed real human hair, most of it purchased from Italy. The company was very successful and supported the four Schwerner brothers and their families. Elie, to whom most of my father's letters were written during World War II, immigrated to New York in 1936 to establish the New York branch of the fabricated wig business. During World War II, the factory in Broocham was taken over by the Germans and turned into one of their headquarters. Luckily, after the war, the family was able to take back the factory and resume the business, though it had been stripped of its machines and furniture.

In 1914, after the birth of their sixth child, the Schwerners moved into a lovely home on Lange Leemstraat #328 in Antwerp. It was similar to a New York brownstone, with narrow frontage and a flight of stone stairs leading to the front door and parlor. The three-story townhouse was built of reddish and dark brown stone and had high windows. A trolley ran down the street in front of it. Everyone in the Jewish community was welcome in their home.

My mother and her siblings led a fairly sheltered life and had little contact with the non-Jewish community. They had no Christian friends and did not experience any anti-semitism. My mother, Sonia, and Ruth shared a room. Ella and Alice, the youngest girls, shared another bedroom, while Norbert had his own. There was also a sleep-in maid, Alice Englander, a Christian, and a laundress who came once a week to wash and iron clothing and linens. There were no pets in the house.

In 1914 at the age of 8, my mother was sent to visit her maternal grandparents in Lubek, Germany. During her stay there, World War I began and she could not return to Belgium so she was sent to Fulda. She remained there with her aunts, Bella and Gittela, until 1916. During that time she attended school and was cared for by her aunts, who were single at the time. My mother was the center of attention and happy to be there. Eventually, Bella and Gittela did marry. Gittela married Mr. Mueller, a teacher, and Bella married an older gentleman with whom she eventually had a daughter, but I wasn't able to learn his name.

Four of the sisters attended an excellent private girls' school, *College Marie Jose,* on *Lamoriniere Straat.* Girls from mostly rich Jewish families attended the school. For some reason, only Ruth and Norbert went to public schools. The girls in the private school wore uniforms consisting of navy jumpers with white blouses and pleated skirts, and unlike the public school, *Marie Jose* experimented with departmental programs, using specialty teachers for different subjects. In most public schools, one teacher taught all of the subjects, but my mother and her sisters had separate teachers for math, French, music, and so forth. It was expensive, of course, but Moses wanted his children to be well educated. A female tutor also came to the house to teach religion. The girls' education was comparable to several years in a university. My mother told me, perhaps because she wanted me to be a good student as well, that all the Schwerner children enjoyed school and were good students, and that the children had few toys and games.

The Schwerner family lived an Orthodox family life with a strictly kosher home. A maid cleaned and prepared the food which Leah then cooked. There were two preparation tables and two sets of dishes in the kitchen, one for dairy and one for meat. On Sabbath, they attended synagogue and refrained from doing any work on that day or during other Jewish holidays.

Moses was a leader at the Eiseman Synagogue, named in honor of its founder and primary investor. It was a small private synagogue and had no Rabbi. Moses was also president of the religious community organization. In those days, none of the girls were Bat Mitzvahed. Norbert was Bar Mitzvahed in the traditional manner.

In my grandparents' home, Sabbath preparations began on Thursdays and continued until sunset on Friday evening. It was much like preparing for the arrival of a special guest. The best dishes and tableware were set, and a festive meal was prepared, cooking enough food to last until Saturday evening. Timers were set for the lights in the house. In my mother's house, they would sit for a few hours on Saturday evening, singing songs as they waited for Moses to come home from synagogue and make the prayer that officially ended the day of rest.

My mother's family very strictly observed all of the holidays. On Friday evenings Leah lit the Sabbath candles. On the Sabbath and other Jewish holidays, my grandfather would often bring someone home to share dinner. Activities that were performed on the Sabbath included praying in the synagogue, studying the Torah, reading, taking a nap, playing games with the children, taking a walk in the park, and visiting friends or relatives.

During the summer Moses had some large pieces of ice delivered to their cellar in order to preserve butter and a few perishables. Summer temperatures rarely exceeded 70 degrees Fahrenheit. Storage was not a problem for meats and fish since they were purchased daily.

My grandfather spent his leisure time reading or having conversations with friends and family. After the war he would take me to the synagogue in a small building nearby that always seemed crowded to me. He taught me about Judaism, including a little bit of Hebrew, and the blessings for washing hands and eating bread. He told me a little bit about Jewish holidays, such as Rosh Hashanah and Passover and introduced me to some important people in the synagogue, including its president, Mr. Prince. Moses wore a top hat in shul (synagogue) on the Sabbath and holidays, and left it there for safekeeping. During the week he would wear his *homburg*.

My mother's family became naturalized as Belgians in the 1920s, which cost a considerable amount of money. Before 1940, Antwerp was a way station for Europeans going to America by ship, and there were approximately 35,000 Jews there. It was a compassionate, middle-class Jewish community with wealthy merchants and diamond dealers. They supported a Jewish health and charity institution called the *Centralle* that helped immigrants and the poor set themselves up in business and had a soup kitchen where Leah worked twice a week. My grandmother's birthday was the biggest occasion of the year for the family, celebrated on February 5th. Her children saved all year to buy her gifts, like embroidered pillows and curtains. Once, they purchased silver candlesticks and living room furniture with money provided by my grandfather.

Moses and Leah did not attend concerts, but the children did, usually on Wednesday and Thursday nights at the Antwerp Zoo, where they learned to appreciate classical music. All in all, the family lived in a wholesome environment conducive to bringing up happy and well-balanced children. These strong roots were the source of my mother's strength, generosity and kindness. Moses insisted that my mother and grandmother visit his elderly mother, Jennie Landau, every day. After eating her meals at home, my mother would often stay overnight with her.

My mother's sister, Sonia, took private courses to become a physiotherapist and worked with children who had polio. She married Louis Suskin, a diamond dealer, and had one son, Sylvan. Ruth and Ella were administrators. Through a *shadchan*, a matchmaker, Ruth met Maurice Schild, who was in the import/export business. They married and had two sons, Willy and Ronnie.

At the beginning of the war, Ella married Nachum Landenberg, an engineer. He was deported to Auschwitz in 1942 and never returned. To avoid the same fate during the war, Ella fled to Liege, where she met people who worked for the Belgium Information Bureau, a front for Belgium's espionage agency. She offered them her services for love of country and was asked to become a spy for Belgium.

She received orders to return to Antwerp where she assumed the name Leonie Renard, and recruited several agents. She submitted weekly reports about activity in the Port of Antwerp to her superiors and was quite a successful *Mata Hari*. Many years later, her contribution was recognized and she was honored for her work by the government of Israel.

Alice was also very adventurous. She befriended an orphan girl, Tanya Abramsohn, whose parents died in Russia. The child had been sent to Antwerp to live with her uncle, Halevy, a wealthy man and ardent Zionist, and his niece, Amelie. He offered to send all three girls—Alice, Tanya and Amelie—to Israel to attend a pioneering agricultural school. Moses consented to let Alice go, although she was only 16 years old, and he felt comfortable with his decision. The girls immigrated to Palestine in 1936. After Alice left, Moses said to the family, "Why did I let her go? I must have been *meshuga* (crazy)."

In Palestine, Alice thrived and became a physical education teacher. She eventually married Myron Abramsohn, Tanya's brother, who had immigrated to Israel several years previously becoming a career officer in the Israeli Army. They eventually had three sons, Danny, Uri, and Odet.

Norbert, my mother's only brother, went into the doll manufacturing business, married Hilda Gruber, and they had one daughter, Margot. The three of them were deported to Auschwitz in 1942 and killed.

My mother was the oldest, and when she finished high school, she was brought into the business where she learned hair processing and clerical skills. She went to night school to learn how to sew, and was also tutored by a woman who was the family's seamstress. All the sisters eventually came into the family business. They were paid pocket money, because my grandparents provided all their other basic needs.

My mother was 20 when she met my father at *Maccabi*. She was there because she was interested in gymnastics and Zionism, in that order. Her sisters were good at swimming and at playing a Belgian form of basketball called Korfball—played with six players on a side, three men and three women. My parents dated secretly for about two years, because on occasion, Moses could be quite a tyrant. My father was not really acceptable to my mother's parents because he was not religiously observant and did not have a high paying job. Then there was the time my grandfather shouted at my mother when she came home late from *Maccabi* with my father and a Mr. Samuelson. For all his tolerance and intellect, Grandfather did not think it proper for his daughter to be seen in public with two men.

My father was six feet tall, thin, good-looking and very popular. He never dated anyone but my mother. To this day, my mother does not know why he chose her. Their "dates" consisted primarily of participating in sports activities at *Maccabi* and taking walks together in a park on weekends. My father would also visit my mother in the evenings when she was staying with Grandmother Jennie. These were the only times they were free from either school or work.

After asking my grandfather's permission, my parents were married by a Rabbi Rothenberg in an Antwerp hall on a rainy Sunday, November 2, 1930. My mother's dress was custom-made, and fairly tight at the waist. My father wore striped pants, a double-breasted jacket and a top hat. They had a very large wedding attended by approximately four hundred family members and friends from *Maccabi* and the Jewish community. My mother and grandmother spent days preparing food and various desserts for the wedding. The day before the wedding, my father's friends took him out and tried to get him drunk, but they couldn't do it. He did not drink much but could hold his liquor fairly well. After the wedding, my parents honeymooned in Brussels for two days.

**Miriam and Joseph Pressel on their wedding day,
November 2, 1930**

**Joseph and Miriam Pressel with her parents
Leah and Moses Schwerner**

For their first two years of marriage my parents lived in a little apartment in a private house in Antwerp, then moved to an apartment in the Anderlecht section of Brussels. They were not observant, nor did they keep kosher, but one of the gifts they received for their wedding was a beautiful pair of ornate silver candlesticks that they treasured. They were from Helen Pressel, my father's mother. The candlesticks are the only precious pre-war possession that survived with us.

My father tried to become successful before they married by going into the soap business with two partners, but they were not good businessmen, eventually leaving him with debts. Later, while my father worked as a transcriber and translator, my mother worked as a dressmaker. They occasionally attended the theater and concerts. They lived a fairly confined and calm life until I livened it up on June 22, 1937, seven years after they were married. I became the focus of their attention, with Maman working at home, while taking care of me. I was told I was a beautiful baby with a full head of long dark hair. In fact, my mother said a photo of me at six months was used by the Baby Kadom Soap Company as an advertisement, although she was never paid for its use!

As I said, I made life interesting, so interesting, that Mother had to save my life even before the war began. When I was just 2 years old, I was running around the apartment when I brushed against a very large mirror leaning against a wall and it started to fall on me. Mother lunged to push me away and caught the mirror on her right arm, where it broke. She cut an artery, and blood was spurting everywhere, so she grabbed a towel and wrapped her arm in it. My father whisked her off to a hospital. She would save me, and my father, several times during the course of the war.

# 2

# THE WAR STARTS

**Marseille, August 5, 1940**

Dear Uncle Elie,

When the bombs came unexpectedly on the 10th of May in Brussels (two houses of three stories each were demolished right next to our dwelling), we decided to be prudent and to move away. We entered France on the 18th of May. After a trip partly on foot, partly luckily by rail, we were in the middle of endless convoys of refugees, many of whom unfortunately died on route, we got to Paris on the 21st of May with our three-year-old child.

Jos

In 1938, my mother's first cousin, a dermatologist, Dr. Friedl Amster, was among those in Germany deported to the Dachau concentration camp, existent since 1933. Until his detention, the doctor had been a politically active Socialist and ardent anti-Nazi. Most of Dachau's early inmates were political prisoners from Munich, Social Democrats, Communists, Catholics, and Jewish doctors and lawyers. Many of them never went home again.

From the beginning, abuse was the guards' way of life. Dr. Amster was literally crucified in Dachau. He was left on a cross for more than twenty-four hours, and when he was taken down, his head was swollen to almost twice its normal size. Amazingly, he survived and eventually escaped. I don't know how he left Germany, but he made it to Antwerp. My grandfather picked him up at the train station and brought him home, where he gave the family his eyewitness account of what was happening to the Jews in Germany. A few years after the war, Dr. Amster established a dermatology practice in New York.

My parents were also aware from newspapers and radio that things were not good for Germany's Jews. They were especially concerned, since others in my mother's family still lived there. They read and heard the anti-Jewish propaganda, Hitler's speeches, and what had happened on *Krystallnacht*, November 9-10, 1938. During those two days, almost 7,500 Jews were rounded up and deported to concentration camps. In September 1939, Germany invaded Poland.

Shortly after, the war in Belgium started on May 10, 1940 when the Germans invaded. This was one month prior to my third birthday, and it astonishes me that I remember that day. Thousands of airplanes flew overhead. The sky was black with planes. I woke up at around 5 a.m. because the house was shaking and there was thunderous noise. I ran to my parents, with my hands over my ears, screaming, "What is boom boom?" The explosions were constant. My parents calmed me down and took me to a shelter, deciding then and there that it was time to leave Belgium.

They knew that our best chance of survival was to go either to England or France. My father's employer, La Floridienne, had already suspended the consortium's business in Belgium, so my parents decided to cross the border to France. The French weren't yet under attack and Paris had a Polish Consulate that sponsored and trained a military unit. My father felt that it was his duty to enlist in the Polish Army to fight against Hitler. My mother agreed.

When we left Belgium we had just one valise, very little money, a loaf of bread and one change of clothing for me. All of our possessions were left in the Brussels apartment. I suppose my parents felt with our lives at stake, our material possessions meant very little. My father wore a pair of dark slacks and a jacket, my mother wore a gray suit, and I wore very short shorts and a shirt. My parents had just enough time to say goodbye to their remaining relatives, some of whom later fled to France, too.

We took a train to the Belgian seacoast city of Lapanne, the city closest to the French border. Two of my mother's sisters and their families, the Suskins and Schilds, went their own way. We didn't see them again until we reached Marseille later in 1940.

My father's cousin, Nuna Torczyner, met us in Lapanne and gave my father 1,000 Francs. This was a very fortunate and kind act, since we fled spontaneously and didn't have much money. It was remarkable that we simply walked over the border and had no problems with the French border patrol.

The roads were filled with thousands of people fleeing Belgium. We hitchhiked and walked our way to Paris. We took trains, coal trucks, and horse drawn wagons, taking us three days to get there. The trip was a nightmare, and people were dying all around us. There was no milk, and so for the first time my mother fed me wine diluted with water. I drank this beverage, along with coffee, until close to the end of the war— because milk was always scarce. There was one time, along the way, in one French village, that a woman gave us a little milk to drink and allowed my mother to wash me.

The transition from a proper, ordered middle-class life to life on the run was difficult for my parents, who found it heartbreaking to see me poorly clothed and fed. Regrettably, things didn't get much better for years.

As soon as we got to Paris, my father went to the Polish Consulate and enlisted in the Polish Army. My mother went to find us a place to live and rented a room for us in someone's apartment. She hired herself out as a seamstress working at home. As the Germans took over northern France and approached Paris, my mother decided to leave immediately by train for Bayonne, a city near the Spanish border. My parents figured that if the war in Europe continued, they would try to get to Spain and go from there to England. They would rendezvous in Bayonne. My mother and I rode in wagons and a train caboose to avoid paying the train fare. We also hitchhiked in coal trucks and I remember sitting for many hours on my mother's lap. We traveled for three days and nights with many other refugees, many of whom were wounded, barely alive. When we finally arrived in Bayonne, my mother went to the American Consulate, where she tried to buy us a visa for United States immigration. Unfortunately, she did not have enough money and we wound up living in a refugee camp. Many other Jews from Antwerp with money were more successful and were able to obtain passage to free countries.

**Marseille**

**August 5, 1940**

Dear Uncle Elie,

I served in the Polish army in France until June 18. On the 23rd after I made a non-stop march of 2 days and 2 nights with many unpleasant circumstances, I reached Miryam and our child who had traveled for 3 days and 3 nights in a wagon packed with refugees and wounded who were barely alive.

Jos

My father trained with his unit in France for a few weeks until Marshal Petain, head of the Vichy government, surrendered to Germany in mid-June 1940. Upon the Vichy surrender, Papa's unit was demobilized. Petain negotiated with Hitler that the Germans would directly control 60 percent of the country, mostly northern and western France. The French government at Vichy, under Petain, would administer the rest.

When the Polish Army in France dissolved, my father began walking south. As he walked mile after mile after mile, he was terrified that the Germans would arrest him because he was a Jew. He was still on the Gestapo black list because of the Zionist work he had been doing in Belgium. He destroyed his Polish military papers and then proceeded on a non-stop journey of two days and two nights walking and hitchhiking a distance of 460 miles. When he arrived in Bayonne, finally finding us, he looked like a corpse. My mother was so scared by how terrible he looked; she thought he was going to drop dead. When he felt better, they tried getting into Spain, which turned out to be impossible, so they went to Marseille hoping to recuperate and find jobs.

We were on the train to Marseille when the French Gestapo boarded it. They were looking for Jews and others whose papers were not in order. Before they could reach our compartment, the train began to move and they left. This was our first narrow escape. If they had checked our papers, they would have found our Polish passports, since we never applied for Belgian citizenship. We would have been removed from the train, taken with the others who were removed, and sent to Gurs. Located near Marseille, Gurs was the main transit camp for the deportation of French and German Jews to Auschwitz and other camps. My Uncle Maurice, Ruth's husband, was held there and in two other camps run by the French—Camp St. Livrade and Camp Lesmilles, also near Marseille.

We finally arrived in Marseille in late June of 1940. With the little funds we had, my parents found shelter in a one-bedroom furnished apartment. It was awful, dirty, and the toilets were disgusting. It was located in the red light district on a narrow, alley-like street called Rue des Petites Maries. I slept on a daybed in an alcove, and my parents slept in the bedroom. Other than some very strong impressions, like the planes flying over our house in Belgium, my childhood memories begin in Marseille.

Although the Nazis did not occupy the Southern part of France, there were many collaborators and Nazi sympathizers in the region. My father reported to a company affiliated with La Floridienne to look for work, but as my mother told me much later, the colleagues he spoke to told him that as a foreigner (and a Jew), he should get the hell out of the place. My father staggered under the blow of this rejection, and my mother again resumed her job as a seamstress, counting on the hundreds of refugees in the city for business. She rented a sewing machine and within two weeks was busy enough to hire extra women to assist her. She put the sewing machine in the alcove and would sit on my bed to work.

My mother's income paid for our sustenance, since refugees like my father could not find a job. Occasionally, he was able to give private language and stenography lessons, but he was afraid to go into the streets for fear of being picked up in a police roundup. The French secret police, the *Milices*, was just as nasty and cruel as the German Gestapo. My parents and other Jews were uncertain of their status because, at the beginning of the Vichy regime, policy toward the Jews was somewhat haphazard. Jewish refugees might or might not be arrested. If they were arrested, there was always a possibility for them to bribe their way out of trouble.

**Joseph, Philip and Miriam Pressel, Marseille, 1941**

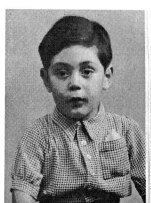  

**Passport photos, 1941**

My father wrote a succession of letters to America and England from Marseille and Lyon over a twenty-one month span, from August 1940 to April 1942. My mother's Uncle Elie was already in the States, and they asked him for help, primarily to obtain exit visas. Soon after the Battle of Britain, which began on July 10, 1940, my father wrote:

**Marseille**

**September 2, 1940**

Dear Uncle Elie,

Again we ask you to do everything you can to help us to emigrate. It is impossible here to know what the large emigration organizations are doing and what to do to get in touch with them. Could you please urgently inquire and sign us up so that we may make the quota. If we are allowed to earn an honest living anywhere, we have no doubt that we could manage.

We are told of the camps where the Poles are interned. It will be an untenable situation if the war continues for much longer. The news that we get from the camp (GURS) where Maurice and the uncles are is very bad; the hygiene situation is deplorable, there are several cases of typhus with death inevitable.

Jos

Dear uncle and aunt,

Do everything you can to get us out of this misery to give us the chance to resume a normal existence. Thank you in advance. Forgive all the bother. Many kisses to you all.

Mirya

It was difficult to live in an apartment with no gas, no stove, and only one electric bulb in the ceiling. My mother cooked on an alcohol burner and used it to heat water to do the wash. She found a large piece of white paper and used it as a tablecloth, so we didn't eat off of a bare wooden table. Maman tried to inject a little civility in our lives. It was a primitive way to live, but we managed. Everything was rationed. My mother stood on lines for hours only to buy food and alcohol for the burner. Supplies often ran out before she made it to the counter, and she would have to wait in line all over again the following day. Sometimes, all we had to eat was bread. Many of my first memories were of our sad days in that tiny apartment. My clothes, the same ones I wore day after day, were taking a beating. My mother tried to keep them clean, and of course, I wasn't allowed to play outside. I would amuse myself in different ways. When my mother found time to knit, I would hold the skein of wool while she wound it up, and I treasured any coloring pencils that I got.

## Marseille

## October 10, 1940

My dear aunt and uncle,

We were so happy to receive your letter of September 21; it gave us a great deal of emotional comfort; not that we lack courage, far from it, but in the circumstances we live in and the upheaval and confusion, we get revived when we get such a nice letter as yours from the land of Stars and Stripes.

We don't sleep very much because we pass part of the night in caves or shelters.

Jos

Early in 1941, a U.S. lawyer named Leon Kubovistsky notified my parents that a "danger" visa was being granted to us. Uncle Elie would pay for our passage to America. We went to the American Consulate in Marseille with our valises packed and a doctor's certificate stating that we were healthy. When we arrived, the consul told us, "I'm sorry you're not getting the visa; your parents are still in Belgium and the Germans are going to make reprisals."

That consul lied about the reprisals. We later learned that he was just giving us an excuse to keep Jews out of the United States. This was consistent with the anti-semitic policies of the State Department. It was also a question of money, money we didn't have. Only Jews with enough money were, in fact, allowed to enter the U.S.

Then, we received a letter from Uncle Elie in New York. He told us he tried to send us money, as well as to his brother, Jacques, and sister, Malsha. But, Elie was told it was not allowed because officials in the U.S. were afraid that any money sent to any occupied country during the war would be impounded by the Nazis.

My father wrote many letters to his family that described the suffering of the Jews in Europe. As I read these letters, a lump forms in my throat, my eyes well up with tears and I become enraged. Since we didn't have a slip of paper called a visa, we were forced to live on the edge of a precipice. My parents were increasingly desperate to leave France, knowing that the Nazis could deport them to a death camp at any moment.

It wasn't long before my mother's sister, Sonia, her husband Louis, and their son Sylvan, (a year older than I) arrived in Marseille and took a room in an apartment one flight up from ours. They had also taken the risky train ride from Belgium and were lucky the three of them were able to stay together all of the time.

Eventually, we all moved to slightly larger apartments on Rue Elemir Bourges, a more pleasant street. I went back to Marseille recently and saw that the street today has reasonably nice apartment buildings. The house we lived in still has the same glass and metal ribbed double doors at the entrance, and there are food shops and restaurants nearby.

Uncle Louis and my father tried to get us all to England. They paid someone who was supposed to get us on a boat to England from Spain. My father and Louis were to wait in Marseille on the Canebiere, the major avenue, for the contact to arrive. He never did. The man was a con artist and the money was lost.

After that, Louis, who had two brothers and a few friends from the Antwerp diamond community living in Nice, moved his family there. He figured he could earn money by cleaving diamonds for them, and he did, earning enough to obtain Cuban visas for his family. Louis, Sonia, and Sylvan left France for Madrid by train and from there went to Barcelona. They left for Cuba on an old cargo ship at the end of October 1941, and wound up living in Havana for four-and-a-half years. They finally immigrated to the United States on May 10, 1946, six years to the day after the war started in Belgium.

My mother's sister Ruth, her two boys, and sister in-law came to live with us when Maurice, her husband, was taken to Gurs. The boys, Willy and Ronnie, were one and two years younger than I. I still have a picture from 1941 of Willy, Ronnie, and I in front of the glass main doorway of the apartment house on Rue Elemir Bourges. Maurice was eventually released from Gurs and was able to get visas to Cuba. My parents accompanied them to one of the last boats leaving Marseille for Casablanca and then to Cuba.

My parents were never able to earn enough money to join them. My mother's earnings as a seamstress barely covered our meager lifestyle. Although my mother hired two girls to work for her as seamstresses, the money earned by my parents was barely enough to pay for rent and ration tickets. Ration tickets were required for everything; including food, coal, and soap. To get the ration tickets, you went to the city hall with your identity papers. Since most foreigners were being arrested, we purchased our ration tickets on the black market to avoid city hall. Buying them illegally cost us a fortune. My mother even had to sell her engagement ring to get food.

By then it was too late to get visas to Cuba, let alone America. We also couldn't go back to Belgium because the Germans had occupied it and opened the Breendonck concentration camp there. We were now stranded in France for the war's duration.

We were still in Marseille in May 1942 when the first news of the Jewish massacres by the Germans reached London. The underground Jewish Socialist Party in Warsaw leaked news out of Poland telling of the mass murders, nearly three quarter of a million Eastern European Jews. This included the slaughter of men, women, children in orphanages, people in old age homes, and the sick in hospitals. Most were shot by machine gun after digging their own graves in nearby woods.

By June 1942, our situation became desperate.

**Marseille**

**June 1942**

Dear Uncle Elie,

The months pass and we unfortunately do not see anything happening. We have previously explained to you that our situation here is without any hope. Couldn't you make an ultimate emergency effort to accelerate obtaining a favorable decision?

I hope that you will do your best so that our case will be re-examined, because we are certainly living in sinister and desperate times, and time is running out for us to be finally granted the requested permits.

                    Jos

By August 1942 Belgian Jews were being deported to Auschwitz from internment camps in Malines, Belgium. I have read that more than 25,000 Jews were deported, and only approximately 1,000 of those survived the war. Luckily, over 25,000 Jews hidden by Belgian Christians were saved. Also, during that summer of 1942, the Swiss government started to turn back Jewish refugees at their border. They no longer accepted refugees running from religious persecution.

My father's letters seemed hopeful about escaping France, at least until this point. Despite all the efforts made on our behalf to obtain visas, it is sad for me to say that nothing ever happened. We never got visas, and therefore spent the rest of the war in hiding and in constant danger.

There is anger inside me still, when I think of how the people in the State Department deliberately prevented Jews from coming to America. It's pretty well known by now that Breckenridge Long, the man in charge of visa policies, was a rabid anti-Semite. His actions amounted to a death sentence for thousands of Jewish refugees.

I have several letters from lawyers and from the State Department detailing the visa application process, the red tape, and the State Department's cheapness as they ask for a refund for the cost of a telegram. Some of the people who signed the State Department letters were H.K.Travers, Chief of the Visa Division and Harold S. Tewell, U.S. Consul in Cuba.

From Dr. Otto Schirn, a lawyer working on our behalf,
to Robert Watson, a lawyer in Washington, April 9, 1942:

"Concerning Joseph Pressel and Family, in the first days of January 1942 the Department of State informed the President's Advisory Committee on Political Refugees that the application for an emergency visa on behalf of Mr. Pressel has been rejected on the basis of a preliminary examination and that the case was, therefore, referred to the Interdepartmental Visa Review Committee."

From the Department of State, Washington, August 4, 1941:

"Under date of June 16, 1941 the Department on your behalf incurred an expense for one telegram to the American Consul at Marseille, France in regard to the visa cases of JOSEPH PRESSEL, wife MIRYAM & son Philippe, amounting to $7.44. It will be appreciated if a check drawn payable to the order of the Secretary of State of the U.S. might be forwarded to this office promptly in settlement of this account & ACCOMPANIED BY THIS BILL to assure prompt credit. Case

811.111 PRESSEL, Joseph. Signed by: D.W.CORRICK, CHIEF DIV OF ACCTS."

From Harold S. Tewell, American Consul in Cuba, to Elie Schwerner, January 7, 1942.

"An applicant for an immigration visa must be sponsored by relatives, friends, or other interested persons who are either American citizens or legal permanent residents of the United States. For this purpose a form B, statement of biographical data and either form C, affidavit of support and sponsorship or form D, affidavit of sponsorship in the case of persons not requiring assurance of financial support, should be obtained from the Department of State, Washington, D.C. and completed according to directions."

In 1943, Henry Morgenthau, the Secretary of the Treasury received President Roosevelt's approval to form the War Refugee Board. For us to ask for help at that time-had we even known about the War Refugee Board-would have meant revealing we were Jewish to the authorities. This would have probably been fatal for us. We had been caught between a rock and a hard place. However, had our visas had been issued by the State Department during the war, we would likely have been spared the suffering, terror, and hardships we endured. Perhaps Papa would have lived longer, as he died seven years after the war due to a heart condition. His heart certainly was affected by the stresses of the war's day-to-day life, the constant fear of being discovered, arrested by the Gestapo or the French secret police, and the tragic deaths of his parents and his sister.

My mother had made some friends among the local people. Three times these contacts rushed to our door to warn us that the police were coming to arrest us. Three times we grabbed one little valise and hid in the apartments of the people who had warned us. Several days later we would be told the danger was gone and we could return to our apartment. Each time, we were told that we had escaped capture by minutes.

It was necessary to see if we could get false papers, and my father met with someone from the underground who said he could get them for us. Without them we didn't dare walk the streets of Marseille. The false papers stated we were born in Lille, France. Lille is a city near the Belgian border, thus our accents matched the region we "grew up in." The man who got us the papers was a decent person who didn't charge very much. The papers were simple. Our last name remained the same. Only my mother's first name was changed from Miriam to Marie.

It was getting dangerous in Marseille. There were constant roundups in the streets. There were massive arrests of Jews and people without proper documents. With jobs and food scarce, my parents felt it was safer to move to Lyon. They were wrong.

# 3

# LYON

You'd better leave quickly.
The Gestapo is coming for you.

*A neighbor in St. Foy*

In the fall of 1942 we arrived in Lyon, then part of Vichy France. The city is situated on two rivers, the Rhone and the Saone, with the business section located on an island between the two rivers. The residential area is on the east bank of the Saone, with the old city of Lyon to the west. Papa took a job as a secretary and translator at a French firm, *Prat et Fils* (Prat and Sons), which had moved to Lyon from German-occupied Paris. At first, we lived in an inexpensive apartment on the second floor of a private house in a suburb called St. Foy, high on a hill that overlooks much of the city, a short commute from his work.

Soon my parents found a private school for me. Now that my father was working, my parents could begin to provide me with a good education. One of my teachers was Mrs. Renee Sabathier, who, in addition to her other job, worked at my school part time. The rest of the time, she was a teacher in a nearby village and later be a large figure in my life, but I didn't know it then. Neither did she.

The company soon provided us with a rent-free furnished apartment on the second floor of a yellow brick building they owned in the center of Lyon. The imposing front entrance to the building had a high archway with dark brown wooden doors, and was set between two other buildings with red roofs. It was situated on the Quai Fulcheron, a major street running along the west side of the Rhone. It was one of those old fashioned apartments with two rooms and a kitchen/dining area with high ceilings and tall windows. The living room windows opened onto a balcony that was about twenty-five feet wide and two feet long with a black metal grillwork railing. It overlooked the river and street below. The apartment was always cold and dark and the furniture was very old. Yet, I was proud to be able to locate my house by my neighbors' red roofs every time I crossed the Rhone on one of its many bridges.

Soon after we moved to the city center, a woman who was a neighbor of ours in St. Foy came to warn us. She'd overheard the landlady at our former apartment building telling the French Secret Police that she thought we were Jewish and had moved to Quai Fulcheron.

We had no choice but to flee. The only logical thing to do was take the train to Argenton sur Creuse, a small town about 250 miles from Lyon. Here, my mother's Aunt Jeanne, Uncle Jacques Schwerner, and their three children, Ady, Edmee, and Harry, had gone into hiding. They lived in an apartment house and put us up until my parents felt it was safe to go back to the apartment in Lyon, which we eventually did. Again, miraculously, we had been warned in the nick of time.

Because it made more sense, I changed schools and attended second grade at a co-ed school almost directly opposite our apartment on the other side of the Rhone. The name of the school was *Lycee Ampere*. We didn't wear uniforms. My female teacher was very strict and would hit us over the knuckles with a ruler when we misbehaved.

I did my best, always one of those obedient and good students, with top grades in conduct, workmanship, and progress. I was still in short pants and knee socks, and when it was cold, my mother would bundle me in a thick mohair sweater. I still didn't have much in the way of clothing, and most of my clothes were dark blue or gray, but my mother always kept me spotless. I didn't get to wear long pants until we arrived in New York in 1946.

I have memories of learning to write the alphabet with old-fashioned nibbed pens and ink. I remember the swatches of cloth sewn together that I used to wipe excess ink from my pen after I dipped it into the glass inkwells provided to us by the school and how, to my mother's consternation, I would get lots of ink on my fingers. I used those same swatches until well after the war. We would also color pictures with pencils that needed constant sharpening—which I did with a knife. I kept my pen and colored pencils in a little cloth sack, treasured as my most valuable possessions.

By this time, my parents were prepared for any emergency. There was always a small packed suitcase near the door. Whenever the air raid sirens went off, usually around 11 p.m., my parents grabbed that bag, a loaf of bread and a sleepy me, and dragged us to a shelter. The bombings and sirens terrified me. At the start of an air raid, the sirens alternately wailed high and low. The all clear was a continuous one-note wail. For many years after the war, in the United States or wherever I was, when I heard a fire engine or ambulance siren, I would cringe and start to look for shelter, biting my lips and freezing still until they stopped. Today, I still detest sirens.

As 1943 turned into 1944, Allied bombing increased. We were bombed every night, occasionally during the day. They were destroying railroads, bridges, factories, troop concentrations, and munitions dumps. In other words, anything that was of use to the Germans. The shelter was a block away from the apartment, and was really a cave tunneled into the hill behind our apartment building. I remember many nights huddled next to my parents with a candle for some light or none at all. I could hear the bombs exploding around us and then, after a few hours, we would hear the all-clear siren and go back to the apartment.

Once we came back and found the building right next door was bombed. The collateral damage included the balcony windows and the collapse of an interior wall in our apartment. Not enough harm was done to prevent us from staying there. I was not allowed to go near the windows at night in case I inadvertently opened the curtains—which had to remain tightly shut because of the blackouts.

Wherever we were, my parents kept an eye out for trouble, especially if there were French police and German soldiers or officers around. We could never relax. We were always on the *qui-vive*, on our guard. Literally it means, "who lives." I could not go outside to play, so I kept busy by helping my mother with household tasks, coloring sketches or doing schoolwork. I had no toys.

By the end of 1944 most of the bridges in Lyon had been bombed, so I was taken to school, with other children, by rowboat. We reached the boat by walking down a stairway leading from the sidewalk to the river's edge. The war did little to prevent the teachers from letting our parents know how we were doing. In fact, I still have my two report cards from the school in Lyon.

Maman, made dresses, hats, and fur items for clients in Lyons and its outlying countryside. Her country clients paid her with food, while her city clients gave her cash. Occasionally, we received eggs and a bottle of milk and once in a while, cheese. One time she went to see a merchant in Vourles, seven miles south of Lyon to collect payment and by chance again met Mrs. Sabathier, the director and teacher of the local village school, and my first teacher in St. Foy near Lyon.

To maintain her business, my mother traveled to the countryside at least once a month, a dangerous enterprise because she was on her own with false papers. At first she did it without realizing how dangerous it was. Later she did it because she had to. She was courageous and strong, all five feet of her.

There was one client who gave my mother a live rabbit that she kept in a box on our balcony. For a time, I would feed it carrots and greens. After several months, my mother announced it was time for us to eat it, because food was so scarce. She brought it to a butcher who slaughtered it and cut it up for us. I didn't really feel too bad eating it, since it wasn't really a pet, and we *were* close to starving. But to this day that is the only rabbit that I have ever eaten and probably will ever eat.

For other foods—bread, carrots and spinach—my mother bought ration tickets with the money she and my father earned. We had no meat for months at a time. Potatoes were also a luxury, and when we had some, my mother used to cut them very thinly, to fool me into thinking there was more to eat.

The food we had to eat at times would be called garbage today. Still compared to others trapped by the war, we were very lucky. I remember that in the later years of the war, I had intestinal parasites. My mother was able to get some medication to destroy them. Today, so many years later, I enjoy food but find that as a rule, I still "eat to live" rather than "live to eat."

My family didn't spend much time outdoors for the first year and a half we lived in Lyon, so I treasured the few times I walked hand-in-hand with my parents along the city streets. My father also helped me with my reading and writing, and taught me a little bit about nature. I thought that tree branches swaying in the wind actually caused the wind by their flapping. He told me that the opposite was true, that the wind caused the tree branches to sway. That shocked me. I asked him where the wind came from, and he explained it was caused by changes in air pressure. I didn't really understand what he said but it sufficed at the time. In his spare time, in the evenings, he taught me his steno system, and how to write short sentences in French.

Throughout 1943 and 1944, my parents remained justifiably terrified of being picked up by the Nazis or their collaborators. They were afraid someone would report them as Jews or that their papers would be recognized as fakes. Most people who were caught outside were caught in what the French called *une raffle*, a roundup. There was a method to the French and German madness. The soldiers and/or the French Secret Police would suddenly block off several square blocks of the city's streets and trap everyone inside. If you didn't have papers, or if they thought your papers were forged, you were arrested, taken to a transport camp, and eventually deported.

I remember one beautiful Sunday, when the three of us couldn't resist going out for a walk in the park. My father wore a long, tatty black coat, my mother a blue dress and sweater. I wore my usual short pants, shirt and sweater. Suddenly we saw a whole group of German foot soldiers heading for the park with several truckloads of soldiers. Papa immediately recognized that *une raffle* was about to begin.

A tram was passing at just that moment, and my mother pointed it out to him. My father hustled us onto the streetcar, which was allowed to pass. We got away. My parents' quick thinking had saved us again.

By this time, I was 7 years old and aware of the war and its dangers. Each time I saw German soldiers or agents of the French Secret Police, I was scared, really scared. What I didn't know, and would have made me cower in hiding at all times was that there were collaborators everywhere. But I had no idea I was a Jew! My parents did a very smart thing-they hadn't told me we were Jewish. I could easily have told other kids in school-and with so many collaborators around, they could tell someone who would turn us in. It wasn't until after the war that I became aware of my religion.

I would often hear my parents talk about bad things that happened to people, like one story told to them by the man who had gotten us our false papers. This story was especially meaningful. Someone had warned him that the French were going to conduct a raid on a hidden press in someone's basement, a press the *Resistance* used to forge documents. He went to warn the partisans only to find that the Gestapo was there first and were dragging his friends out and arresting them. He turned, walked quietly away, and never heard from any of them ever again.

Our situation was precarious, and my parents decided that in order to assure my survival, I had to get out of the city for a while. I stayed with my Aunt Jeanne in Argenton sur Creuse, approximately 250 miles west of Lyon. At the train station, we all cried, since there was a good chance it would be the last time we would see each other. My mother made the journey with me. My aunt met us at the train station, and my mother returned to Lyon with a heavy heart.

My heart was in my mouth while I was away from my parents, and not for the last time during the war. Luckily, I was staying with family. They provided comfort and took excellent care of me. I remember that I ate pretty well in Argenton, having foods like eggs and meat. One of my aunt's visitors even entertained me once by doing magic tricks that made things appear and disappear under a bed.

The joy we felt when my parents and I were reunited several weeks later is indescribable. Unfortunately, this bittersweet experience was only the first separation of many from my parents. The fact is, since those days, I don't enjoy being alone even now, and certainly never in the dark.

There are also times, even today, when a street scene strikes me as familiar or my nose catches a smell familiar from those days, and a flood of memories washes over me. Some of the smells I distinctly remember are underground smells—the smell of caves, of old subway tunnels, musty and damp, and of old interiors and fireplaces. I actually enjoy the smells of a subway or being underground—somehow it makes me feel safe.

The regular tribulations of childhood made their appearance during wartime, too. While in Lyon, I developed tonsillitis and was taken to a doctor to have them removed. His office was on the other side of the Rhone, and my mother took me there to have the procedure. We were leaving his office in the afternoon, after it was done, when the air raid sirens suddenly began to wail. My mother grabbed my hand and we ran, as fast as our legs could go, across one of the remaining bridges. By the time we got to the shelter near our apartment, waves of planes had darkened the sky overhead.

My parents amazed me. Somehow they managed to get ice cream for me to eat the next day, to help me recover from the tonsillectomy. All I ate that day was ice cream and spoonfuls of condensed milk out of a can.

My mother never wanted to be separated or caught far away from home or my father. My father worked at home and stayed indoors most of the time. In fact, he and I were both very pale from our lack of sunshine. Because we didn't have a radio, he sometimes went out to try to catch the news about the war through the open windows of our neighbors who might be listening to the BBC. He would go out at dusk and walk around the block, and my mother would be frantic until he got home. Later in the war, when the Allies were chasing the Germans out of France, once in a while, he would take me with him.

There was yet another reason for my father's walks. He was on a tobacco hunt. Tobacco during the war was extremely expensive and hard to get—especially for smokers who were poor. When my father was finished with a cigarette, he would save the butts and put them in his special pouch and would roll his own from his butt collection, which he gathered when he walked the streets; that's how desperate he was for his smokes!

My mother's birthday is August 1st, and one fine summer day my father took me out to the fields to pick violets, her favorite flower. We found enough time to write her poetry.

I still have the letter that I wrote to my mother on her birthday in 1943:

**August 1, 1943**

My dear Maman,

Today according to what Papa told me, you are 37 years old. I wish you a happy birthday, good health and a long life, and I hope that this ugly war will soon be over. I promise you my dear mother that I will always be good and obedient. To make you happy I will do everything and kiss you on both cheeks.

Philippe

When the bombing of Lyon became intense in March 1944, the city government decided that an underground shelter at night was not the healthiest environment for children. The mayor decreed that all children must be evacuated or their parents would not receive their ration tickets.

I had to leave town, but I couldn't go to Argenton. It was too far away for my parents to visit me should there be an opportunity to do so.

The only person my mother trusted outside Lyon and felt was reliable enough to take care of me was Mrs. Sabathier, my teacher from St. Foy. She, her husband Alfred, and their son Jean, who was a year younger than I, lived in Vourles, about seven miles south of Lyon. It was close enough for my parents to visit me whenever possible.

People outside Lyon were told that they had to take a child from people living in the city. So the Sabathiers were happy to take a child they already knew. The Sabathiers did not know we were Jewish, just that we were from Lille, near Belgium. My parents packed my few things and brought me to Vourles by taking a streetcar to the edge of Lyon, and then walking about three hours to get to the village.

The day we left for Vourles was the beginning of many months of agonizing separation from my parents, and it was a place where I was subjected to many unexpected dangers.

# 4

# VOURLES

*"I nearly died of fright when I peeked through the curtains and saw German soldiers manning machine guns in back of an open truck that suddenly appeared around a corner of our house."*

*My thoughts one day in Vourles.*

Vourles had approximately 500 inhabitants and was located on the crest of a small ridge. The Sabathiers lived in an apartment on the second floor on the right side of the town hall. The town hall had a gray masonry exterior, and four windows on each side of the front door, with the word *"MAIRIE"* (Town Hall) inscribed above it. Most of the streets in Vourles were narrow and cobble stoned. The buildings on both sides of the streets were of a yellow-brown rough masonry, none of them more than two stories high.

The Sabathiers were a family of four: papa Alfred, maman Renee, their son Jean, and Renee's mother. Jean was a very nice boy and we got on well. The apartment was given to them because Mrs. Sabathier was the town's school director and the girls' teacher. The Sabathiers' living room was in the back of the building and overlooked the valley. There were mountains in the distance and small homes with red-tiled roofs peeking through the trees in the foreground. The dining room and the bedroom that I shared with Jean were in the front of the apartment and looked out on the Town Square. There was no bathroom. We washed ourselves in the kitchen sink and the toilet was downstairs in the courtyard.

The *Mairie* faced the town square on the south side. St. Bonnite Catholic Church faced the square from the west side and a marketplace faced the former Mairie from the north. The church, which hadn't changed in centuries, was typically Gothic. Its heavy wide front doors, at the top of four wide steps, were painted black and were ornately carved with deep swirls. There were two columns on each side of the doors that have recessed alcoves on each side housing the statues of the town's patron saints. The right corner of the church has a tall square clock and bell tower that chimes the hour on the hour.

There was a narrow street between the apartment building and the church that led to the back of the building, out to the countryside and down to the valley. The two-room schoolhouse, was where Mrs. Sabathier taught. Jean and I took our classes every day with the boy's teacher, Mr. Marcel. It sat right between that tiny street and the church, and had its own little garden, surrounded by a low stonewall. Mrs. Sabathier's mother tended the garden.

On most Sunday mornings, I would accompany the Sabathiers to Mass, and we would usually sit in a pew in the back. I would sit quietly—unobtrusively—trying to make myself invisible. No one tried to explain the Catholic religion to me and I really couldn't compare it to anything in my experience. My parents, to that point, had never taught me anything about any kind of religion. I had the sensation I really did not belong there, without quite knowing why. Surrounded by the heavy scent of incense, I would stare at the statue of the man nailed to the cross as I listened to the people quietly praying. I knew they were praying to Jesus Christ, and that he was the man nailed to the cross. I was fascinated whenever the priest would walk up the spiral staircase to the pulpit and deliver his sermon. At the time, the only language I could speak or understand was French, and sometimes, the words in the priest's sermon would scare me. He gave his sermon in French, while the rest of the service was done in Latin. I just followed along without understanding the rituals.

Several times, after a wedding, I would exit with everyone and stand on the steps to throw rice at the newlyweds. There were times I was envious of the boys and girls who were wearing really good clothes when they celebrated their first Communion. The boys wore their best suits and a white bow on their arms, and the girls wore beautiful white dresses. The older boys and girls who celebrated their Confirmations were also very well dressed, and I soon realized that I wasn't getting Communion or being Confirmed.

After I lived with the Sabathiers for a while, I discovered Mr. Sabathier was in the French military. He was also one of the leaders of the Maquis, the French freedom fighters, who waged guerrilla warfare against the Germans. Their local headquarters was in Vourles and was a source of anxiety, fright, and danger to everyone.

That wasn't my only source of anxiety. As a youngster, I was very impressionable. Every evening, from the front window, we would watch a man dressed in dark clothes come out of the church's side door carrying a big black sack. The sinister-looking man would walk toward the town square and then disappear down a side street and Mrs. Sabathier told me not to worry, he was just the sandman making his rounds, putting little children to sleep. For years, I believed her story, but eventually someone told me he was just the church maintenance man, and a childhood myth exploded.

During the time I lived in Vourles, I was of the age where I lost several of my baby teeth. The Vourles' tooth fairy custom, at the time, was one where the child left the tooth behind a loose rock in the garden near the church at sunset, and a mouse would come during the night and leave a coin in its place. Amazingly, it worked every time! It was the one innocent childhood belief of mine that was not corrupted by the war.

The town square, in addition to being the center of town life, was a playground for Jean and me. At times, we played with Jean's marbles made from little balls of clay that broke easily, and would require us to frequently renew our stock. We would also kick a ball around the square in our own version of football. On one particular afternoon, which I cannot ever forget, I was alone, on one of the narrow streets, when a violent hailstorm blew into the village. I was caught in a torrent of hailstones that seemed to be the size of bird's eggs. I ran as fast as I could back home. Mrs. Sabathier explained that they were pieces of frozen rain. I first thought that pebbles were falling down from somewhere. Luckily, the only ones that hit me were small and did not hurt.

Even in Vourles, in the countryside, there were occasional air raids that would force us to take shelter in the school cellar. The cellar was an almost empty room that was entered by running down steps through a double set of wooden doors. The room was always quite dark and we would sit on the floor with several candles burning. There were no windows, but you could hear the noise of the planes and bombs.

After one of those air raids, the Sabathiers and I were in the garden when a soldier suddenly came running around the corner of the church, brandishing a revolver. He was an Allied pilot who had been shot down and parachuted to safety. Now he was asking the Sabathiers to hide him from the Germans. Mr. Sabathier put him in the school cellar, where he stayed until the Maquis were able to smuggle him out and ferry him back to England.

What overshadowed everything I witnessed or did was how much I missed my parents, especially Maman. Every morning, when I opened my eyes, I hoped she would be sitting at my bedside, but she wasn't there, and I would get a hollow feeling in my belly and an ache in my throat. Then I would spend some time crying into my pillow, bereft with loneliness. When I wasn't busy with schoolwork or chores, playing with Jean, or sleeping, I was miserable. I often sought solace at night by curling up tight in the fetal position before I could fall asleep.

I spent many months with the Sabathiers. On the few weekends my parents were able to visit, we slept on cots that were placed in the two-room schoolhouse so we could be together. When they would come to Vourles, they would always be dressed the same way. My mother always wore a dress or a skirt and blouse. My father wore a dark suit, a shirt and tie, and his dark rimmed eyeglasses. Clothes hung on him loosely because he had lost weight from the lack of food. In fact, we were all pretty skinny.

Once, while my parents were visiting, there was a huge air raid in the middle of the night. The Allies were bombing the Germans, who were camped out in the valley behind Vourles, and it was frightening. The Allies lit up the valley with flares deployed on parachutes. One of them landed on the schoolhouse roof. The noise from the bombing woke me, and through the window I could see part of the parachute draped over the edge of the roof. I was terrified because I had been told that the flares could blow up. I started screaming, "We have to get out, it is going to explode." My parents tried to comfort me and insisted that it was ok. There was no need to go to the school cellar that night because the Allies were ignoring the village and concentrating on the German troops in the valley. When the raid was over, I went back to sleep. The next morning, after some men took the parachute off the roof, my mother, seamstress that she was, helped some women make blouses out of the silk. One of them she gave to Mrs. Sabathier.

I dreaded the Sundays when I had to see my parents head back to Lyon. Their eyes would fill and shine with tears. I was insecure, afraid and lonely, and didn't want them to leave. Today they call that condition "separation anxiety." I would have called it "separation terror." Every time my parents left me, it broke our hearts because we never knew if we would ever see each other again. I shed rivers of tears and developed physical pains in my chest. Even now, when I become nostalgic or say good-bye to a loved one, I get that same sensation. I often fear it will be the last time I see them, but I try hard not to show it.

Though it was clear that our time apart was difficult for Maman, she took the situation with her usual aplomb and strength of character. On the other hand, Papa had a very difficult time of it. I can only imagine the torment and sadness my parents felt when they had to leave me in Vourles. They had to walk the seven miles to the outskirts of Lyon, and that took several hours, before they could catch the bus home. It must have been so difficult mentally and physically for them to go through that. Of course, for me, the weekends we had together were wonderful.

I don't remember when I realized it, but each time my parents came to see me, they were taking risks. It was dangerous because they never knew who was going to ask for their papers or whether they would be arrested on trumped up charges. There was one time that Mr. Sabathier took me along while he went on an errand to Lyon, so that I could spend some time with my parents. We went on his motorcycle, and I sat behind him, hanging on to his waist. After I spent a few happy hours in Lyon, I cried my eyes out before leaving. But I dutifully climbed back on the motorcycle, again put my arms around Mr. Sabathier's waist, and we were off. About half way to Vourles, a German roadblock appeared in the distance.

My protector, partisan that he was, had no intention of being stopped or questioned by the *Boches* and having his papers examined. He was determined to get through it. He told me to hang on tight because he was going to speed up and either crash through the barrier or go around it. I closed my eyes, squeezed him as tightly as I could, holding my breath until I could feel the blood pounding in my head. I concentrated everything I had in making sure that my arms wouldn't budge from around my human anchor, even if we went flying through the air.

**Philip and Jean Sabathier in Vourles, 1944**

**Jean and Mrs. Sabathier with Pressel family in Vourles, 1944**

And that's exactly what Mr. Sabathier did. He gunned the motor and practically flew that motorcycle around the barrier. I heard yells of surprise behind me, then seconds later the unmistakable sound of gunshots, as we sped away, zigzagging down the road to avoid the bullets aimed at us. Luckily the Germans missed and never bothered sending troops after us, so we managed to arrive safely in Vourles. It was more than enough excitement for me. That was the first and last time I ever rode a motorcycle or was shot at.

From the hills around the town, the Maquis constantly harassed the German troops by sniping at them with high-powered rifles and guns as they passed through the valley. I even remember doing my fair share for the resistance by once carrying a bandolier of machine gun bullets for the good guys.

The Germans didn't take the attacks passively. They responded with vicious reprisals. One afternoon, Jean, Mrs. Sabathier, and I were sitting in the dining room when we heard the ominous rumble of trucks and armored carriers approaching. We peeked through the dining room curtains at the scene unfolding in the town square below us. I stood to the right side of one window, behind the wall, trying not to be seen from the street. The sounds were coming from the road just to the left of our building.

An open truck filled with German soldiers manning four machine guns entered the square in front of the church. The machine guns were aimed in all four directions, one on each side of the truck. I knew they were German by their helmets, the well-known German helmets. These were the helmets where the bottom portion around the back of the head curls out slightly to ward off rain. American helmets came straight down. The soldiers manning the guns were either lying prone or kneeling, their eyes glued to the sights of their guns. Several armored cars followed the open truck, packed with soldiers and machine guns. Other troops on foot marched into the square behind them.

I was so petrified I could hardly breathe. We did not make a sound. I remember the thundering noise the trucks made as they rolled through the town and the thumping of marching boots on the pavement. The Germans crossed the square and continued down one of the side streets that led north through the village. A minute or two passed, the motors got quiet, and then we heard the staccato blasts of machine gun fire.

A few minutes later, when the shooting ceased, the rumble of the trucks echoed through the alleys and then faded in the distance. When we were sure the Germans were gone for good, we went out, and saw about a dozen villagers lying dead in the side street—men, women, and children. The Germans had mown them down without mercy in reprisal for the Maquis' actions. They wanted to prove that resistance was futile. They failed.

It was sheer luck that Jean and I were in the apartment and not playing in the square when the Germans came. The terror of those moments still lives with me. There are times I imagine I can smell the odor of burnt sulfur, the acrid smell of gun smoke that filled the air in the aftermath of the slaughter. I developed an extreme hatred for the German-style helmet, and to this day, if I see a motorcyclist wearing a Nazi-style helmet, I get angry towards him or her. Unfortunately, those helmets are part of the current "biker" fashion scene.

Jean and I remained lucky. Whenever the German army came through the village on foot or in troop carriers, Jean and I were never outside. German officers riding in motorcycle sidecars escorted the soldiers. I remember vividly that we had to stay absolutely quiet and that no one was allowed to speak as long as the Army was around. If we had to urinate, we had to do it silently, something that was not so easy to accomplish.

As the Allies advanced from North Africa through the South of France in 1944, there were more and more air attacks by the Allies on the German convoys passing through the valley. We would stand in the living room during the day and watch the planes drop their payloads onto the convoys. The big dark shapes that seemed to float to the ground, then explode, entranced me. The planes also used machine gunners to strafe the troop columns. I was sitting on the sofa in the living room when a stray bullet came through the open window on my right and imbedded itself in the wall above my head. We instantly hit the floor and stayed down for quite a while. Then we went back to watching the attacks and saw many disabled German vehicles burning. Smoke rose from spots all over the valley.

The day after the Allies destroyed the German vehicles, Mrs. Sabathier took Jean and me down the hill, fairly close to the site of the devastation. We avoided the bomb craters, but the smell of smoke permeated everything, along with the stench of burned rubber from the overturned remains of vehicles and the dead soldiers thrown about the valley. The sight was similar to a scene I saw many years later in the film "Patton." There, the infamous general observes the remains of destroyed and smoking vehicles on a battlefield in France.

The German convoys were always intent on moving forward, and the Maquis were just as intent on harming them as much as possible. They continued to snipe at the German troops from the hills and detonate mines as the German trucks passed over them.

Then there was the weekend my father saved the town from certain destruction. My parents were staying with me in the two-room schoolhouse when a German convoy began passing through. The phone in the *Mairie* rang, and was answered by people who spoke no German. It was the German commander in charge of the troops that were passing through, and he wanted to deliver a message to the Maquis.

My father was the only one around who spoke German. Since that was known in the town hall, and he was literally next door, the townsfolk asked him to take the phone call. I remember clearly that my father was very reluctant to do so, but did it anyway. The general told him he was issuing a warning to the people of Vourles. The sniping had to stop immediately or he would stop the convoy and use cannon fire to destroy the village entirely. My father relayed the German threat to the Maquis leadership, who in this instance, held their fire until the convoy went through.

One afternoon in Vourles, Jean and I were playing in the square and heard aircrafts buzz overhead. We looked up and saw two planes chasing a third. By then, we could tell the difference between Allied and German aircrafts, and we realized we were watching two Allied fighters shooting at a German one. They were so close we could hear the machine-gun chatter. As we ran into the house for safety, we looked up and saw the German craft take a direct hit. Black smoke was spewing from the plane as it started spiraling down. Then, it smashed into the bottom of the hillside near the railroad tracks, about half a mile from our house. Jean and I and some of the men from town rushed down to the crash site to examine the wreckage, but there was no sign of life. The men kept Jean and me away from the plane, but I did find a button I assume came from the pilot's uniform. I kept the button for a long time, but over the years somehow managed to lose it.

After D-Day, June 6, 1944, and the liberation of France, the Maquis were no longer afraid of reprisals. They continued their guerilla warfare more intensely than ever. They once caught two young German soldiers, stragglers from a convoy that had just gone through the valley, shot them on the spot and invited the men of the town to view the bodies. Jean and I went down there with some of the men. We saw the bodies lying on the ground face up. I will never forget how some of the men unbuttoned their flies and urinated on the bodies.

There was joy as the liberation progressed. The American troops coming up from North Africa came through the valley. Maman had given me a small cloth French flag, three vertical stripes of red white and blue fabric that she had stitched together. With a blue colored pencil, I drew General Charles DeGaulle's Cross of Lorraine, the symbol of the Free French Army, on the central white stripe. It consisted of one vertical line and a short horizontal line about one third down from the top and a longer horizontal line one third of the way up from the bottom. Then I went down to the valley with other townspeople to wave at and cheer the American troops as they went by. I waved that flag with all my might, and they threw Hershey bars at us. It was unforgettable. I still have that flag—it is a little tattered, but it's the only souvenir I have left from Europe—other than my memories and my father's letters.

Another holdover in my mind from those days is the theme song of the Maquis, which I learned soon after coming to Vourles. It is a lovely song and occasionally I hum or whistle it to myself. The words translated from the French mean the following:

> *Friend, do you hear the black flight of the crows on the plain?*
> *Friend, do you hear the deaf noise of the country that one is chained in?*
> *Oh supporters, workers and peasants, this is the alarm!*
> *This evening the enemy will know the price of blood and tears.*
>
> *Climb out of the mine, descend the hills, friends.*
> *Get out the rifles, machine guns, grenades out of the straw;*
> *Oh marksmen, use the bullet and use the knife, strike fast!*
> *Oh saboteur, dynamite your burdens!*
>
> *It is us that break the bars of the prisons, for our brothers,*
> *At the heels of our troubles and the hunger that pushes us, misery.*
> *It belongs to countries where people in the hollow of their beds dream*
> *Here you see, we marched and we killed and we died*
>
> *Here each one knows what he wants, what he does as he goes along*
> *Friend, if you fall, friend get out of the shadow of where you are.*
> *Tomorrow black blood will dry from the large sun on the roads*
> *Whistle companions, liberty listens to us in the night.*

From the beginning of July 1944 until near the end of August I did not see Mr. Sabathier. I found out much later the reason for this. He had been denounced. A collaborator told the Gestapo that he was working with the Maquis. One of his tasks with the Maquis was to be a liaison person and deliver documents. He hid these in the heel of his shoes. He was arrested by the Gestapo and imprisoned in the Montluc prison. There, Mr. Sabathier was interrogated and beaten. He was put in a cell and was only let out for 15 minutes a day. Near the end of August 1944, the Allied armies coming up from Northern Africa were liberating France. There were approximately 1200 prisoners. On the evening of August 24, 1944, at around 8 PM, they were released by the remaining Wehrmacht guards. I was not aware of the joy for the Sabathier family, but was told later when he arrived home, and walked up the stairs, Mrs. Sabathier remarked upon his absolutely white complexion. He had not been in the sun for his total time of imprisonment of 55 days. He had also lost about 40 pounds.

Mr. Sabathier had been scheduled to be either executed soon or to be deported to a camp in Germany. As a matter of fact, in the middle of August, the Nazis killed and deported many people from the St. Genis-Laval area nearby. It turned out that three members of the Maquis and citizens of Vourles were killed by the Germans. Mr. Sabathier was lucky to survive.

# 5

## JOYFUL RETURN TO MY PARENTS

The time finally came when children were allowed back into Lyon and I could leave Vourles to return full time to my parents. I left Vourles for good on August 28, just four days after Mr. Sabathier returned from prison. I know that my parents were eternally grateful to the Sabathier family for sheltering me, and for most likely saving my life. What joy for me and for my parents! We were finally back together again!

Life in Lyon was a little easier once the hostilities ended, though food rationing was still in effect and many basic provisions were scarce. My mother still gave me half red wine, half water to drink, and I continued to drink coffee with condensed milk. In fact, I liked to eat condensed milk by the spoonful, right out of the can. That wasn't my only pleasure. Now that the arrests and deportations were almost over, my father would often take me to the park. I went back to the school across the Rhone, taking the little boat to cross the river because the bridges were still down.

My biggest thrill came soon after I returned, when I finally received my own toys. Somehow my parents had managed to buy me my very own bicycle, with training wheels that I immediately wanted removed. My father took them off, and I quickly learned to ride. Until then, I had had no real toys, only makeshift or make-believe ones. In many ways I had been robbed of childhood joys, its normal activities and joys, but I tried to make up for it. Soon our daily routine became post-war "normal."

There was still danger. My Aunt Ella, my mother's sister, decided to leave Belgium to visit us in Lyon and her Aunt Jeanne and Uncle Jacques in Argenton. She made the trip by train and by hitchhiking. Along the way, she had a narrow escape. She was on a streetcar near Lyon when it was caught in "*une raffle*." A German officer boarded the streetcar from the front and another one boarded from the back. She had her false papers, but was afraid to be interrogated. She was very near the middle of the streetcar, and when the first officer asked for her papers, she told him, "The other officer already looked at them." What chutzpah! And she got away with it!

The liberation was not bomb-free. There were occasional air raids and several prolonged bombardments of the city. One afternoon, I stood on our narrow balcony and watched a procession of coffins pass by our apartment house. The coffins were transported in open–bed trucks, all different sizes; I was shocked to see so many tiny ones, obviously for children. The procession went on for hours. My mother explained to me that most of the deceased had been killed during the Allied bombings. They could have been innocent bystanders or French or German workers and soldiers in the factories, railroad trains, or German troop concentrations that were targeted. It made me very sad to see so much death. By then, I understood that to die was the end of life and everything that goes with it. I knew nothing about heaven, hell, or an afterlife. Then, in late 1944, as we stood on the same balcony, we watched an endless retreat of German troops in trucks, armored carriers and tanks.

In the summer of 1944, weeks after D-Day, we heard Jewish orphans were arrested in the Paris area, deported to Auschwitz, and gassed. It was pure luck that our false papers were never detected and that no one knew we were Jewish. In fact, I *still* did not know I was Jewish.

As the liberation came closer to Lyon, the police asked us to come to headquarters. My mother wouldn't allow my father to go, and determined to handle whatever the matter might be in her own way. She dressed up in her finest clothes, put on her makeup and a hat, ready to face her adversaries. She walked into the police station, with lots of bravado, and demanded to know: "What is this all about?"

The police office told her our papers were not in order. They could not find proof of registration in Lille, the northern city close to Belgium that we listed as our place of origin. Maman, who kept her stoic composure, asked a basic, logical question: "What do you expect me to do about that? They probably bombed Lille and the original papers were destroyed."

Instead of arresting her, they agreed with her logic, and said they would continue to see if they could find the registration. They kept our papers, and Maman walked out with her head high. She had grown up in a lovely, sheltered, generous, calm, upper-middle-class Jewish Orthodox home in Antwerp, Belgium, but had backbone and knew how to keep cool under stress and think on her feet. My *"Yiddishe Mama"* was anything but the stereotype meek little old Jewish lady with a nagging accent. She presented herself as a strong French housewife. Her resolve to keep us alive and together made her aggressive, self-reliant, and instantaneously responsive to crises. She came home and told us what had happened. Then she rhetorically asked Papa, "What are we going to do when they find out that we didn't come from Lille?"

There was a man of their acquaintance, a sympathetic Christian in the neighborhood, who frequented the barbershop nearby. Mother thought he could be trusted, so she went down to the barbershop to look for him and then invited him to come up to the apartment. My parents explained to him that our papers were false and that we were being closely watched by the police. They asked him if there was anything we should do, and he told them "Don't do a thing, I will take care of it."

Mother asked how much it would cost. "Nothing," he said. He apparently had some connection to the police. He went into their headquarters, found our papers, put them in the stove and burned them. That evening, my father took some ham, cheese, and wine given to him by his co-workers, and gave it all to the man. The food was worth a fortune, but he had saved our lives. This all happened just one month before the Germans began their final retreat. During those few harrowing weeks, without our papers, we could have been arrested at anytime.

After the Germans marched through Lyon for the last time, it was no longer necessary for us to hide our identities or get false papers. Lyon was liberated on September 3, 1944.

My father wrote two letters later that month, one letter to Uncle Elie, and one to his niece Susi. They were the first news that anyone had received from us indicating that we were still alive.

On September 28, 1944, my father wrote to Elie.

```
J. Pressel
24 Quai Fulchiron
Lyon, France
September 28, 1944

Mr. E. Schwerner
539 Ocean Parkway
Brooklyn, N.Y.
```

Dear Uncle Elie,

"They are still alive!..."

Yes, we are still alive and we can finally breathe in freedom. We have lived in Lyon since the end of 1942. The city was liberated on September 3. We feel like the survivors of a cataclysm. The joy of feeling free is profound, but we have seen too much suffering, and we worry a great deal about those dear to us whose fate is unknown, before our joy can be complete.

It is almost a miracle that we were able to survive safe and sound from this torture. For the past two years, human life has counted for nothing. Perhaps later we will have the opportunity to tell you in more detail all that we went through.

On November 11, 1942, we saw the arrival of German troops in Marseille, and we had to wait until August, 1944 in Lyon, to see the withdrawal of this army, in endless ranks in front of our house, while being routed and pursued by the Allied armies coming up from the south of France.

What a relief! We waited for so long, and so fervently hoped for deliverance. Our son was evacuated to the countryside last May under mandatory order to be sheltered from the bombings. We joined him on the 28th of August to be together no matter what would happen. The village where we found ourselves was already in the hands of the French resistance.

The French Army of the Interior was all around us, attacking the German troops. Also, in the distance we could see the Allied planes diving and strafing the German convoys and dropping their bombs on the enemy trucks. The village was caught in a cross-fire and for several days we lived in an agonizing situation.

Anyway, the essential thing for the moment is that we can tell you that we three are safe and sound and happy that we were able to save our little Philippe - who is now 7 years old and who never lost hope— and who had confidence in everything that we had to do to shelter him from harm.

Concerning other members of the family:

Since the battle for France, postal communications were halted and are still not normal, so we are waiting for news from various places. We were therefore very happy to a letter today with the news that Jacques and Jeanne Schwerner are in good health. They are still in Argenton- sur-Creuse. Ady is still in Toulouse and intends to rejoin her parents soon. Edmee is in Switzerland.

Harry (Schwerner), as you probably know, was arrested in 1942 at the Spanish border just as he was intending to resume his Belgian military service; he was interned for several months in a camp in Drancy (near Paris) and was subsequently deported. We have not heard from him since.

Licy, the eldest daughter, and her husband and two children are also safe and sound. We have not heard recently from the

Kincler family. You probably don't know it but unfortunately their daughter was deported in August 1942; little Irene stayed with her grandparents during the whole time. Jacques was also arrested but was able to escape in time and went underground; we last heard from him about two months ago. We hope that we will soon learn that he too was able to celebrate freedom with his parents.

We have not heard from Belgium for about 6 months. At this time my in-laws, as well as Ella, were still there and we hope that they are safe and sound. My mother, unfortunately, was deported in 1942 and I have not heard about her fate; my sister and her husband were also taken in 1942 to "a destination unknown."

Will I ever see them again?

Norbert, his wife and child underwent the same sad fate, as well as Ella's husband, Naphtali Landenberg. Prior to their deportation, he and Norbert were able to communicate several times. My wife's uncles, who were in France, were deported... It is an unending list. My wife would have liked to go to Belgium immediately to see her parents, except that train travel is not yet possible, and going by road is an expense that we cannot afford.

Since I have only your address, Uncle Elie, I cannot write to any other members of the family, therefore I ask you to please send this letter to my family in New York, to Miryam's two sisters, and to all the good friends who have asked about us during these hard war years.

We would like to know how you all spent these last few years, if you are in good health, what you are doing, and what are your plans for the future? Where are Ruth and Sonia? How are the children, etc.?

We do not intend to stay in Lyon long, but we do not know yet where we will go. Like before, we do not know how long it takes for correspondence to go from France to the USA and back, so I ask you to please note that all correspondence sent to us should be temporarily sent to: Societe Emile PRAT & FILS, for J. Pressel, 24 Quai Fulchiron, Lyon, France. If we leave here, the Societe will forward our mail.

Hoping that we soon receive detailed news from you, we send you our best wishes and kisses,

Yours,

Jos, Mir and Philippe

My dear all,

We have returned to life; let us hope that our dear parents are also safe and sound, as well as brother, sister, sister-in-law, and brother-in-law, mentioning only the immediate family. You cannot realize the good fortune of all those who did not have to live in Europe for the last two years. As far as the future is concerned, we cannot make any plans, but I want to return to Belgium as fast as possible.

Write to us quickly if possible, it has been so long since we have heard any news from the family that every letter gives us a great deal of pleasure.

A thousand kisses to divide among you all.

Yours,

Mir

I would like to see you all again. I send you lots of kisses for both cheeks.

Philippe

On September 26, 1944 he wrote the following letter to Susi:

**24 Quai Fulchiron**
**Lyon**
**September 26, 1944**

Dear Susi,

I just learned that postal communications with England have resumed. Therefore I am writing to you immediately and hope that I remember your address correctly and that these lines reach you.

So many events happened since our last correspondence during the first half of 1942! *(Note: No letters exist or were received by Susi after the one dated 4-20-41).* How are you dear Susi and what did you do during all of this time? We hope that you are in good health, as well as you husband, your in-laws and the whole family, and that you valiantly held up emotionally. Write us quickly because we would like to know if you are safe and sound. You can obviously write to us in English if that is easier for you.

I know quite well how worried you must have been about the fate of your parents from whom you probably haven't heard in two years. Unfortunately we also cannot reassure you of their fate because we ourselves are without news about them since August 26, 1942. During June 1942 I visited them in Nice and we were together for two days. On August 8, 1942 in the "non occupied zone" of France, thousands of people were taken and interned for several days in camps or buildings and then deported. I was able to learn that your parents were on a list of people who were transferred to a destination unknown, probably in Germany or Poland. Since then, without stop tens of thousands of people suffered the same fate and despite all efforts to determine the fate of those deported, it is impossible to learn what is going on. Even the Red Cross was not able to get the least bit of information about them. The end of the war is approaching; let us hope that that your parents were able to survive the suffering and that you and us will hear that they survived unharmed through the terrible upheaval that shook the continent. My father died at the beginning of 1941 at the hands of the boches; unfortunately my mother was also deported around the months of October or November 1942, without me having gotten any news about her fate. Will I ever see her again? Thus in all families there are cruel voids that have been formed and we do not know yet the extent of the disaster that the Nazis perpetrated on the world.

I will not write to you now all that we went through for the last two years; perhaps later we will have the occasion to tell you all of that. But it is a miracle that we were able to survive, my wife and child (whose is now seven years old) and me, to come out unharmed from all of the innumerable dangers that menaced us day and night. Needless to tell you the relief that we felt, thanks to the advancing Allied armies, when the German troops of occupation started to pack their baggage and then flee. For 15 days, we saw uninterrupted caravans of the German army coming up from the South, withdrawing, and file by our house. This was followed by the joy of finally being able to breath freely. Lyon, where we lived for the last two years was liberated on September 3.

We are waiting anxiously for news of my wife's parents, who approximately six months ago were still in Belgium; however since then we have received no news about them. It is still very hard these days to go to Belgium; otherwise my wife would already have made the trip. I am working here as a secretary/administrator in a company that has affiliates in London. It is La Societe Prat Daniel Ltd, but I do not count on staying with them for long. We will probably leave for Paris or Brussels, but meanwhile you can always write to me at the address at the top of this letter.

For today, I will end this first episode of contact, hoping that this letter finds you in good health, and send you, dear Susi, and all of you dear ones, our best wishes and many kisses.

Jos Pressel and family

We were hoping that the war would be over before the year was out. Our lives were no longer at risk. We were not afraid of getting arrested or deported every time we ventured outside. My father's firm moved back to Paris, and it was time for us to move there, too.

# 6

# PARIS & ASNIERES

**Paris**
**February 20, 1945**

Dear Susi,
    We were very happy to get your nice letters, especially with the news that you had a little daughter. Congratulations and happiness to you and the family. Without this horrible war, our little Philippe who is already 7 1/2 years old would probably have had a little sister. We are happy for the three of us to be together because we escaped many dangers.
    We are feeling alright, considering how much we suffered from the cold this winter

without any coal. Also uncle Jos' hands and feet suffer from frostbite and he has bronchitis. All will heal with better weather hopefully soon.

Philippe is feeling fairly well. Unfortunately he lacks many ingredients of basic nourishment. Susi you ask if the little one lacks anything. Happily you cannot imagine what we lack in France; especially for growing children. However we don't complain because we always think of those who were deported whose fate is a thousand times worse. I don't know if we will ever see my brother Norbert with his wife and adorable little daughter who were deported, and so many other young cousins without even speaking of the adults.

Myriam

In November 1944, we moved from Lyon to Asnieres, a suburb north of Paris, approximately fifteen minutes away by commuter train. We rented a room in an apartment two blocks from the railroad station, at #5 Rue Waldeck Rousseau, a house of large horizontal stones and yellow-brown bricks. We were on the second floor of a six-story building that had black grills about eight inches high on all the windows. Mademoiselle Louise Poupard, a spinster in the classic sense, was our landlady. The apartment consisted of her bedroom, a narrow kitchen, a small living room, a bathroom and a bedroom for us. My small bed was at the foot of my parents' double bed.

At first, my father, who commuted to Paris daily, continued working at *Prat et Fils*, but several months later quit to take two jobs. He translated copy in a publisher's office and worked as a journalist for a local newspaper.

My mother was having a difficult time because of our lack of privacy. If we wanted to find a better place to live, it would cost us thousands of francs, and that was out of the question. Food was still rationed—there were major shortages and coal was scarce. It didn't help that the approaching winter gave all signs of being a harsh one. Our heat came from a wood and charcoal stove in the middle of the living room that left a smoky smell in the air. We were always very cold and often sat around the stove, bundled up in our heaviest clothes. That's probably why, to this day, I hate being cold and have never enjoyed the "advantages" of a fireplace.

```
Paris
March 21, 1945

Dear Susi,

    For three weeks we haven't touched a
gram of meat, etc. It is like a great
penance, as you can see, and yet we are
happy to be rid of the Boches. For that
alone it is worth the deprivations, and yet
we know that in this murdered Europe there
are many others who suffer more than we.

                                    Jos
```

My diet remained meager. Meat, eggs and chocolate were rare treats. Once, I was given a small pack of chewing gum and was able to savor it for weeks by chewing one stick at a time. When I had enough, I put the ABC (already been chewed) gum back in its wrapper for a few days and then chewed it again. Toilet paper was a luxury. We used cut up newspapers for that. If we felt sorry for ourselves, we reminded ourselves that there were others, who suffered much more. This always put things in perspective. It could have been much worse, and we knew it. I was almost 8 years old, in my seventh school. My father was suffering from bronchitis and frostbite, and my mother desperately wanted to get me proper food.

My parents sent me to a school called *College Giband*, located in Bois Colombes, the adjoining suburb. The school had yellow concrete walls and was surrounded by a high, spiked metal fence. If you want a "feel" for what the town was like, the soccer match in the movie "Victory," starring Sylvester Stallone and Michael Caine, was filmed in the stadium there, and nothing much has changed in the intervening years.

Although many schools required children to wear uniforms, the *College Giband* did not, so I wore my usual short pants and high socks. My mother occasionally trimmed my full head of dark brown hair. I combed it myself most of the time, and parted it on the left side.

When we first came to Asnieres, I was still afraid to be alone and wanted my father to bring me to school and take me home. After a few weeks, I became daring and decided I wanted to go to school by myself. Usually, I would walk, but once in a while I would take the train for one stop. By today's standards, I guess I remained a good student and Maman saved the report cards and gave them to me. Some of the written comments include: "good worker," "serious worker," "he can do better," "good behavior," "sloppy handwriting," "too much talking." Schoolwork kept me so busy I had no time to feel lonely.

A few years ago, my wife, Pat, and I visited *College Giband*, and impressed the headmistress with my saved report cards. She gave us a tour of the school, and from what I remembered of it in my childhood, it had barely changed. The desks were the same—with wood tops that tilted open to store school supplies inside. The *pissoirs* (urinals) in the courtyard were still there, too.

Because we were in the suburbs, thankfully, we didn't get caught in the final battle for Paris. There were still blackouts almost every night, and we had learned to live by candlelight. During the few hours a day that we had electricity, my father listened to our landlady's radio to see if he could get the BBC from London and hear about the advances of the Allied armies.

Some relatives and friends, who had escaped to France from Belgium or survived deportations, came to visit us. I met many people with concentration camp tattoos on their arms. One of them, my parents' old friend from Belgium, had been a champion runner. He came back from Auschwitz near the end of war and I have never been able to figure out how he found us. We sat down by candlelight to our little bit of supper, and he told us about his experiences in that hell-hole. He described a nightmare that was worse than anything we could imagine, and he told us what people did to survive.

Though I was a little kid, I had seen, experienced, and heard plenty about the war but these stories were shocking. I heard what he was telling us, but I had trouble believing it, it was so horrible. I had been having occasional nightmares, but after that night, I had them more often and my mother would comfort me when I woke screaming in the night. She would rub my back, until I fell back asleep.

My father had been corresponding with his niece, Suzi, in London for several months. In April 1945 he wrote to her and included a comment about U.S. President Franklin Delano Roosevelt's death.

**Paris
April 14, 1945**

Dear Susi,

...Yesterday we got the sad news of President Roosevelt's death. We joyfully welcomed his armies.

Imagine! It has been years since we have had any real soap; the brick of American soap you sent in the package was received like an old friend whose face was almost forgotten.

On V-E Day, May 7, 1945 he wrote to her again:

We have finally come to the end of this long and awful nightmare. We congratulate you for having escaped the danger and to have reached this memorable day safe and sound. On the Place de la Concorde, we took part in the proclamation of the end of hostilities, followed by national anthems, sirens blaring, artillery salutes, bells chiming in all the churches of Paris. Immediately after that we walked up the Champs Elysees to the Arc de Triomphe and the tomb of the Unknown Soldier from the other war. It was a sea of humanity, augmented by innumerable airplanes flying overhead. Numerous youths boarded Jeeps and military vehicles and roamed all over Paris. Unfortunately our thoughts cannot be separated from all of those whose lives were taken from us during this horrible storm, and it is of them that we think,

> more of than the victory that we wanted
> them to share.
>     ...Along with huge crowds we saw the
> military marching with flags. The whole
> city watched. You will see these
> celebrations in the newsreels. Among
> hundreds of thousands of people, I am here
> with Philippe on my shoulders, but do not
> try to find us in the enormous crowds.

I remember very well sitting on the curb in my short pants, in front of my father, and then being lifted and riding on his shoulders at the famous victory parade, when General Charles DeGaulle marched down the Champs Elysees. There were thousands of people, including many who climbed what was left of the trees for a better view. The French marching music was loud and joyous.

For my eighth birthday, my parents gave me *Chasseurs De Fauve,* a wonderful set of four books about the jungle and big game hunters. I used to lie on my belly on a small thick multi-colored rug in front of the living room window, reading endlessly. I was so engrossed in the material that I had to be called several times before I would come to the dinner table. My other entertainment was to play cards with our spinster landlady, Louise. I had no friends my own age because I was still afraid to go out alone, and just after the war things were still not conducive to socializing.

Whenever I went out with my parents, I always held their hands. When we were walking outdoors, if we became separated, instead of calling us, my mother would whistle at us in her own distinctive manner. Like a code, it was four quick notes, high-low, high-low. She used this call until her old age.

Occasionally my father would take me to the park, where I would play on the swings or on the merry-go-round you pushed yourself. Our outings were very precious to me. We would sit on a bench and he would tell me very inventive stories, many of them about cowboys, and Buffalo Bill in particular.

One time, as we walked back home from the park, we saw two cars sideswipe each other. One flipped over and came to rest on its side, with its wheels still spinning, which absolutely fascinated me. People came rushing up to the vehicles to help the passengers and drivers climb out. Any fear I felt right then was like nothing compared to the fear I felt in

Vourles during the bombardments. I was starting to learn about perspective.

With the war finally over, my parents felt it was time to tell me I was a Jew. It took quite some time for me to understand the concept of religion and being Jewish. My father told me about the important Jewish holidays and gave me two books to read. One was a book of Hanukah stories and the other was about Jewish biblical legends, both in French. Frankly, I preferred to read about Babar the elephant and the wild animals in my jungle books, and I didn't know whether to believe the stories—but my father somehow managed to instill me with pride in being Jewish.

The years of malnutrition had taken their toll on our bodies, but we were fortunate not to have gotten seriously ill. When Papa had bronchitis, my mother used a very old-fashioned remedy—glass ampoules, which were small jars, filled with cotton soaked in alcohol. She lit the cotton, let it burn a bit, blew it out and placed the hot ampoules on my father's back. The heat and the vacuum generated were supposed to draw blood to the area to help heal and loosen the congestion in the lungs. He eventually recovered, but I don't know if it was due to my mother's treatment. I have since learned that these ampoules are called *bankes* in Yiddish, and they were a traditional remedy.

My father's immune system wasn't working well; he was prone to infections and developed boils on his neck. Maman and I just didn't have enough food for strength and energy, but somehow, Maman was very tough. Despite her weak physical condition, she worked very hard and did the shopping, carrying all the bags herself. And as food and meat became more available and affordable, we slowly regained our weight and strength.

One of my parents' post-war treats was to take me to the movies. I got to see some Charlie Chaplin movies and enjoyed them a lot. I found the newsreels interesting, even when they showed awful things, like the collaborators who were caught in France being shaved, paraded in front of jeering crowds and, in some cases, shot. The terrible newsreels showing the liberation of the concentration camps caused my parents' agonizing pain.

My mother learned from Ella that her parents had survived and she was desperate to go to Belgium to see them. In late spring of 1945 we hitchhiked to Antwerp because traveling by train was unaffordable and unreliable. We still had no identity papers, but no one seemed to care, at least for the moment. We looked rather ragged—Papa's clothes still hung on him, and Maman had patched all of our clothing many times.

When we arrived at my grandparents' house, none of that really mattered. The reunion with Maman's parents, Moses and Leah Schwerner, was very emotional and joyful. I didn't remember them from my early childhood, but I loved being hugged hard by Aunt Ella and my grandparents. It was a little odd being kissed by my grandfather, who had a beard and mustache, but it was still wonderful. We found out that my mother's sisters Ruth and Sonia and their families had gone from Cuba to New York City soon after the war. My father's brother Jules, who was a medic on cargo ships, survived and returned to Belgium. We reunited with him and some other relatives and friends. Sadly, many others did not survive.

We also found out that Uncle Jacques and his family in Argenton, France, where I had stayed for a while, had survived. His daughter Ady wrote a letter to Uncle Elie in New York after the war in which she said:

```
Dear Uncle Elie,

    Did you know that I left mother, father,
and Edmee in 1943? The police of Argenton
were very friendly, and they warned that I
better "disappear". I lived under false
identity. I "became" a teacher in a convent,
then with a private family. After numerous
adventures, I joined the Resistance (the
army of DeGaulle). After the August
liberation I entered the OSE (Oeuvre de
Secours aux Enfants-Work to Rescue the
Children), where I was an administrative
assistant- very interesting work- with
amicable relations with my bosses and
colleagues.


                     Ady
```

At the time, my grandparents lived at 303 Lange Leemstraat in a three-story brownstone. It was almost across the street from #328, where they had lived before the war. That place had been completely ransacked by Germans looking for hidden valuables. The Nazis had ripped up the floorboards and destroyed the house. I couldn't blame my grandparents for not wanting to go back there. Their home at #303 was wonderful anyway and I loved it. During the war they were sheltered by the Queen of Belgium, along with many other elderly Jews, in a home for the aged.

The living room had a Delft fireplace and leather chairs. A shiny wooden banister ran down three stories from the top floor to the front foyer, and I used to slide all the way down, slowing only for the sharp turns. There was a redwood-lined veranda with a large window and door leading to a small back yard that boasted four rattan easy chairs. I used to put two chairs face-to-face and then turn the other two upside down directly over them to create a shelter where I could hide.

My grandparents were able to get enough food for all of us, and we made the best of it. Between the veranda and dining room/living room was the kitchen, a little piece of heaven. There was a wonderful aroma of rich cakes in the air. My grandmother, a terrific cook, was always preparing meals or baking cakes and would let me help. She used lots of eggs, cream and sugar, delicacies I was not used to. She was a wonderful kind lady who let me lick the bowls after she was done. Sometimes I even helped her decorate her mocha cream cakes by squeezing the cream out of a tube. To this day, mocha cream cake remains my favorite.

We stayed with my grandparents. My parents had their own bedroom, and I was given the spare bedroom on the third floor. There were some life sketches of female nudes on the walls that I enjoyed looking at, but I hoped my parents would not come upstairs. I would be embarrassed—and I never mentioned the pictures to anyone—but I realized that someone must have known they were there.

In the few weeks we spent with my grandparents, my grandfather taught me much more about being Jewish. He took me to synagogue and taught me some Hebrew and a few basic prayers. He also bought me new clothes and shoes.

After dinner, most evenings, the adults would sit around the table and talk about the war and all the things that had happened to them and their friends. I sat quietly and listened. My grandparents also played host to several neighbors and friends who had been deported and survived. They had tattoos on their left forearms, and that again made quite an impression on me, but I was very shy and didn't ask questions. I just made sure that I sat very close to one of my parents, so I would feel secure.

My parents left me with my grandparents for a few days to go to Brussels to check out their old apartment on the Rue des Adriatique. Their landlord had taken everything that belonged to them and refused to return anything, except my mother's sewing machine. He felt our possessions were due to him in lieu of rent for the war years! Someone else had been living in the apartment all that time, but the landlord didn't care. Now everything my parents owned before the war was gone, including my father's collection of Zionist speeches that he had transcribed in steno, then translated.

When we returned to Asnieres from Belgium, there was still no news from my father's sister, Charlotte (Susi's mother), or his parents. In October of 1945 he wrote letters to Susi that showed his diminishing hope for his parents, sister, and brother-in-law. The letters still bring tears to my eyes. My father's nature was optimistic and he tried to be strong.

**Asnieres (Seine)**
**October 3, 1945**

My Dear Susi,
.... You, who were in England during the war, may not realize how little human life on the continent meant to the bands of Nazis who invaded it. We saw and learned things about the enemy's fierceness that followed us throughout the war. We were resigned to eventually suffer the worst.

Since the end of the war, day after day, we have learned not to count on the return of our parents or the millions who perished these last few years. Despite this, we still maintain some hope, although it diminishes more and more. Having endured all our experiences and knowing that our lives hung by a thread, we can probably accept more easily than you the misfortunes which befell our family.

We want you, who have the whole future to look forward to, to accept your pain. There is not a single family in Europe without a cruel void; parents without children; children who lost their parents; women who lost their husbands, etc., without counting among the survivors those who lost all that they possessed.

A parents' biggest hope is always to know that their children are happy and it was certainly your parents' desire to know that you were sheltered without worries and that you were happy. If your happiness is temporarily shaken, recover your control and don't get sick by thinking too much about what is irreparable.

I don't know anything else about your parents that I haven't written to you, and so I do not send you my condolences. Considering the immense loss of Jews known to us, tell yourself that your dear parents have gone to a better world, and have left behind them unanimous regrets. Tell yourself that we could not honor their memory in a better way than to give our children the love with which they enveloped us.

I think now of my mother and that she will probably not come back to me. May your dear child, whose name she carries, perpetuate her memory.

Be courageous, dear Susi, and support yourselves in dignity, just as we force ourselves to support ourselves...

Jos

After the war was over, we discovered that my paternal grandfather Samuel Pressel had died at German hands in Belgium, and in 1942, his wife (my grandmother) Helen, was deported and died in Auschwitz. Others deported and gassed in Auschwitz included my mother's brother Norbert, his wife Hilda, and their baby girl, Margot. Also deported were Ella's husband, Nachman Landenberg, my father's sister, Charlotte, her husband Naphtali Hamel (Suzi's parents) and, all of my maternal grandmother Leah's siblings, except three. There were so many dead in our family.

My father kept his emotions locked inside. He was a serious, steady person, and wasn't a type who yelled, or spoke about the war. He'd occasionally use some light French cuss words, mild enough for me to hear, such as nuts and darn. He rarely smiled, unless I said or did something that pleased him. When he found out that so many of our relatives were dead and that millions of Jews had died, he became even more serious.

Even after we arrived in the United States, he didn't smile often and rarely laughed. I am sure this depression contributed to his heart problems. Maman, on the other hand, had no trouble expressing herself, and she laughed easily. In America, at parties, or family get-togethers, I could recognize her laugh from across a room—it had a high-pitched squeal to it. When I wasn't alone, I was a happy kid who loved to laugh. I loved my parents very much and knew that they loved me. Later, I understood and appreciated my father's tenderness and sensitivity. Mother could be strict, but she was also very warm and loving. I was so dependent on my parents that I was well into my adulthood before I finally broke loose. I freely admit I was a mama's boy for a very long time.

Maman was still unhappy in Asnieres and wanted to go to America to join her sisters in New York. She felt that there was no future for us in Europe because the Germans had wrecked it. To her, it didn't feel good to be there. It was heartbreaking for her to leave her parents, but her sisters in New York told her life there would be much better.

My parents both grew up in an environment where education was important and encouraged. My father had always been a Zionist and his enthusiasm was contagious to my mother and eventually to me. They always stressed the importance of learning about Judaism and Zionism, telling me why we had to support Israel and be proud of being Jewish and being an accomplished person. To them this was different from being religious or believing in God. Their heroes were Theodore Herzl, Chaim Weitzman, Abba Eban, Moshe Sharrette, and Harry Truman.

The only time my father ever mentioned living in Israel was in a short sentence in a letter to his niece Suzi right after the war ended in 1945 saying: "We are not sure what we will do next. There is nothing for us in Belgium. Miriam wants to go to New York to be with her sisters. I am thinking perhaps of *Eretz* (Israel)."

My mother has repeatedly told me she would not have agreed to go to Israel. She only wanted to go to New York, and my father reluctantly agreed though he did not really want to live in America. He was very idealistic and did not like the materialistic mentality of America.

I think he did eventually become happy living in America. His goal was to visit Israel, and that we did in the summer of 1951. With the difficult health problems that he had, he knew that he really could not have lived in Israel. It would have been too difficult, and he understood that the best place for him was in New York. When he found out that the United Nations was hiring translators to work in New York, he took the exam and passed.

The publisher in Paris, where my father was still doing translations, offered to match the salary the UN offered, but Maman had had enough of living in one room without privacy. She was also fed up with rationing, so my father accepted the job translating French and Spanish into English for the United Nations Journal and Bureau of Information.

My father left for the States alone so that he could establish himself at the United Nations and find a suitable place for us to live. He was going to make contact with relatives, including my mother's sisters. He sailed for New York City aboard the *USS Washington*, with a diplomatic passport, on September 6, 1946. I still have the wonderful 37-page letter he wrote telling us of his journey. We would follow him a few months later.

# 7

# AMERICA

My mother and I left Cherbourg on the *Ile de France* in the middle of November 1946. I had not been to the seashore since I was 3 years old, so the view of the Atlantic Ocean from the port was new to me. The ocean was so big and the horizon was so far away! The *Ile de France* had been converted into a troop ship, and when we left for New York, it had not yet been converted back to a passenger vessel. It still had very poor accommodations on the lower deck, where we shared a stuffy cabin with two women. After a few days at sea, Papa was able to make arrangements through the United Nations and the ship's purser moved us to a private cabin.

Halfway through the trip I became seasick, and Maman, who, of course, didn't have one bad moment, put her hand on my forehead and held me tightly whenever I threw up. Somehow it always seemed to help.

When I felt better, we spent much of our time in a makeshift lounge or sitting on deck.

We weren't docking at Ellis Island, instead we were going directly to a pier on Manhattan's West Side, and we faced the skyline as we approached the dock. I never did get that first glimpse of the Statue of Liberty that is so much a part of the immigrant experience. Rather, I was taken back by the size of the buildings in New York City.

Papa had used his diplomatic papers to gain access directly to the dock, and I was thrilled to see him waiting for us at the end of the gangplank. He was easy to spot because he was taller than most of the people there. When we finally made it into his arms, he hugged us tightly, and choked back his emotions.

Our luggage had been deposited under a sign with the letter P painted on it, and Papa went to gather our bags, leading us through customs. Afterwards, my mother's two sisters, Sonia Suskin and Ruth Schild, my father's maternal uncle, Henry Piper, and his wife were all there to greet us. The Pipers, amazingly, were long time residents of New Jersey, and somehow, some way, Papa had managed to find them. What tears of joy flowed that day, especially from Maman and her two sisters.

We stood on the street talking for a long time, until finally, Papa took us, by train, to our new American home, a room in a private home in Great Neck, Long Island, near Lake Success—where the UN was first located. The UN didn't move to Manhattan until 1951.

Since housing for UN personnel was not yet ready, we lived on the second floor of a one-family house owned by the Mandels. They weren't very welcoming or pleasant, and refused to give us advice, or help us get accustomed to the local culture. They tried to ignore our existence. My mother found work as a seamstress at Harriet Ligety, a fashionable dress shop in Great Neck, located on the main street, Middle Neck Road. Maman's specialty was fitting dresses for the shop's clients. Both of my parents went to work by bus, because they absolutely could not afford a car. They never learned to drive.

I first attended the Arrandale Elementary School and, by necessity, learned English very quickly. Before he'd left for America, Papa taught me basic English words like thank you, hello, good-bye, and so on, and how to pronounce them. In Europe, I had practiced speaking and reading English with my parents. Now I was forced to use my English and really learn it so I could keep up with my studies and socialize. My teachers seemed quite impressed. I must have had a strong French accent, but it eventually disappeared as I became more "American." It is amazing how being forced to speak and read English helps people learn the language quickly! Now, in my older years, I disapprove of teaching children in their native language instead of in English.

With my parents inculcating me with a love of learning, I became a conscientious student who did my homework immediately after coming home from school. When my homework was done and the weather was nice, I would take a book, find a nice secluded spot in the empty grass lot across the street and read. I also amused myself at home by making plaster animals from molds in an arts and crafts kit one of my aunts gave me. Getting "chores" like homework out of the way became a habit for me, so that even now, I find I always try to take care of business as quickly as possible to free up my time for other things. I became "Americanized" in my manner of dress. For the first time ever, I wore long pants and it felt a little funny, but it also made me feel more like an adult and more like all of the other kids. I was happy about it.

We lived with the Mandels until spring, 1947, when two new apartment buildings were opened for UN employees. We moved to the second floor of 46 Schenck Avenue, a three-story U-shaped red brick building. The entrance to our apartment was by the dining room, which led to a long living room. To the left of the dining room were the kitchen and an alcove. Next to the kitchen was a hallway leading to a bathroom and the bedroom. The windows in the bedroom and the living room overlooked the backyard of a private house.

My parents had saved money to buy furniture and chose simple modern pieces: a sofa, two round chairs and two glass end tables. A rectangular coffee table sat in front of the sofa. We are now in the 21st century and my mother still has one of those round tables! They also purchased a desk so that my father could do some of his work at home. We had a dining room set, a double bed for them, and a single bed for me. For the first time I could remember, I had my very own space—the alcove next to the kitchen. There was no elevator in our building, but that was fine with me.

What amazed us most about America were the supermarkets. Maman was dumbstruck! The abundance of food items and choices was almost overwhelming, but wonderful. We began to eat healthy foods and soon stopped looking like skinny refugees.

For my first birthday in America, in June 1947, my parents thrilled me by getting me an English racer with thin wheels and handbrakes. Most of the kids in the neighborhood were riding around on little Schwinns with fat wheels and foot brakes. To the envy of some of my schoolmates, I often rode my bike to school, instead of taking the school bus. I locked the bike at one of the bike racks. Another sign I was growing up was that my parents began giving me an allowance of 25 cents a week that I squirreled away in a little toy safe.

There was one place in the apartment house where I did like to spend some time—the basement. My bicycle was in a storage room, so I could easily get it to go riding. Next to the laundry room the building management had provided tenants with a recreation room that, even then, had a television set. The screen was tiny, so there was a thick magnifying glass hanging over it to increase the picture size. Since my parents didn't get a television set for another three years, I went down to watch "The Howdy Doody Show" with Buffalo Bob, Clarabell, Mr. Bluster, and Princess Summer Fall Winter Spring. I especially loved watching cartoons.

I would go bike riding around the neighborhood, alone, since most of my friends lived too far away from the house for me to bike or walk there. On weekends, Papa took me on walks and to play in the park. Papa, who was still quite strong, used to demonstrate how to swing on the parallel bars, and he was very good at it. Occasionally I'd ask him to flex his biceps for me, and I was always *very* impressed with his muscles.

Papa knew absolutely nothing about baseball, so I taught him everything I learned from the kids in school and my cousin Sylvan. We played catch in the park. Once in a while, Papa and I played tennis at the neighborhood courts, or he'd take me swimming at the local YMCA. He never got into the pool because he was modest and the men were required to swim naked, so he taught me how to swim from the side. It wasn't until we went on a summer vacation that I realized just how good a swimmer he was. Yet, since we were living on a tight budget, my parents rarely went on vacation.

I do remember one train trip we did take, to St. Agate, Canada, a city north of Montreal. We had come to the U.S. on UN diplomatic papers, and it was time for us to "officially" enter the U.S. so that we could apply for citizenship. That required us to leave the country and then come back in. In addition to the legal reasons for going to Canada, my parents wanted to have a few quiet days to relax. In St. Agate we stayed in a nice large old hotel on a lake. We played ping-pong, went rowing, and took long walks together. Then we "re-entered" the country at Rousses Point, N.Y.

Papa was very lucky. Because of his work at the UN, he had media credentials and got press seats to sports events. They were always good seats, often right up front. He would take me to outdoor track meets on Randall's Island, indoor track meets and boxing at Madison Square

Garden, boxing and soccer matches at the old Polo Grounds, the home of the baseball Giants before they moved to San Francisco.

Some of the famous athletes he took me to see were runners Mal Whitfield, Andy Stanfield, Harrison Dillard, and Bob Richards (all future Olympic gold medal winners). We watched ringside as middleweight boxers Sugar Ray Robinson and Carmen Basilio slugged it out. We saw Irving Mondschein, the national decathlon champion and Henry Laskau, the national race walking champion and world record holder, both future Olympians, in action. Papa knew Henry Laskau because they were in the *Maccabi* athletic club in Antwerp together, and I got to meet him.

My father also took me ice-skating in the winter, to an indoor ice rink in Great Neck. We'd go fishing several times a year—taking the bus to Glen Cove on the north shore of Long Island. We'd rent a rowboat, I would row and we would fish for flounder using sand worms as bait— and I learned to bait my own hook. The fishing in those days was excellent. Several times we came home with multiple dozens of fish. We carried them in several canvas sacks and fed all the neighbors. Maman showed me how to cut, scale and clean the fish, a job that soon became mine. Then Maman would sauté the flounder in butter and it was delicious. She'd also freeze some of the fish so we could enjoy it out of season.

Papa was an avid chess player and collected books by the great chess grandmasters. Chess was his favorite hobby after sports, and he taught me how to play. Sometimes he would take the Long Island Railroad into the city to play at the Manhattan Chess Club on 42$^{nd}$ Street. Once, he met Larry Evans, the American grandmaster, and obtained his autographed photo. It's now one of my treasured possessions, along with Papa's chess books.

I often read or built things with my new Tinkertoy set. Eventually I was given a set of American Flyer electric trains, and I must say, I appreciated those toys with all my heart. Yet, I still hadn't forgotten what life had been like in Europe and how miserable we had been.

Even in those days of budding television, the media was important and always looking for an angle. And so I came to have my first fifteen minutes of fame. Before the television set ruled the universe, there was radio, and many of the personalities on the radio later became television stars. Among them was Allen Ludden, who later became the host of the popular TV game show, Password.

In the mid-1940s, he hosted a radio show called "Mind Your Manners," a program where kids got to talk about their lives, interests and problems. I was invited to participate as one of four panelists in a program featuring the children of UN employees. They asked me what it was like in France during the war and how it felt to come live in America and learn English. After the show was over, Ludden gave me his autograph, and I've saved that, too. The radio show was taped at the UN in Lake Success and aired the next day. When I heard myself on the radio, I thought I sounded just like an American kid.

I remember the huge snowstorm of 1948 more than any other because it was the first time in my life I had ever seen a significant amount of snow. It snowed almost twenty-four inches and the schools were closed. The tree branches were heavily laden with snow and when the sun came out, everything was bright, clean and sparkling. It was beautiful. I walked in the unplowed street with the snow up to my chest. On that snowy day my father stayed home and worked most of the day at his desk. He did go out once to help me build a snowman, and to show me how to throw snowballs. All he told me about snow was that it was frozen water.

Although my parents sent me to public school, Papa continued to teach me about Judaism and the Jewish holidays. For my educational benefit, my parents joined Temple Israel, the Conservative synagogue in Great Neck. They were still not at all religious and the war certainly had a tremendous negative effect on their faith, especially on my father. The loss of his family hit him hard and he lost any belief in God he may have ever had.

On occasion, in future years, when I was an adult, Maman told me of her own disbelief, but she always felt it was important to realize and be proud we were Jewish. She stressed being supportive of Jewish causes and Israel, even if we were not observant or true believers.

Maman rarely went to synagogue other than for weddings and bar mitzvahs. We did, however, celebrate Hanukah at home. I lit the candles and she made the traditional *latkes*, potato pancakes. For the New Year holiday Rosh Hashana, we would normally have dinner at her sister Sonia's house and Maman would make her carp dish. On Yom Kippur, the Day of Atonement, she fasted (my father tried to fast but did not do so for the whole day).

On Passover, a holiday celebrating Moses leading the Jews from Egypt, we attended the Seder at Aunt Ruth's house and Maman again prepared her delicious carp. Ruth's husband, Uncle Maurice, was Orthodox and ran the service very strictly. He would sit at the head of the table in a white robe, leaning on some pillows. He made sure to recite each word in the *Haggadah* and it took forever. The wine he used for the service was sweet, unlike the watered down table wine I was accustomed to drinking. At the start of the service he would break a matzo in half and hide one piece, the *afikoman*, between the pillows. My cousins and I would have to figure out how to steal it so that we could ask for "ransom," because you can't end the Seder without that piece of matzo.

Of course, we were somehow always able to take it and hide it until the grownups needed it for the ritual, then we would bargain with them for the "ransom" before giving it back. Our "loot" over various years included tickets to "Peter Pan", "Where's Charley?" (with Ray Bolger), the Ice Capades or a Yankee game, and we always got what we asked for.

My cousins and I would also have a contest to see who could eat the bitter herbs and the horseradish without choking, coughing, or complaining. The bitter root was a symbol of the suffering of the Jewish slaves in ancient Egypt. My favorite *Seder* food, however, was Maman's cold boiled carp in its jellied sauce, eaten with matzo and mayonnaise. My mother still prepares carp for certain holidays and it's still a favorite of mine.

During various weekends of the year we got together with my mother's sisters, Sonia and Ruth, and their families. They both lived in Manhattan, and between them, they had three kids. I was very close to Sonia's son Sylvan. My parents and I would ride the Long Island Railroad into Manhattan, then take the subway uptown. I loved to stand at the front window of the first car and look into the dark tunnel ahead of us. I also enjoyed playing with the penny gum machines mounted on the subway station support columns. Sometimes, on Saturday nights, I would stay at Sylvan's apartment on Riverside Drive and West 96th Street in Manhattan. Riverside Drive remains a choice location with a magnificent view of the Hudson River, the Palisades, and the George Washington Bridge. Broadway, with its cornucopia of stores, is just two blocks away. The apartment was on the twelfth floor and was essentially a long hallway with all the rooms off to one side to take advantage of the view.

Uncle Louis worked at home as a diamond cutter and polisher. His worktable was against one wall of the dining room and I loved to watch him work. He would sit with a large apron slung between his waist and the worktable to catch any diamond dust and chips. The diamonds he worked were stuck in wax at the end of a wooden rod that he held in one hand, while he held a cutting diamond on a similar rod in his other hand. A lit candle on the worktable was used to melt the wax whenever he had to reposition or remove the diamond.

Sylvan was a bright kid, and he and I played board games or games that he invented–like flicking poker chips along a circuitous path along the dining room table. We did lots of things with poker chips, even using them to play our own version of knock-hockey. Eventually Sylvan was given a set of Lionel electric trains that I loved to play with. When it was time for me to go home, Sylvan's parents would put me on the LIRR and my parents would pick me up at the train station in Great Neck.

Although I was adjusting fairly well to life in America and had some Jewish friends, I still felt somewhat like a stranger and ill at ease. I was living a new and relatively easy life, but I still felt different and suffered a great deal of inner turmoil. I was extremely nervous and had facial tics. In some ways I was a mess. A European doctor, familiar with our family history and our wartime experiences, told my mother to ignore my symptoms and they would eventually go away. He was right, but it took years for them to disappear.

While days away from my parents were not a real problem for me, spending the night away from home still caused me severe separation anxiety, often to the point of hysteria. This was all probably an emotional holdover from my time in Vourles, when I couldn't see my parents regularly. I was afraid to be alone, until I was a teenager and that caused my parents to hire babysitters for me if they had to go out in the afternoons or evenings. My primary baby sitter was a wonderful, single, middle-aged Dutch lady, Suzanne Van Gelderen. She was my father's colleague at the United Nations and lived right next door. Because she had trouble walking, Suzanne and I entertained each other by playing cards. She taught me an essential life skill—how to play gin rummy.

There was concern about my teeth. I had an overbite that made me look like Bugs Bunny, so my parents regularly took me to Manhattan for visits to Dr. Zimmerman, the orthodontist. His office was on Broadway at West 72nd Street. When we'd leave his office, we would explore the city—go to museums, take walks on Fifth Avenue or go down to Times Square, a place that was absolutely awesome. All the moving and stationary lights, the constant activity, the mass of people and cars moving around the square fascinated me then and they still do now.

I was a loner who shied away from socializing with individuals or groups. Once I was invited to a birthday party in a private house, and the kids decided to play the daring game of the day, Spin the Bottle. For those too young to know what this game is—the group sits in a circle. Usually, it's boy, girl, boy, girl. In the center of the circle is a soda bottle lying on its side. The hostess gets the first spin of the bottle, and has to kiss the person of the opposite sex closest to where the bottle is pointing. Then, that person has to spin the bottle and get it to aim at a girl, and so on and so forth. It was a very risqué thing to do, in those days, anyway. I was extremely shy, but I did get one kiss. I once took Lotte Rahman, the daughter of a man who worked with my father, on a date. The date consisted of going to a park on Long Island Sound with our parents. I went to a school dance with a girl named Margo Fleer in my class, but I don't think we really danced. Her mother drove us there in the family car. Boy, was I jealous! I wanted a car of our own!

My parents enjoyed entertaining their colleagues at our home, and they would dress rather formally for those occasions. Papa would wear a jacket and tie, while Maman was always *tres chic*. I would help Maman prepare and serve the snacks, then sit and listen in on the conversations. For the sake of clarity, they were held in English and were interesting, covering almost every conceivable topic, especially politics. There was a couple from France, one from Haiti, one from India, and two "White Russians" who were vehement anti-communists. The American couple that visited was Mr. and Mrs. Morrow. Mr. Morrow worked at the Sperry Corporation, the gyroscope manufacturer, in Lake Success—located in the same building as the UN.

We rarely ate out, but I remember once going to a Chinese restaurant and enjoying everything, even the hot mustard. Often, when I wanted a snack, I'd butter a piece of bread and pour chocolate sprinkles on it. This was a big treat for me, because I had been so chocolate-deprived during the war.

I visited my father at work many times, a few times first at his office in Lake Success, and in his ninth floor office in the Secretariat building in Manhattan. My father's office in Lake Success was a simple cubicle in a large room with many other cubicles. Later at the Manhattan UN building, his office was quite nice, large, private, and overlooked the East River. He always wore a dark suit and a white shirt to work and only removed his tie after he came home. On weekends, he wore casual clothes.

When the UN was in Lake Success, I went there by bus from Great Neck. I went by train to visit him in his Manhattan office after school, and was always fascinated when he let me attend various meetings in either the General Assembly, Security Council, or when committees such as the Trusteeship Council, or the Economic and Social Council met. Thanks to my father's press credentials, I would usually sit in the first row of the press section, and occasionally in the interpreter's cubicles.

During the many times that I visited him in his Manhattan office, he took me to the delegate's lounge where I either met or saw some of the more famous UN delegates such as Andrei Vishinsky and Andre Gromyko of Russia, Madame Lakshmi Pandit of India, and Moshe Sharrett of Israel. These people were the newsmakers of the day and I was very impressed. The two Russians never smiled, seemed very stern, unfriendly, and ignored most people around them. They were always dressed in dark suits. Madame Pandit wore beautiful saris and had a pleasant face. Moshe Sharrett wore striped gray suits and was friendly and animated.

In the evenings, Papa would sometimes take me to lectures or concerts at the UN. At one event, I met Sir Edmund Hillary later of Mt. Everest climbing fame. I was among a few people who asked him some questions, and he was friendly enough to take the time to answer them. We also attended a wonderful concert given by Victor Borge, a master of comedy and music. At one weekend soccer/picnic outing for UN employees at a park, I sat next to Trygve Lie, then Secretary General of the UN and near the President of the General Assembly, Mr. Entezam of Iran. Since they were wearing casual clothes, they did not appear quite as formidable as they did when in session. They were all smiles and very friendly. Some of the delegates teased me and let me kick a soccer ball around with them during practice.

The United Nations, in those days, gave their employees and their families free trips to their countries of origin every two or three years. So my parents and I were able to go back to Europe in the summer of 1948. We sailed on the *Queen Mary* and returned on the *Queen Elizabeth*, and both voyages were thrilling to a kid like me. In addition to the great accommodations and pleasant activities, there were special people on board. The United States Olympic team, on its way to compete in the London games, sailed with us from New York to South Hampton, where there was a stopover en route to Cherbourg.

I was able to watch the teams do calisthenics and practice on deck. They all wore beautiful white uniforms and it was marvelous to see them, especially the fencers and gymnasts. I took a few pictures of them but never had the nerve to go over and talk to them. On the return trip, Marcel Cerdan, the French middleweight boxer and the lover of the legendary songstress, Edith Piaf, was on board. He was coming to the US to train and fight Tony Zale, then middleweight champion of the world. Cerdan was my idol and I got to watch him play deck volleyball. I didn't have the nerve to approach him, either, but he seemed to be having a good time playing and talking to the other passengers. Papa and I later watched him take the title from Zale on television.

On that UN trip we visited Belgium and France. First, we spent a few days sightseeing in Paris. We stayed at the Hotel St. Lazarre and took the Metro or walked to various parts of the city. We went to the Louvre and I was so impressed with the Mona Lisa because wherever I was in the room, I thought she was staring at me. In the Jardins des Tuilleries, (literally the garden of red roof tiles) my parents rented a toy boat that I sailed in a large fountain, steering it with a long stick. I rode the carousel and caught the brass ring on each rotation! There was no prize, but it was a challenge to collect as many rings as I could. We went to the top of the Eiffel Tower and the Arc de Triomphe. We walked the boulevards, watching men play Boule, a game similar to Bocci, in the Tuilleries.

We left Paris by train for Annecy, in the French Alps. We saw the Mont Blanc and the Aiguilles Vertes, the Green Needles, covered with snow, even during the summer. The three of us went rowing in pristine lakes among green trees, blue skies, black rocks, and white clouds. It was very different from any city or place I had ever been and was very peaceful. It was as if my parents were refreshing their souls and airing out their bad memories.

Of course we went to Antwerp to visit my grandparents and all the rest of our relatives from both sides of the family, including Papa's brother Jules. All the adults did was sit and talk, while my grandmother fed me continually. I loved her dinners! She'd serve carp as an appetizer, followed by a baked chicken entrée with a vegetable casserole as the side dish. I was sometimes allowed to choose our dessert pastries from a bakery a few doors away, where the smell of vanilla, cinnamon and chocolate would smack you in the face and almost knock you over when you walked in the door. It was a delicious, rich aroma that spells heaven to a child, a smell you could never forget!

No vacation would be complete without a trip to the beach. We winded our way to Blankenberg, a Belgian seashore beach resort. It was the third time I had seen the ocean and big waves from the sandy shore. The previous summer, I went to Jones Beach on Long Island, and tested myself by running into the waves. In Blankenberg, we saw Papa's niece Suzi, her husband Joe Pantzer, and their daughters Helen and Carol, who came from London to see us and join us on vacation. I played in the sand with the girls, and later we shared ice cream parfaits in a little cafe. Jules met us in Blankenberg and he treated Papa and me to a boys' night out. The three of us went to a pool hall, where Papa and Jules drank beer and played billiards while I sat there, watching and listening.

After two weeks in Belgium, we returned to the Hotel St. Lazare near the Gare St. Lazare in Paris. I thought it was nice of the hotel to put us in the same room we'd had two weeks earlier! It struck me as silly and odd, but then, what did I know? I realized eventually that all hotel rooms were furnished exactly alike. We took the train to Cherbourg to board the *Queen Elizabeth* for our return to New York. Each of us carried one old-fashioned hard-sided suitcase covered with souvenir stickers from all the places we had been, a tradition that has since died.

In the spring of 1949, I started studying for my bar mitzvah. I was 12 and studied with Mr. Benjamin Weinglass and the now illustrious Rabbi Mordechai Waxman at Temple Israel in Great Neck. On a Saturday morning in June 1950, my parents dressed me up in a fancy white shirt and tie, dark pants, and a gray jacket. We went to the synagogue with our guests and during the service I read my portion of the Torah and sang my Haftorah. When it was over, Rabbi Waxman gave me a two-volume set of books, "The Pentateuch and Haftorahs." There was a kiddush, a small reception at the synagogue with cakes, cookies, wine and punch. Then there was a lunch for twenty family members and close friends at our apartment. Everyone sat at a long table made up of borrowed small tables covered with white tablecloths.

My parents sat at one end with me between them. My mother had done all the cooking. I'd written a little speech with the Rabbi's help and was a bit nervous about delivering it, but it came out all right. One of our guests was my cousin from my father's family, Arthur Gold, a special person in all of our lives. Years later, he got his bachelor's degree from Princeton and his Ph.D. from Harvard, became a Professor of Literature at Wellesley College and book critic for the Herald Tribune. He was a gentle person, who wrote beautifully. Arthur eventually was my older son Allan's godfather and would periodically write letters to Allan about his life philosophies. Arthur had lived in New Jersey as a youngster, and his father owned several movie houses. On one visit, for some special occasion, long before it was trendy to do things like that, we were treated to a special private screening of Pinocchio!

Henry Piper, Arthur's grandfather, was my father's only remaining relative besides Jules and Suzi. Henry's family, kind and friendly people, all their children and grandchildren, had settled decades earlier in Northern New Jersey. When we would visit them, they'd welcome us with genuine warmth and open arms. On one of those visits, one of the family members presented me with a book that I have and treasure to this day. It was all about the 1948 London Olympics, and had photographs of the American athletes who had crossed the Atlantic with us in action at the Olympics.

During part of the summer of 1950, my parents sent me to sleep-away camp in the Catskills. It was the same camp that my cousin Sylvan was attending. It was a hotbed of Zionism called *Ein Harod*. Of course the point was to make me independent. And frankly, I did pretty well. It was sort of primitive and worked on principles similar to those used in the kibbutzim in Israel. Each person did assigned chores, and everybody shared food and work. Chores included cleaning up the bunks, serving food in the dining room, and putting dishes away. Each morning we would stand at attention and salute the American and Israeli flags, then sing both national anthems. After breakfast and lunch we'd play soccer, go swimming in a lake, do some arts and crafts or learn songs. At *Ein Harod,* I learned many Yiddish and Israeli songs and my enjoyment and love of those songs has continued to this day. It's my favorite kind of music. At bedtime we would lie on our cots and lights went out early. During non-group activities, near bedtime, I would get that lonely feeling, but camp lasted only a month, and I was having a good time. Still, I was very happy to be back with my parents.

That fall, I changed schools to Kensington Elementary since it was closer to our apartment. At recess I'd play marbles in the schoolyard. Since I began playing years before with Jean in the market square in Vourles, I won more marbles than I lost. I played two kinds of games. One game set up a "biggie" marble, usually a colorful large marble, in front of me as I sat on the ground with my legs spread to catch incoming marbles as other kids tried to hit the "biggie." I used to win a lot of marbles that way. The other game set up a whole row of smaller marbles in front of me. Each marble hit by another kids' marble, he would get. The person aiming for the marbles in each game was about six feet away from me. I had good aim when I was the shooter. I also remember being a hall monitor at school and was proud to wear the yellow monitor badge because it made me feel powerful.

I graduated from Kensington and attended Great Neck Middle School. I was on the track team and competed in the long jump. I was proud to be presented with a pair of spiked shoes from my coach. They were second hand and quite worn, but I didn't care. I wore white shorts and my mother had sewn red and blue stripes on the side of each leg, just like the American Olympic athletes wore. I'd already won a blue ribbon in the city championship and set a new Great Neck record for my grade with a jump of 13'-9 ½".

Then came Hanukah, 1949. I lit the candles each night, but one evening I became very sad. I was lighting the candles when we heard the terrible news on the radio that Marcel Cerdan, the French middleweight boxing champion of the world, my hero, who had been with us on the *Queen Elizabeth,* had been killed in a plane crash. He was on his way to the United States for a championship fight with Jake LaMotta.

I was devastated and cried for days. Papa tried to console me. He said there was no reason or logic for it, but that it was an accident. I was in denial for days and could not understand why it had happened. And I still have problems understanding why bad things happen to good people.

Living in Great Neck provided my family with a safe and solid transition from France to America. We adjusted to our new lifestyle and its non-threatening environment. We were able to get re-acquainted with family, and, because we were associated with the United Nations, we had a sense of local community.

But about that time, Papa's health started declining. The stress and trauma of the war had taken its toll, and his chain smoking didn't help. It made him a prime candidate for a heart attack. He also suffered from lumbago, and Maman would give him back massages and heat treatments. One morning, he was running to the station to catch a train and fell, breaking his rib. Our doctor, Dr. Brettler, who was a family friend, taped him up, and even lugged his heavy EKG machine up the stairs to check Papa's heart. Papa was no quitter. He continued to go to work at the UN and in his spare time at home worked on a Zionist project that meant a lot to him. I will write about that project which dealt with stenography in the next chapter.

# 8

# JACKSON HEIGHTS

When the United Nations moved from Lake Success to Manhattan, my parents moved closer to New York City. In the spring of 1951, they found a two-bedroom apartment in Jackson Heights, a community in the borough of Queens with direct subway service to New York that made the commute easier for them. We lived at 85-05 35ᵗʰ Avenue, in a red brick three-story apartment house, with an area where I could safely play and bike. The neighborhood was essentially residential, with single-family homes, a few apartment buildings, lots of trees, and grassy lawns. Our apartment consisted of a kitchen, dining room, living room, and two bedrooms.

My bedroom was situated between the living room and my parents' bedroom, and I was thrilled to finally have my own *private* space—where I could do as I liked—read, do my homework and relax. I would set up my electric train tracks in different ways, and would even run them from my room to the kitchen and back—and ask Maman to load the cargo car with cookies as it passed through. Maman commuted to work at high-fashion shops in Manhattan, where she continued her work as a seamstress. I was transferred from Great Neck Middle School to PS 125 in Sunnyside, Queens, several subway stops away from home (we were issued bus passes), and I joined the local baseball team, the Thors. I was the catcher and a pretty good hitter.

I will never forget one game. When I was playing catcher, A batter hit a pop-up between the pitcher and me, so we both went running full speed for the ball and collided. I was slammed so hard that I was knocked out cold. I lay on the ground dizzy for a few minutes, then sat up and realized I was okay, but the pitcher was hurt and unable to continue, so I volunteered to pitch. I pitched, we put in a new catcher, and we won the game. Boy, was I thrilled!

At PS 125 I continued being a good student. I did well in math, science, history, and English. I carried what seemed like a ton of books in a bag slung over one shoulder. Our classes were co-ed, and there was one girl, Gloria Broden, a redhead, was someone I could tease and joke around with. She was a friendly girl and it was easy for a shy kid like me to speak and kid around with her. Yet, I was too scared to ask her for a date.

The school had a playground for outdoor recess, and I would play baseball and a little basketball. I was really bad at playing basketball. I had never learned the rules about double dribbling and would lose the ball each time because I would stop dribbling and then resume. I also never learned to fake the other players out or shoot baskets.

We would eat lunch in the school cafeteria, and I would bring chicken or jelly sandwiches Maman would make for me. Occasionally, I would treat myself to that all-American snack, Twinkies.

And then there was stickball. That is where you hit a pink rubber Spalding ball (they bounced higher and longer than their cheap imitations) with a broomstick and use manhole covers and other assorted things, like parking sign poles and cars, as bases. Once someone hit the ball so hard, it went smashing through a candy store window. All the players ran from the scene of the "crime," but I didn't run, because I didn't think I had done anything wrong. The owner of the store came out, and he was fuming. He asked me what happened, and I told him. Instead of holding everyone on the "team" responsible, he took my name and phone number, called my parents and demanded payment of $10. They gave him the money and weren't angry with me, but I realized I was naive compared to my "city-slicker" buddies.

Then one day, in the early 1950s, in a most unlikely yet predictable way, we celebrated a new addition to the family. Uncle Louis and Aunt Sonia brought his niece, Raymonde Fisher, from Belgium and adopted her. Her parents had been deported and hadn't survived. She had been cared for and hidden by a very kind and sensitive Christian family, named Frans and Joanna Van Lommel. Ray, as we called her, was two or three years younger than Sylvan and me. When she arrived in New York with Uncle Louis, we were all there to greet her in the Suskin's apartment and presented her with flowers. She was only able to speak French and Flemish, but Sylvan and I made sure that she learned English quickly. She adjusted fairly easily and we all fell in love with her, for she was a wonderful person.

When she became a young woman, she married Henry Katz and had four children with him. However, tragedy struck when she contracted breast cancer, the plague that takes so many good women, and she died at 39, in 1979. We were all devastated because she brought so much joy, kindness and love into the family. We remained friendly with Henry after he remarried to another lovely woman, Joan Sadinoff, and in my mind, Henry and Joan are special. There is a word in Yiddish, *mensch*. This word is used to describe compassionate, decent human beings. Of all the people we know, Henry and Joan fit that description best.

In 1951, Papa, Maman and I took another long vacation, courtesy of the United Nations. By this time, I was 14 years old and had a better appreciation of the trip. We again boarded the *Queen Elizabeth* in New York and sailed to Cherbourg, then took the train to Paris. We did some sightseeing there, as we had once before, then headed to my grandparents' home in Antwerp. The clean smell of freshly washed streets early in the morning, and the delicious scent of different foods being prepared in various kitchens escaping into the street from open windows and from food vendors' carts in the marketplace remain embedded in my memory.

Every Shabbat when we were in Antwerp, my grandfather, who was Orthodox, took me to the *shul* (synagogue), where men and women are seated separately. He taught me as much as he could about Judaism, told me what the prayers were about and tried to impress upon me the importance of being a Jew. A few days before we left Belgium, we went to the beach in Knocke, where Suzi and Joe Panzer and their two children joined us from London.

**Sisters, seated Miriam (left), Ruth, Sonia,
standing Alice (left), Ella**

**Joseph Pressel at his desk at home**

Next, we boarded a train to Northern Italy, to a resort hotel on Lake Molveno, where I spent lots of quality time with Papa. He took me boating, swimming, and we played tennis. The resort was the most elegant place I had ever seen in my young life. The service in the dining room was impeccable, and I was amazed, as I had never seen "French" service before. The waiters served the food from their platters by gripping the food with two spoons and depositing it on our plates. I couldn't figure out how they did it until I was older and understood the use of chopsticks! I still remember the peaches they served. They were the largest and juiciest peaches I ever ate in my entire life!

Because my parents appreciated art, we went to Florence for a few days, where they took me to all the museums and explained famous statues and paintings. We traveled on to Genoa, where the most anticipated and exciting part of our trip began. We boarded the Italian ship, the *Grimani*, and crossed the Mediterranean to the three-year-old brand new country that was born from the ashes of the Holocaust. We were going to Israel for three whole weeks.

Papa and Maman, especially Papa, wanted very much to visit Israel. I still remember the day when Israel declared Statehood in 1948 and when it was admitted to the United Nations. Papa was at his post in the General Assembly during the vote, and translated Israeli Ambassador Abba Eban's thanks to the world. Papa also had a dream, and he worked on it in his spare time. I've mentioned a number of times that he was an expert stenographer. He also invented a shorthand system for Hebrew, written from right to left, like Hebrew is written. The only stenography available in Israel in those days was written from left to right. He spent many hours perfecting and developing the system into a book. The book included paragraphs to be translated either into steno or from steno. He wrote them in French, English, and Hebrew because those were the languages that he was primarily interested in being able to use in his system. He wanted to discuss his system with people in Israel.

Maman went to Israel to see her sister, Alice, and her family. Alice had married Myron Abramsohn. Tanya was Alice's childhood friend whose uncle had sent her to Israel in her teens. Alice, a physical education teacher, and Myron, a career officer in the IDF (Israeli Defense Force), lived in Rehovot, a town south of Tel Aviv on the Mediterranean coast. They had three boys, Dani, Uri, and a newborn, Odet.

Alice and Myron came to meet us at the dock in Haifa, but there wasn't a vehicle large enough to hold us all and the luggage, so we had to split up. Maman rode with Alice in her friend's car, and Papa and I rode in Myron's army Jeep. Papa sat in the front with Myron and I was jammed in the back with the luggage. The sun was so hot, I couldn't touch the metal parts of the Jeep, and I got bounced around like a rubber ball, but I really didn't care about that—I just didn't want to burn myself.

Before we left Haifa, Myron took us to the top of Mount Carmel to show us the magnificent panoramic view of the city and the harbor. It took about two hours to get from Haifa to Rehovot, and the scenery, for me, was amazing. Things looked so modern in such an ancient land. I was surprised to find that the house in Rehovot was spacious and had lots of land. Olive trees were growing on the property, and a barn housed goats and rabbits. There was a small gym, a basketball court and a small swimming pool, and we put it all to good use during the three weeks we were there. It turned out that in addition to their regular jobs, my aunt and uncle had opened a part-time day camp for Israeli children.

Dani, Uri, and I slept on cots in the gym, and the two of them would sing Israeli songs to put themselves to sleep. One song in particular caught my fancy. It was called "Finjan," which is a Turkish coffeepot. I loved that song so much, I ended up singing it to my own children as they grew up.

After a few days of rest and relaxation at the house in Rehovot, my parents wanted to travel around the country to see all the important sites from biblical history. Uncle Myron took some time off, piled us into his Jeep, and for approximately a week gave us the grand tour. Papa sat with Myron in the front, and Maman and I bounced around in the back. As a precaution, one that is still necessary more than 50 years later, Myron strapped his rifle to the front support of the Jeep.

Our first stop was Jerusalem, where we couldn't even get close to the Old City or the Western Wall, the only remnant of Herod's Temple, because they were under Arab control, and would be until 1967. We were taken to the old Knesset building, the Parliament, where my father introduced me to a Mr. Princetzak, President of the Parliament, who happened to be the son of Mr. Prince, the leader of my grandfather's congregation in Antwerp. He had changed his last name when he moved to Israel to make it sound more Israeli and less European, as did many others who came to live in the Land of Milk and Honey.

We stayed at a very old hotel, and Uncle Myron took us on long walks through Jerusalem, an amazingly beautiful city set on a series of hills. The buildings looked very old and were made of large stone blocks that looked ancient, although scores of them were built in the 1880s. As the sun set in the west, the light would bounce off the walls and give the city a golden glow. But you didn't have to look hard to see that many of them were pockmarked with bullet holes and scarred by artillery shells from the battles with the Arabs during the War of Independence. We visited the King David Hotel, a large, beautiful stone hotel not far from the Old City walls, famous today for being the choice of world leaders whenever they come to visit the city. It is also notorious for being the headquarters for the British Occupying Forces before independence and the site of the bombing by Menachem Begin's underground fighting force, the *Irgun*.

Papa asked Uncle Myron to take us to see Theodore Herzl's grave. Herzl had developed the idea of secular Zionism and a home for the Jews in Palestine as his 19th century answer to European anti-semitism. His burial site, topped by a magnificent monument, is in a beautiful park on a mountain overlooking the city, in a place called *Bayit VaGan*, then on the outskirts of the city. Zev Jabotinsky, another fierce Zionist who warned the European Jews that they were facing a Holocaust and pleaded with them to leave for Palestine, is also buried there, as are other distinguished Zionist leaders. This was particularly meaningful as my father had translated many of Jabotinsky's speeches. In fact, it is interesting that the link between Zionism and the establishment of the State are emphasized today on that same mountain, now also the site of the world's most important Holocaust memorial and center for Holocaust research, Yad Vashem.

Papa was fascinated by the mix of different ethnic groups in the city and the clothing that distinguished them from one another. There were Arab men in red and white checked scarves and long white robes; Arab women in brightly embroidered long dresses who wore scarves on their heads, and even over the lower parts of their faces; Greek Orthodox priests in the high black hats and long black robes who wore huge crosses on their chests, Hassidic Jews who looked like Polish noblemen from days of yore, wearing long coats, long sidelocks and big black hats, Catholic priests in their traditional black garb with white collars, nuns from many different orders wearing different habits, and the old Jews of Meah Shearim, an ultra-Orthodox Jewish section, who still wear striped satin robes and are often called, affectionately, the zebras.

Most of the time, we ate fish because there wasn't much beef or lamb available. But the smells in the streets of Jerusalem coming from the food vendors tickled my nose and made my mouth water. Coriander, cumin, cinnamon and Turkish coffee spiced the air almost everywhere we went. And once, I remember that when Papa noticed an old Jewish beggar sitting on a curb, reading Psalms, he bent down to give him a few coins.

We spent a few days exploring what we could of Jerusalem, and then headed up north to the Galilee, to see Nazareth and Lake Kinneret, which feeds the Jordan River and where the New Testament says Jesus walked on water. Unlike the dry hills of Jerusalem and the desert beyond it, the Galilee was green and fertile and served as Israel's breadbasket. We passed through different villages and cities, some of them prosperous and modern, some of them ancient, destitute or abandoned. We experienced a dust storm called a Hamsin, a sort of mini-monsoon, a hot wind, but we didn't stop. Groves of orange and olive trees dotted the landscape. The farmers, who were innovative and ingenious, terraced all the hills surrounding the valleys. There were saplings planted everywhere, as the Keren Kayemet, the Jewish National Fund, began its campaign to grow trees everywhere in Israel.

We visited Safed, a hilly city with twisted narrow streets filled with Jewish history and the legends of the mystics that is now a center for artists and artisans, musicians and Kabbalah (mysticism) students. On our way through the area, we also visited several kibbutzim, the collective farms—now fading from the scene—that had been responsible for draining the Hule swamps, preparing the people and the land for the future state. Besides working the land, each kibbutz had products exclusive to them that were sold to sustain their communities. Products could be anything from fruits and vegetables, breads and baked goods, leather goods, arts and crafts, jewelry, kitchen items, machinery, to all the other items necessary to bring a state into being and provide for a burgeoning population. I felt a particular affinity for Kibbutz Ein Harod, because it had the same name as the Zionist summer camp my parents sent me to back in the States. Kibbutz Ein Harod produced fruits and arts and crafts.

We never did make it to the northern border or even to the Dead Sea, way down in the south. When we finished our tour of the Galilee, we took the coastal road south through Haifa and small towns where they were beginning to develop banana plantations, wineries and fish farms, and headed back to Rehovot to rest for a few days before we sailed on the Kedma from Haifa to Marseille. Immediately after war, the Kedma had been used in the *Bricha*, (underground smuggling of Jews into Palestine) like the ship *Exodus*, to bring Jews into Palestine before statehood was declared. (In the spring of 2003 an Israeli movie called "Kedma" was released and told the story of the Kedma as an Exodus ship in the 1940s.)

When the family said goodbye, the air was fraught with emotion, and both my parents' eyes were moist. It would have been even worse had we all known that this was the last time Uncle Myron and Aunt Alice would see Papa.

Our voyage was quite an adventure. We were hit by one of the roughest gales to ever smack into the Mediterranean. It was so rough that if we had to walk from one place to another, it was necessary to hold on to the railings that were fixed along the bulkheads. Luckily, we didn't get seasick, but it was difficult to eat with the ship pitching and rolling from side to side. The crew would wet the tablecloths so that our plates wouldn't slide off the tables. I remember seeing very heavy seas with huge waves and lots of rain hitting the decks at a sharp angle. Some of the waves crashed so hard against the ship that a few went over the decks. The wind was howling. We could not go out on deck, although once I tried. I took a few steps out then had to sit down on the deck to avoid being swept along. I crawled back to the exit doorway to go back inside. The storm lasted for about one and a half days. When we finally docked in Marseille we heard that several ships sank during the storm and that many people were lost at sea. Shaken by our narrow escape, we took trains to Paris and Cherbourg for our trip home on the Mauritania. It was time for my parents to go back to work and for me to start high school.

# 9

# LOSING MY FATHER

While we were in Israel, Maman had received a telegram with very sad news. Papa's best friend, Haskel Balken, whom he had known since his youth in the *Maccabi* club in Antwerp, had died suddenly in New York. Because our trip was about getting Papa to relax and get rid of some of his stress, Maman did not want to spoil his trip and so she didn't tell him about it until we were almost home. The news did not help Papa's health. During our trip Papa was laughing more than usual and was happy, especially during our visit to Israel. After he heard about his friend Haskel's death, he once again became serious, less talkative, and sad. He was not upset at missing the funeral and thought my mother had done the right thing by delaying the news. Soon after our return, we all went to see Haskel's widow, Ethel, who had also been a childhood friend of Maman, and remained a friend until Ethel's death in 2002.

In my last year at PS 125, the ninth grade, my teachers recommended that I take the entrance exam for Stuyvesant High School, on East 15th Street and First Avenue in Manhattan. This was one of three special science and math schools in the city, and I was accepted. When we came home from our vacation, I began as a sophomore, and commuted daily into the city from Queens. In those days, and maybe now, too, students were issued bus passes and given deep discounts for shows and sporting events through what the schools called the students' GO, or General Organization. The subways and buses were free when we showed our passes (the going fare was fifteen cents; today it's $2.00) and entrance fees to sporting events was sixty cents, which was cheap, even in those days.

Papa's love of sports never died, even when his heart was crippling him. He enjoyed art, classical music and all that, but sports were his passion. He introduced me to and taught me about track and field, boxing, gymnastics and soccer. In addition to watching sports on TV, he and I also attended sports events whenever possible. He also taught me how to play chess—and sometimes I would win, but I was never really sure if I had won legitimately or not. Maybe I *did* win, but I'll never know, because he never told me.

But Papa had had two heart attacks since 1946, when we had arrived in America, and he had been hospitalized each time. Maman would sneak me into the hospital to visit him, because in those days, children weren't allowed to visit—even if a parent was terminally ill. He still hadn't stopped smoking cigarettes and it wreaked havoc with his health and heart. I believe that the stress from the war added to the problem. For several years, Papa worked on the United Nations Bulletin, a magazine about major UN happenings. In 1951, his assignment was press officer for the Ad Hoc Committee on Forced Labor, established by the UN and the International Labor Organization. He was also in charge of translating the material. The committee investigated Genocide during World War II.

The meetings were secret and covered the terrible things that happened during the Holocaust. The subject of his work was depressing. Daily, he had to listen, write, and translate the terrible details that occurred to the Jewish people, including the members of his immediate family. I believe that this final stress probably contributed to his final and fatal heart attack.

Medications and treatments for heart disease have changed drastically in the last fifty years. Then, the main method of keeping people alive was through rest. Papa needed "rest," so we bought a

Dumont TV set and he and I would sit and watch TV together in the evenings. We especially enjoyed the Friday night boxing matches sponsored by Gillette. Papa's other main enjoyment came from sharing quality time with Maman and me. They bought one of those old fashioned record players that played at 33, 45 and 78 rpm and quite a few classical albums and we loved to listen. It was because of Papa and Maman that I developed some knowledge and love of classical music.

Papa was dedicated to his work and was often praised. In July 1952, he received a copy of the following memorandum from Manfred Simon, Secretary of the Ad Hoc Committee on Forced Labor to his chief, Leonard Berry, Press and Publications Bureau.

Second session of the Ad Hoc Committee on Forced Labor, Press Officer - Mr. Joseph Pressel. July 1, 1952.

The purpose of this memorandum is to thank you most sincerely for the considerable help you have given to the Ad Hoc Committee's secretarial staff and to the Committee itself by placing at its disposal Mr. Joseph Pressel as officer in charge of all press releases and relations with the press and radio correspondents.

In his closing speech Sir Ramaswami Mudaliar, Chairman of the Ad Hoc Committee expressed his deep satisfaction with the services rendered by the Administration to the Committee, and he also specifically mentioned the press officer, Mr. Joseph Pressel. You will find a summary of Sir Ramaswami's remarks in the summary record of this morning's meeting, E/AC.36?SR.26. Sir Ramaswami's colleagues, Mr. Paal Berg and Mr. Garcia-Sayan, shared the opinion of the Chairman.

I wish to add that personally I was particularly satisfied with Mr. Pressel's services. Not only did he take charge of the Committee's relations with the press and radio correspondents, thus relieving me of a very delicate task for which I am not very well prepared, but also during the

**Joseph Pressel, far left, at
ad hoc UN committee meeting, 1952**

technical crisis which occurred, he was good enough to take verbatim notes of the Committee's proceedings and to produce very excellent summary records from his notes. This work obliged him to do much overtime.

As for his press releases themselves, they were objective and at the same time comprehensive without, however, revealing those parts of the proceedings which the Committee wished for the time being to be kept confidential.

Approximately eight weeks after I started Stuyvesant High School, my father suffered a fatal heart attack at home. It was Sunday November 2, 1952, and my parents were celebrating their twenty-second wedding anniversary with my mother's sisters and their families.

I wasn't home. I was in Manhattan at a Jewish youth group meeting. When my Aunt Ella came to the door of the meeting room and motioned for me to come out, I knew immediately that something terrible had happened. She hadn't come alone—Uncle Elie was with her, and that, in itself was not a good sign at all. They had a taxi waiting to take us back to Queens, so I knew it was going to be even worse than anything I could imagine. Hardly a word was said on the half-hour ride home. I stared out the window, willing myself not to think, looking at, but not seeing, the city as it passed me by.

When I walked into the apartment, Maman greeted me at the door with a long and sad hug, told me to be strong, that Papa had died and was in the bedroom. When Papa collapsed, he was in the midst of his family, celebrating his love of Maman. She summoned a doctor who lived in our building, and he had tried everything to revive Papa, including the injection of adrenaline straight to the heart, all to no avail. I went in to see Papa there, lying on his bed. I cried for a long, long time, while Maman covered the mirrors and prepared to sit *Shivah,* the traditional week of mourning.

The service the next day was at a funeral home in Flushing, Queens. All of our family, many members of the Jackson Heights Jewish community, and my father's associates at the United Nations attended. Members of the UN and the Jewish Congregation eulogized him. I was just 15 years old. My father was only 51. I decided to honor my father by thinking about him every day and trying to do my best at school. I dove back into my schoolwork and life continued. Maman, being the strong person she was, resumed her work for the high-priced clientele.

Papa had died much too young. He was a wonderful man and I miss him terribly. I have missed his counsel, company, and love from that day to this. He was such a good role model. He was gentle and sensitive in so many ways, empathetic to other people's feelings and respectful. He rarely raised his voice. He was respected by all of those who knew him. He was a good athlete, fair and honorable, and he carried himself in a dignified manner. He was intelligent. He was generous with his time and dedicated to his family, work, and Zionism. I wish that my wife and children could have known him. They would have all loved each other. We received many condolences, including telegrams from UN dignitaries.

> Mrs. Joseph Pressel:
> The United Nations has lost an able and devoted officer in the death of your husband. On behalf of the Department of Public Information I send you heartfelt condolences. Please also accept my deepest personal sympathy.
> Benjamin Cohen, Assistant Secretary General.
>
> Mrs. Joseph Pressel:
> Associates of your late husband deeply grieved at the passing of a good colleague and friend. He had the affection of all who worked with him. Please accept our deepest sympathies. Ilder Foote, Director Press and Publications Bureau, (and signed by sixteen of his colleagues).

The Zionists praised Papa, too. One of their representatives read the following at his funeral.

> On November 2, 1952 the Jackson Heights Zionist District suffered an irreparable loss through the untimely death of Joseph Pressel, a member of the Executive Committee of the District.
>
> Mr. Pressel was an indefatigable worker in the cause of Zionism, and before his fatal illness, gave of himself unstintingly to the services of

Zionism as a whole, and our District in particular. During his late trip to Israel (the summer of 1951) accompanied by his wife and his son Philippe, he studied Israel with an unparalleled intensity. Even on bus sightseeing trips he took voluminous notes in shorthand, for which he had an unusual facility. It is as if he had tried to crowd into his short lifetime as much of the love for Israel and Judaism as a person who had a premonition of an impending curtailment of his stay on this earth would be tempted to do.

His devotion to Judaism and Zionism was lifelong. A native of Belgium for many years, he was born in Poland while his parents (also Belgians) were on a temporary visit there. At the age of three months he was returned to Belgium. His life was hard, and his self-discipline began very early. A self made man, he pursued his higher studies after graduation from high school, in the evenings, after his daily work. He acquired a perfect facility of French, Dutch, German and English languages with the ability to take shorthand notes in all of them. He also had a knowledge of Hebrew and Yiddish which he acquired by himself. He was an original thinker and up to the time of his death was working on an unpublished original system of shorthand for the Hebrew language, which it is hoped, will one day be of benefit to the Jewish people.

During World War II he enlisted in the Polish army in France. Shortly thereafter France surrendered, and he and his family spent the war years in hiding under harrowing and frightening circumstances, as all Jews under the Hitler regime did.

When the United Nations was organized Mr. Pressel was appointed to the United Nations, served as a reporter, translator, stenographer, editor and writer for the United Nations Bureau of Public Information from September 1946 until his death.

At the age of 18 he joined the Zionist Movement and was a leader in young Zionist groups for many years. He was intensely interested in awakening the Jewish spirit through sports, and he was one of the organizers of the Jewish *Maccabi* organization; from 1920 to the War, he was Secretary of *Maccabi* and its Athletic Director.

The indefatigable industry and unusual facility which Mr. Pressel possessed for taking shorthand, was utilized by the World Zionist Organization which commissioned Mr. Pressel as the only person in Holland and Belgium to take verbatim notes of important speeches in those two countries by such men as the late Chaim Weitzman and Zev Jabotinsky, Nachum Goldmann, and others. Mr. Pressel transcribed these speeches for his personal library, which would have been of inestimable historical value had not the fury of Hitler resulted in destruction of this treasure by fire.

The Jackson Heights Zionist District is grieved at his untimely death, and extends condolences to his bereaved family.

BARUCH DAYAN EMES!

Members of our family and the Jackson Heights Jewish community, as well as some friends and UN colleagues, visited my mother and me in the apartment during the following week. There seemed to be little left of me emotionally. I attended the local synagogue as the dutiful Jewish son, to recite *Kaddish*, the traditional prayer for the dead. I was not comforted by doing it, and soon stopped.

I thought about Papa every day. Perhaps, I felt he was special because I was his only son and only child and we had been through so much together. Maybe, it was because I was forced into world events even after the war, and managed to travel to Israel with him and watch his dream about Israeli statehood come true. I thought he was special because he always had time for me and set an example with his kindness, stability, and sense of social responsibility. He also managed to inject me with an appreciation of the finer and applied arts, as well as a sense of pride. Maybe some folks would slough me off as being a spoiled kid, a bit standoffish, a loner—but then, maybe they didn't understand that I grew up in a hostile environment with gentle parents who valued my life above all else.

When Papa died, I felt as if I had lost my rudder—and I was more alone and lonelier than ever. As a father and husband now in my senior years, I realize even more how much I miss him and what we missed by not sharing his life for over fifty years. For years, Maman and I periodically visited Papa's grave. We both felt that we could honor him daily, and not just graveside. We tried to emulate him as much as possible.

I had no idea what I would do with my life, but now the chance to discuss these things with Papa had evaporated. We used to discuss various professions and different kinds of subjects—ranging from boxing to chess, Zionism to science, history to current events. What I understood, without being told, was that I had to continue to do well in school for the sake of his memory.

Unfortunately, Papa passed before finishing his book on Hebrew stenography, leaving much of the development and organization undone. Years after his death, I tried in vain to get someone to work on it in New York or Israel, either as a doctoral thesis or as a paid project. Later, I was told that stenography is dead in the computer age. I still have his original manuscript and, though it gave him great satisfaction and pleasure, I feel badly it fell far short of completion and it was never published. He had dedicated his work to the people of the State of Israel.

I did the best I could at Stuyvesant, and was an average student there—although they say that average at Stuyvesant is better than good elsewhere. Mrs.Vaughn, my algebra teacher, and Mr. Blue, my chemistry teacher, were two of my favorites, and they made an impact on me, because I still remember them.

I joined the Stuyvesant swimming team coached by Dr. Sigfried Meyers, who was also a physics teacher. He took me under his wing and acted as a surrogate father, persuading me to study engineering and to swim at college.

With Papa gone, Maman continued to work at *haute couture* shops, like Martha's on Park Avenue and East 56th Street in Manhattan. She made dresses for celebrities like Zsa Zsa Gabor, Claire Booth Luce, Twiggy, and Mrs. Perry Como. To reduce our expenses, we moved to a one-bedroom apartment a few blocks away from where we were, and Maman gave me the sole bedroom. She kept the alcove off the kitchen for herself, cooked, cleaned, and encouraged me to continue my studies. In fact, she still bought me most of my clothing. I took a job as a part-time delivery boy for the local deli, carrying orders for people who came to the store and didn't want to schlep the stuff themselves, or for those who called in their orders. Often I would be given soda bottles to return for their deposits, and ended up making a fairly decent amount of tip money—enough for me to make occasional deposits in my savings account at the Bowery Bank in Manhattan. From my first paycheck, I bought Maman a bouquet of flowers.

I've been an avid fan most of my life of track and field. Papa had certainly given me a feeling for the sport, and I admired many of its heroes. In the spring of 1954, I had the thrill of a lifetime because I was in the right place at the right time! It happened that the Stuyvesant swim team practiced at the Madison Square Boys Club on First Avenue and East 22nd Street in Manhattan. A few weeks earlier, Roger Bannister broke the record for the four-minute mile in England. When he came to New York for interviews and awards, his first stop was the Boys Club—where I managed to stay after practice and watch him go through his paces for the gentlemen of the press. Then I walked over, shook his hand and asked him for his autograph—which he gladly gave me and is a possession I still cherish.

My best friend at Stuyvesant was Michael Langsam, who lived in Forest Hills, not far from Jackson Heights. Often, on hot days during the summers, we'd take the bus to the beach in Far Rockaway, on the peninsula along Long Island. It was [and is] the most unlikely "beach resort" in the world. The strip of land, easily visible if you are landing or taking off from Kennedy Airport or LaGuardia, was filled with hotels built in the 1920s and 30s, still housing many old Jewish people—many of them Orthodox Holocaust survivors.

One day that Michael arrived at a party with a smart young woman named Carol. Barbara, his first cousin, had introduced them, and it wasn't too long before the lovely lady became his bride and I his best man. Though we now live on opposite sides of the country, he and I still stay in touch, and through him and college friends, I learned the true value of friendship.

I was still a loner at heart, though. I spent lots of my free time on my bike, pumping the pedals to the edges of Long Island, to Rockaway Beach, and Great Neck, distances as far as 30 miles. I was pushing myself to the max, and felt that a bicycle was something under my control—unlike the life that whirled around me since my childhood. One of my favorite rides was the one that I'd take through LaGuardia Airport. It was only about five miles from the apartment, and was a straight, long, paved stretch of land, much easier to negotiate than the hills of Brooklyn or the traffic on Queens Boulevard.

There was no security in those days, and a kid on a bike never generated much interest. The airfield was a great place to get some exercise, and also to experience history. I was coasting along the field when a military aircraft landed and the first prisoners of war from Korea disembarked. I was standing right next to the "welcoming" party, and the next day, when I saw the newspapers, I realized I was standing right outside the frame of the photograph they had taken of the event.

It wasn't as if I was miserable all the time. I devoted my evenings mostly to staying home, doing my homework, or reading. Sometimes Maman and I would watch TV or play cards together. Sometimes we would go to the movies or theater together—we saw "The King and I," and even visited Times Square one New Year's Eve, but left before the midnight chaos broke loose.

In those days, Stuyvesant was an all boys' school, and the chance to meet girls was almost non-existent. Besides, there was always baseball, *real* baseball, to distract you. My cousin Sylvan and I would go to Yankee games in the Bronx, and got to see the all-time greats: Mickey Mantle, Joe DiMaggio, Whitey Ford, Yogi Berra, Hank Bauer—and some of the Dodgers, too—like Duke Snyder. After one game at Yankee Stadium, I stood at the players' exit and managed to collect a great bunch of autographs from the Yankees, including one from Mel Allen, the legendary game caller and official voice of the Yankees. Billy Martin, on the other hand, simply shoved me aside when I asked for his signature. Interesting how a personality comes through in the little things!

Amazingly, the hair processing business my grandfather in Antwerp had founded so many years ago was now thriving in New York City! My mother's relatives continued to run the business, including Uncle Elie. Later, when synthetics, like *Dynel* and *Allura*, took over the business, the market for human hair began to shrink and eventually the business was dissolved. One of my cousins in the Schwerner family was Michael, a civil rights worker, the same Michael Schwerner who disappeared with Andrew Goodman and James Cheney, also civil rights workers, during the upheavals down south in 1964. The story of how my cousin and his colleagues were heinously murdered in Philadelphia, Mississippi was aptly told in the film "Mississippi Burning."

In the Spring of 1953, Aunt Ella, Maman's sister, who was married to Arthur Fink, a businessman in the chemical and dental supply industry, called us when an apartment became available in the house they were living in, and convinced us to move to the Bronx. It made sense for us in the long run because the NYU School of Engineering was only four blocks away and that was a factor in my choice of college. I'd been accepted at Columbia and City College, both in Manhattan, but the convenience of living near the NYU campus couldn't be overlooked.

In June of 1955, my mother attended my Stuyvesant High School graduation. My classmates included some illustrious and brilliant people, including Edmar Mednis a future international chess grandmaster, and Roald Hoffman a future Nobel Prize winner in Chemistry. Among all of the talent at school, I thought I did ok by winning a Bronze Scholarship Certificate. I am very proud to be an alumnus of such a prestigious high school—where I believe close to 100 percent of the students go on to college.

The following fall, I began at NYU and never regretted my decision to attend the school. I attended the freshman fall dance and met Eugene Sferrazza, another engineering student who was so broke I had to lend him $20 for the admission fee and other incidentals. Hazing was something that freshmen had to go through. Before the dance could begin, all of us freshmen were forced to parade down University Avenue in our pajamas and hike back to the campus. Once there, we had to run a through a gauntlet of water hoses aimed at us by the upperclassmen. Well, Eugene and I considered this a bonding experience, and became friends for life. I tutored him whenever he needed it, and he taught me to drive and let me practice on his car before I went for my driving test. For a while, we even worked for the same company. He gave up engineering for the insurance business, but we still took fishing trips together. Gene has passed on and I miss his friendship.

I was doing well in school and after a first semester of straight A's, and as the only son of a widow earning little as a seamstress, I was given a scholarship that covered half of my tuition. I took five courses every semester for my four undergraduate years and decided to concentrate on mechanical engineering, since I loved math and mechanics. I was a little bit off the mark, because I only allowed myself to take one liberal arts/humanities course per semester, and now I feel I deprived myself by neglecting the breadth of my education.

After taking lots of the basic engineering courses, I decided mechanics, stress and dynamic analysis were my favorite subjects. I was doing well enough so that in my senior year, I was invited to join Tau Beta Pi, the national honorary engineering society (equivalent to Phi Beta Kappa), and Pi Tau Sigma, the national honorary mechanical engineering society. I became the secretary of both organizations, which looked good on my resume. But money was always tight. In order to make some spending money, I tutored other engineering students in math, physics or mechanical engineering courses. I also tutored some high school students in French, earning $4.00 an hour, which was considered good money back then.

My dream would have been realized had I made the track team, but I just wasn't fast enough to make the cut on either the sprints or the long jump. Instead, I joined the NYU swimming team and discovered that working out relaxed me, giving me something to look forward to. It even helped me boost my grades! My events were the 50- and 100- yard freestyle and breaststroke races. In my senior year, the team took a three-day road trip to compete with Union College, Hamilton College and Syracuse University. The Syracuse meet was down to the last relay, and I swam fast and hard, and when we won the race, we won the meet. In fact, we won all three meets, and I was the team's high scorer for the weekend. We'd taken the bus through upstate New York, but after we beat Syracuse, the coach flew us back to the city. It was a thrill in more than one way—we took off in a DC-3 in a vicious snowstorm and landed at Newark airport. It was the first time that I ever flew.

During my four years competing at NYU, every year we won the New York City college swimming champions. When the season was over, the coach would take us to mid-town Manhattan, to the theater and restaurant district and treat us to a feast at Mama Leone's Restaurant. The portions were huge, the waiters noisy and wild, and the décor as campy as you could possibly imagine. It was in the basement of a brownstone in what used to be Hell's Kitchen, now part of the theater district, and called Clinton Hill. Mama Leone's was festooned with plastic garlands and chains made from the tabs of soda cans. They served, literally, mountains of spaghetti, and gallons of tomato sauce, not to mention half-gallon pitchers loaded with your favorite beverages, including sangria or beer. Mama Leone's, where they invented "super-sizing," is long gone, but the legend lives on!

As I grew older, I began to appreciate more and more how fortunate I was to have escaped the worst of the war and survived. I was determined not to waste my life on inconsequential stuff, and worked hard to succeed. I earned the balance of my tuition, about $1,500 a year in those days, by working summers as an office boy, doing clerical work, deliveries, as a trimmer in a leather company, an architectural firm's gopher, and mainly as a bellhop in the Catskills—once at the Green Acres Country Club and another season at the Alamac Hotel in Woodridge. I made extra tips by parking cars, moonlighting as a lifeguard, and setting up card tables for the guests.

At first, being up in the mountains, I missed Maman, but I soon made some friends, ate well, and kept busy. There were also two summers, when business was slow among the elite corps of New York's *haute couture* ladies, and Maman went to Swampscott, Massachusetts. She was *the* society seamstress in great demand and still able to enjoy a bit of a vacation. Our mode of transportation in those days was the bus. She took one to the north shore of Boston, and I took one to the Catskills. We stayed in touch via the U.S. Postal Service, writing as often as we could. Around this time I started calling her Ma instead of Maman, as it seemed the more adult thing to do.

Life on campus wasn't always about peace on earth. When I turned 18, I had to register for the draft. The Cold War was raging all around us; Vietnam hadn't happened to the U.S. just yet. I went down and registered at the recruiting station that sat in the shadow of Yankee Stadium. For the first two years at NYU, I was in the ROTC, the Reserve Officers Training Corps. We were like weekend warriors. We learned how to handle M-16 rifles, how to march, and took courses related to the military. I received promotion to corporal, but did not want a future in the military so I didn't re-register after my sophomore year.

My winter treat was to be able to attend several annual indoor track meets at Madison Square Garden. The best, the one I enjoyed most, was the Millrose Games. In forty-three years I missed just four games, until I had to give up the tickets when I moved out west in 1999. I'd often invite neighbors and friends to come to the meets with me, and I kept working on getting better tickets. Eventually I had four tickets, first row trackside at the starting line. I don't exaggerate when I say it was thrilling for me to see so many of my favorite athletes perform at their peak.

NYU's limited social opportunities were really hard to deal with and no better than Stuyvesant's. The Bronx campus was not co-ed. I began to date girls I met at dances, while working in the Catskills or through Jewish organizations. Occasionally, I'd let someone fix me up on a blind date. I even got myself an old 1952 Pontiac Catalina (a two-door green coupe with a white hardtop). I would take my dates to see movies at the Loew's Paradise on the Grand Concourse.

The car turned out to be very cantankerous and gave me huge problems, especially in cold weather—even when I covered the engine with a blanket to absorb moisture and retain some heat. The AAA was sick of seeing me, but had to start her up for me anyway. It didn't really matter to me how cranky the car got. Even with the signal turn lever popping out of its socket and a constantly-dying battery, I loved that car.

In the fall of 1958, I showed up early for a Halloween Dance at Hunter College in the Bronx. Marion Levy, whom I had never met before, pressed me into service and got me to work the coatroom with her. She had gone to the Bronx High School of Science, so I knew she was intelligent. She was an attractive shapely brunette, and friendly; she could hold her own in a conversation, was Jewish, and I liked her. I asked her out to see movies and shows. One of my favorite places to take dates was to the Amato Opera Company in Greenwich Village. Tickets cost but a song, and I could afford to listen and see operas like La Boheme and La Traviata when the Metropolitan Opera was so far out of financial reach. If we got to the theater early enough, we could sit right behind the conductor, and enjoy everything, even the scenery collapsing on the stage.

The more time Marion and I spent together, the more I liked her. Marion was majoring in math at Hunter College and lived with her parents only ten minutes from our apartment. Her mother, Gertrude, taught high school French at Evander Childs High School, was an amateur still-life painter, and a voracious reader. Her father was a children's hosiery salesman, who covered most of Long Island, and spent much of his days in his car traveling from one customer to another. He was an avid pipe smoker, a snappy dresser, and a fine gentleman. Things got serious between us after Marion attended my commencement exercises in May 1959.

Marion and I decided to marry, but we wanted to wait until she finished school in January 1960. We did not want to live too far from the city, because we wanted to be close to our parents. We hoped that there would be job openings available to us so that we could start our life together properly. We loved New York and were very reluctant to yank ourselves out by the roots.

# 10

## GROWING UP

The NYU campus was a convenient place to find a good job, because the campus held job fairs, and recruiters would come to the gym to headhunt. Many "high" tech companies in those days were looking for good prospects. My hard work paid off when I earned second place in my class standing among the mechanical engineers. I met company representatives from everywhere, and visited many of the corporation's headquarters and labs. I interviewed with RCA in Camden, NJ, Westinghouse in Baltimore, MD, and Hamilton Standard in Windsor Locks, CT.

RCA gave me an offer I couldn't refuse, even on the best of days. In addition to a hefty salary of $6,500 a year, the highest offer made to anyone in the graduating class, they offered me a full scholarship to the mechanical engineering graduate school at the University of Pennsylvania. I would only have to work a total of three days a week.

The other two days of the week were for studying and attending classes. I took the deal, since no other offers came close to that.

Camden was about two hours from the Bronx, not very far from Philadelphia, Pennsylvania, on the other side of the Delaware River. Just before graduation, I climbed into my not-so-trusty green Catalina and found an upstairs room in a widow's boarding house, about five miles from work.

I was eager to get started. I wanted to prove to myself that I could be independent. This was about the time I realized how far I had come from being an almost-victim in the old country. I was no longer a greenhorn. Compared to other relatives, who spent time in camps and those sacrificed on an altar of hatred, we were fortunate. Still, my family had suffered its own fate, but due to my parents' perseverance, love and determination, we survived. I was an American in America, free to do as I pleased, within the limits of the law, in the land of opportunity. I realized I was in a good place at a good time, and appreciated every wonder-filled moment. I was grateful for the abundance of opportunities and possibilities. I was grateful to Papa and Maman (especially her in my more mature years), working hard to provide me with values that praised the positives of high standards!

I loaded up the Pontiac Catalina with my stuff and headed to my "garret" in Camden. I was certainly disappointed by the simplicity of my first assignment and concerned that it was not in any of my areas of interest. I was to familiarize myself with the electronic testing components for the Hawk missile, and write engineering change orders. I wasn't an electrical engineer, but I was a member of the engineers' union at RCA. Unions were so powerful, I wasn't permitted to use drafting tools to make a sketch, or move a wastepaper basket from one side of my desk to another. If I wanted the wastebasket moved, I had to call a member of the material handlers' union. I got in trouble for making a sketch with drafting tools once, because I didn't call in the drafting union members. Still, though I felt like a fish out of water, I got a five percent raise in salary after only eight weeks on the job due to a union negotiated increase!

A few months before Marion graduated from Hunter College in January, 1960, we spent some time looking for a place to live not far from the RCA plant in New Jersey. We found a garden apartment in Haddonfield, a growing township only eight miles away. With the apartment found, we continued with our wedding plans. The ceremony took place at Temple Rodeph Shalom, a Reform synagogue in Manhattan, which we felt was appropriate for us, as neither of us were very observant or religious. Joan Levy, Marion's cousin, was the Maid of Honor, and Michael Langsam was my best man. Uncle Maurice and his two sons refused to attend because we were having our wedding in a Reform Temple and they were Orthodox. Aunt Ruth attended in deference to my mother. Although my relationship with Uncle Maurice wasn't very solid to begin with, it was non-existent after the wedding!

Our wedding day also marked the day of our first fight as a married couple. The wedding ceremony and reception went very well, but when I went to change the film in my 8MM home-movie camera, the film popped out and was all tangled up. Marion had loaded the film improperly and I lost my temper. But we made up soon afterward, before we traveled to San Juan and St. Thomas for our honeymoon.

We had spent much time finding furniture for the apartment. I wanted to participate in the decision-making, but knew very little about styles and furniture. Marion had to put up with me and was wisely silent, though my actions probably cost us time and money when it came to getting the apartment the way we wanted it. Marion, who finished Hunter with high honors in math and statistics, got teaching jobs—one at Kramer Junior High School teaching math, and one teaching statistics at Rutgers University. Then she applied to graduate school at the University of Pennsylvania School of Education and finished her Masters degree in a single year, in May 1961. She majored in math education.

After four months, I asked to be transferred to a department that made better use of my skills and interests. I was transferred to the RCA Moorestown plant not too great a distance away, and for the next two and a half years, had interesting assignments. I designed gear-train assemblies for ground-based radar antennae for the military, and worked on the design of a steel chamber used in electrical energy experiments in a pressurized nitrogen-based environment.

Stress must have gotten to me, because after just two years at work, and studying for my Masters, I developed intestinal problems. First the doctors told me I was suffering from ulcerative colitis—a painful, stress-related problem. Eventually the real diagnosis was made: I suffered from Crohn's Disease, chronic inflammation of the bowel, and was put on Prednisone for years and years. I still haven't figured out how that happened! Had I really put that much pressure on myself without even realizing it?

It wasn't long before RCA's business began to decline and there were layoffs at the beginning of 1962. I saw the handwriting on the wall, and decided to look for a company where the concentration was on mechanical engineering. I wanted to do more in my areas of interest.

Since I had my Masters' degree by then, I also figured I might negotiate a salary increase. We sure could use it, because Marion and I were expecting our first child. I interviewed with the Avco Corporation in Wilmington, Massachusetts, near Boston. They designed and fabricated missile nosecones. My job would be mechanical engineering and stress analysis. My salary was $11,000 a year, an amazing feat for someone just three years removed from NYU. My friends at college and I had figured it would take us at least seven to ten years to get to that level, and I had made it in three!

We found a two-bedroom townhouse in Bedford, a small development about fifteen miles from the Avco plant. Marion's pregnancy advanced nicely until December 4, 1962, when she went into labor. Her little suitcase was ready to go and so was our new child. Though we lived in New England, the snow had yet to fall, so I made it in time to the Symmes Hospital in Arlington. They took Marion away, and told me I would be better off at home, because it would take sometime for Marion to deliver. In those days, husbands were *persona non grata* in labor and delivery rooms. No sooner had I gotten home when the phone rang, and there was Marion on the other end to announce the birth of a healthy baby boy. I made the two obligatory phone calls— one to Ma and one to Marion's parents. I grabbed my camera, and I was off to the hospital to begin recording the life of my first child. I handed out cigars at work and played the role of the proud papa, although Marion had done all the work.

We decided to call our son Allan Joseph. We both liked the name Allan. The baby's Hebrew name was Leb, after Marion's maternal grandfather (Leopold or Lev) and Joseph for my father. A week later, Marion's parents and Ma arrived for the bris, the circumcision ceremony, performed by a *mohel,* who welcomed my son into the Jewish people. After the ceremony, we shared a toast to life and munched on sweet cakes and cookies.

I have to admit I was worried about my ability to be a good father. Papa had been so special and I had lost him so early. I only hoped that I could affect my children in the same positive way. I knew I had to care for the baby as well as Marion did, and I think we did a fairly good job. I really loved playing with Allan and had lots of fun with him. I just couldn't handle the crying part, so we got him a pacifier and it seemed to do the trick. Then, after his second birthday, I got it into my head to make three-by-five-inch flashcards with the alphabet written on them in red ink. Within weeks, Allan knew his alphabet, so I made new cards with words on them, and before I knew it, he could read simple words.

I spent the next three years at Avco learning all that I could about missile nosecones and stress analysis—and things that came in useful for the rest of my career. Marion had moved from teaching to publishing, and was editing textbooks part-time for Houghton-Mifflin, one of the largest textbook publishers in the world.

Before we'd moved to Bedford, Mass, we dreaded facing New England winters and booked a Caribbean cruise out of Manhattan in the fall 1963. Marion's parents offered to baby-sit, so before we headed to the pier in the city, we went to the Bronx to drop off Allan. We left Bedford at noon on Friday, November 22. About two hours later, as we were driving along the Merritt Parkway in Connecticut, I turned on the radio and heard that President John F. Kennedy had been shot in Dallas. I was so shocked and upset I couldn't drive and I pulled the car over to the side of the road.

After a while, I headed straight to the Levys. We dropped off Allan, since we couldn't cancel the cruise. We boarded the ship in New York, but it was a somber departure, and our whole journey missed that carefree, fun attitude we had so looked forward to. At every port, the assassination was the main subject of discussion, quickly chased away by subsequent events, including the arrest and killing of Lee Harvey Oswald. Our sadness at the loss our country had suffered went deep, but we weren't home to get the full impact of the historical events from the American media. We came home and determined to keep our spirits, to continue working, and raising our family, which within the year, began to grow.

On the morning of October 24, 1964, Marion had a doctor's appointment. Unfortunately I had a 24-hour virus and she took me to the hospital, although she was due with our second child the next day. Her parents came up that night to take Allan home with them until after she delivered. They lived over four hours away in New York. I was released the afternoon of the 24th and Marion went into labor that evening. I brought her to Concord Emerson hospital where the doctor, again, sent me home to wait out Marion's delivery. Early the next morning, as I was preparing to leave for the hospital to see how things were going, the phone rang, and once again, it was Marion announcing the birth of our second son. His English name was David Michael and Moshe in Hebrew. Marion and I liked the name David, and two of our grandfathers had the name Moshe, so both sides of the family were covered. The bris took place eight days later, and the same *mohel* who had welcomed Allan to the Jewish community welcomed David.

I decided to diversify my experience and hopefully boost my salary. So I looked around and interviewed with three companies. Perkin-Elmer in Wilton, Connecticut, maker of optical equipment, Combustion Engineering near Hartford, builder of nuclear power plants, and the last was Brookhaven Laboratories in Brookhaven, Long Island, researchers in nuclear energy. The job at Perkin-Elmer intrigued me, because they were designing sophisticated optical instruments for military and medical use and it seemed to me that there would be growth in that sector. I chose Perkin-Elmer and started making plans.

Marion and I scouted about for an apartment and found one in a brick apartment complex about twenty-five miles from work, in Stamford, Connecticut. Besides being an interesting job, we were much closer to our parents than we had been before. The company paid for the move, and we began our new life with our two sons in a new town.

# ACCOMPLISHMENTS & HEARTBREAK

For thirty years, I worked at Perkin-Elmer, and was fascinated by my work, lots of which was classified and sent into outer space by Air Force rockets or on the shuttle through the National Aeronautics and Space Administration (NASA). I began as a mechanical engineer designing sophisticated optical instruments—cameras and telescopes. I grew to become a project leader, responsible for the design, analysis of optical instruments, and following them through hardware production, testing, system integration and interfacing with various system components. If it sounds complicated, that's because it was.

Later in 1966, I was chosen to join a group of engineers that spent months doing studies and preliminary designs for a large optical system that was going to be shot into space. We took weeks to write the proposal by hand, and eventually after typing, it was the size of a fat telephone book. Two other engineers and I wrote most of the mechanical engineering section for the project, which was then presented to the United States government. We scribbled and dictated until we got it correctly done. Every "i" had to be dotted, every t had to be crossed, then we waited. And waited.

Finally, on a day in October 1966, the team was summoned to a Perkin-Elmer conference room. We sat down at the table and didn't know what to expect until the program manager and the corporate vice president walked in. When the VP pulled a cigar out of his jacket pocket, we knew we had been chosen to design and build what we had proposed. We were ecstatic because we were bringing in millions and millions of dollars for Perkin-Elmer, working for America, and doing some pioneering science to boot. What could be better than that? They even built us a new facility for the project in Danbury, Connecticut so that we could handle the job.

When the program was moved to Danbury, a significant amount of time was added to my commute, so we went house hunting again. This time, instead of an apartment, we bought a house in the northern part of Stamford in the spring of 1968. We purchased a four-bedroom ranch house with more than two acres of land. Part of that land was a pond, about one acre, not far from the house.

Over the next year, Perkin-Elmer hired many support personnel and mechanical engineers to work on the project. Because I had been in on it from day one and was familiar with the project, I was given the large responsibility of being the project engineer for a major part. I oversaw the whole optical sub-assembly, which was a complicated piece of equipment weighing about six hundred pounds. It was my job to lead a group of engineers and draftsmen in the mechanical design, analysis, drawing release, and integration of that assembly with other system components. I was also responsible for interfacing with other disciplines such as electrical and computer systems, test departments, and handling design reviews with the goal of "hardware release" (getting the product fabricated and ready for launch) in a timely and cost efficient manner.

All of the work and paperwork had to be performed in a secure environment because it was all classified. It was Perkin-Elmer's largest project and it pushed them onto the list of Fortune 500 companies. Everything we built worked extremely well, so Perkin-Elmer had its contract renewed, and my technical group received kudos and awards from people at the highest levels of the American government.

In due time, I worked on the design of the guidance system for the Hubble Space telescope, which is responsible for some of the most incredible photographs ever taken of the universe. The system is now so accurate you could, for example, aim a rifle in New York to hit a tennis ball in San Francisco! The problem that caused fuzzy pictures when the

**Phil at Perkin-Elmer**

Hubble was first launched came from the primary mirror in the main optical assembly, not the guidance system, and then in the end, Perkin-Elmer staff had a hand in making the corrective lenses that functioned so well and extended the life of the telescope. We are all extremely proud of ourselves, and our accomplishments. How many scientists around the world use it to study the heavens? How many thousands of people use Hubble photos as their screensavers? When Daniel Goldin was the head of NASA, one of the most spectacular Hubble photos, one he called "The Finger of God," hung in a prized space in his Houston office.

I was the lead or project engineer for mechanical engineering on several other interesting and complicated optical systems. One was a space-based *Star Wars* telescope. Another was a 24-inch aperture ground-based telescope for the U.S. government. One extremely complicated system we designed was a laboratory-based test stand for an infrared detector assembly that was approximately the size of a basketball. The test stand was about seven feet tall, weighed a thousand pounds, and had to spin the infra-red detector at 1,500 revolutions per minute. Also, it had to maintain its rotational position stability to within an angle of less than ten seconds of arc. All that had to be done while we were passing liquid helium (at four degrees above absolute zero) through part of the system, a portion of which was in a vacuum. We were the only bidder on the program and were not sure it would work. Happily, when we tested it, it worked beautifully. All of the systems I worked on were built and operated successfully. I was very proud of my contributions, but I didn't do it alone.

My teams were highly talented people assembled by Perkin-Elmer. I learned a lot from them and from our work. I made great friends and had fantastic colleagues. Most of them are retired or have passed on. One of them was Ed Brelling, a man I still miss. He was the best designer/draftsman I ever worked with, and I have worked with the best. We worked together for almost twenty-eight years and became very close. It saddened me greatly when he died in the spring 2002. Some of the other talented colleagues that I was close to and still stay in touch with are Marty Yellin, Werner Pollack, Joe Prusak, Joe Vollero, Dennis Preston, Frank Sileo, Oscar Berensohn, Paul Yoder, Ted Urban, and Sam Palasciano.

Perhaps it was because I was so proud of my work, or perhaps I thought that I had gone through enough, I wasn't totally prepared for the trials and tribulations that were still ahead. Marion had given birth to our third son, Steven, in 1969. He was just as wonderful as my other two boys and just as beautiful, too. When we moved into the new ranch house with the pond, we had been warned by our neighbors to put a gate around the pond. We thought that a fence around the backyard play area would be sufficient to keep the children safe. Sadly, we found out, on Tuesday, March 23, 1971, just how wrong we were.

When I drove up to the house from work that afternoon, my neighbor, Doris Fowkes, was waiting for me in front of the house. She told me that Steven had been playing ball with another little boy, and the ball had fallen into the water, and Steven was sent to get it. Steven went into the pond, but the child he was playing with disappeared and never told anyone that Steven had fallen into the pond.

Marion came out of the house to look for him and found him floating face down. She pulled him out and gave him CPR and managed to revive him until the ambulance came and took them to the hospital in Stamford. Doris stayed behind to take care of Allan and David. I sped through town and met Marion in the ICU. She told me that several doctors were working on him. She stayed with him around the clock for the first forty-eight hours. I went home both nights, once to get Steven's favorite teddy bear, and to make sure that one of us was around to comfort the boys.

When the doctors finally allowed us to see Steven, he was hooked up to various machines, lying on a bed that was cooled to keep his body temperature low. By late afternoon Thursday we were very apprehensive. I was nervous and had a constant ache in my heart and throat. I'm sure Marion did too. When we heard a voice on the loud speaker calling a cardiac specialist to the ICU stat, the bottom dropped out of my belly, my heart started to pound and my pulse raced. It couldn't be good, and it was much worse than that. It wasn't long before our pediatrician came out to tell us Steven had gone into cardiac arrest and that they couldn't save him. Our rabbi, Joseph Ehrenkrantz, had just come by and was there to comfort us and escort us home.

We had the funeral the next day, Friday. We thought it would be too traumatic for Allan and David, so we asked our neighbors to watch them. After the service in Stamford, we laid him to rest in a family plot in the Cedar Park cemetery in Oradell, New Jersey, about 10 miles from the George Washington Bridge. Later, I realized that "sparing" the boys from the funeral was the wrong thing to do. Being part of the family as it grieved would have benefited them greatly.

Steven's death was the worst, most horrific experience of my life, overshadowing everything from my childhood. Everything. There are those who lock the horrors of the Holocaust deep inside themselves and never confront the pain. I am that way about Steven. I don't like to think about the tragedy of losing my son. He was just two years old, and losing a toddler like that, losing any child, is the worst thing a human being can experience. In a sense, I also appreciated then how hard my parents had worked to keep me alive.

I considered myself a good father, and worked hard at it. I was involved with my kids, helped them with homework, taught and played with them in any sports they cared about and wanted me to be involved in. I built them a go-cart for coasting down the local hill and a tree house in the backyard. We set up electric trains in the attic. We sang or listened to songs together. Perhaps the "quality time" that I spent with them was my way of avoiding the negative relationship that I was having with Marion.

We had good times. We took family trips to several states—Utah, Nevada, Arizona, California, and New York. We even packed up the boys for a trip to Israel. As the kids grew older, we used the backyard a lot. We invented a contest called the Olympics—a decathlon we invented. This included the 25-yard dash, one lap around the house, a ball toss in the backyard, a standing long jump, a hurdles race (I built some low wooden hurdles), and a high-jump unto an old mattress. When the boys were older, we added the 8-pound shot put toss. We even kept records of times, distances and heights.

Occasionally, I did the Olympics with Allan although I admit, these days I mostly watch the kids. My grandchildren are starting to try some of the events. In the summer of 1976, Allan, David, and I went to Montreal for the Summer Olympics. We mostly attended track and field events, but we also managed to get some tickets for swimming meets, volleyball games, gymnastics, soccer, and cycling in the velodrome.

Marion and I were still maintaining our marriage, working at it, and keeping things on an even keel. On February 28, 1972, Marion gave birth to our beautiful daughter, Linda Ellen. Linda was welcomed by the boys, and was included in of all the games and sports, like the Olympics and was even part of the homework crowd. She was as tough and competitive as the boys, especially when we played cards, which I rarely let the kids win. I also enjoyed reading them stories and sharing music with them at bedtime—especially Alvin and the Chipmunks and Israeli music.

We joined the Agudath Sholom synagogue in Stamford so that we could provide our children with a Jewish education. Marion and I were not very observant and attended synagogue only on the High Holy Days, yet on Passover, Marion usually made a Seder, the traditional meal, for our closest relatives and a few friends. Also, I went to synagogue twice a year for *Yahrtzeit* (memorial) services, to say Kaddish for Steven and my father. All the children had a bar or bat mitzvah at Agudath Sholom by the steadfast, loyal, warm, and caring Rabbi Joseph Ehrenkrantz.

After being widowed for fourteen years, in 1966, my mother married a terrific human being, a Mr. Harry Groner. They'd met through mutual acquaintances, Fred and Blanche Katzenberg. Harry worked in the garment industry until he hit his 50's and his wife died. He went back to school to become a teacher, earning his degree at City College of New York at age 55. Then he became a history teacher at Morris High School in the South Bronx. He loved his new vocation and worked until the city forced him to retire at age 70.

I grew to love Harry like my own father. He had a wonderful family, two sons, and their families. Warren is retired from the biomedical engineering business and his wife Rosemarie, is a retired medical administrator. Ed, Harry's other son, is a widower retired from the oil business in Oklahoma. His late wife was named Ellen.

Harry and my mother, who worked until her eyes failed her in her mid-70s, shared a love of art, music, theatre, and playing cards. They traveled all over the world and were a fascinating couple. They could speak with anyone about most anything. They belonged to the Senior Citizen group at the 92nd St. "Y" in New York, where they played bridge. Harry taught American history and my mother taught conversational French, until she was 96 at the "Y"! As such wonderful role models, they were invited by Mt. Sinai Hospital's Geriatric Department to lecture the doctors once a year on what a senior's way of life was like. They also were participants on the topic on the "Today Show."

My mother survived the war very well. With all of the hardships, responsibilities, family losses, and frights she endured, it was amazing that she didn't break down or have a heart attack. She was extremely strong, physically and mentally, and stayed that way. Of her siblings, she is the oldest, and the only one living. Her brother was deported. Her sisters Sonia, Alice, Ella and Ruth have passed. Before Harry died, she said, "We go on. I'm very lucky and very happy with my son Philip and his family and with my husband and his family. My husband and I have been very close and have very nice grand- and great-grand children. We are satisfied with what we have." At 98, she still feels the same way.

My intestinal diseases forced me to be hospitalized several times. I eventually developed pre-cancerous symptoms that required surgery. In August of 1971, I had surgery at Stamford Hospital and made a good recovery. Later, I decided to help others with the same condition by becoming a peer counselor. In the fall of 1972, I attended Enterostomal

Therapy School at Roswell Park Memorial Institute in Buffalo, New York for six weeks, taking some time off from work. I was fascinated with the work and doing hands on care and I subsequently practiced therapy part-time for the patients of doctors in the area. It was gratifying work and I soon became involved in the local and national organizations for Enterostomal therapists and the United Ostomy Association.

Unfortunately, our marriage was not going well. Marion and I tried to keep the marriage alive for eight more years, and tried counseling together and separately. It just did not work. We were like oil and water. In the spring of 1979, I moved to an apartment in Bethel, Connecticut, four miles from my office, and the divorce became final the following year. We both were at fault for making many mistakes and the breakup took its toll on our children.

**Miriam Pressel Groner and Harry Groner**

# 12

# LATER YEARS

After our divorce, I tried as much as I could to spend time with the kids, doing the things we shared in the past, but they were getting older and getting on with their lives. Marion was teaching and going to graduate school at Yale in the School of Organizational Behavior. I was figuring out what I had to do next. My mother was emotionally supportive of me when Steven died, and throughout my divorce. She had been through so much in her lifetime that she was not overcome with sadness. She accepted these things as tragic, but also part of living and kept reminding me, "life goes on."

I was still working on secret projects for the government, and that was sort of exciting—exciting enough to occupy me, and keep my mind off of my difficulties.

Patricia Trudel, a high school teacher from Fairfield, Connecticut, and I met through the ostomy organization. We became friends and she helped me through the divorce in a gentle and non-judgmental way. We later fell in love and were married in August of 1980 at her parents' house in Stamford by Justice of the Peace William McNamara, a math teacher at Pat's high school. Thirty of our family members attended the morning wedding ceremony.

We spent a week of our honeymoon on Long Beach Island down at the Jersey Shore. We were supposed to also spend another week in the Poconos Mountains, but our relaxation was shattered a day after we arrived. We got one of those unwelcome phone calls, this time about Pat's father, Roland Trudel. He had a heart attack, so we rushed back to Stamford. Happily, he recovered quickly.

We'd gone house hunting and found a three-story townhouse in Bethel, Connecticut that we moved into immediately after the wedding. I continued working for Perkin-Elmer. Pat continued teaching history, business, and psychology at Fairfield High School, (formerly Andrew Warde High School). She'd received her BS in history with honors from Boston College, and her MA and a Sixth year certificate from Fairfield University. For many years, she was the teacher in charge of the National Honor Society, where she led the selection process and bestowed the honors to the students. She also co-taught an Advanced Placement (AP) class in American Studies. Her fellow English teacher was Paul Corwell, a talented teacher and motivator.

I spent time with Allan and David on weekends, and Linda came to stay with us every other weekend. The boys attended Rippowam High School, and Linda attended Stamford High School. Allan was a diver on the high school swimming team, David was a wrestler, and Linda played field hockey. They were also great students.

After graduating with honors from high school, Allan went to Brandeis University in Waltham, Massachusetts, majoring in economics and computer science. He was a diver on the Brandeis swimming team and earned "All American" honors his senior year. He spent his junior year at the London School of Economics and traveled extensively in Europe. In Leningrad, USSR, he and a fellow student helped a "refusnik" — a young Soviet Jewish chemist—immigrate to the U.S. After graduation, he headed west to Los Angeles, where he attended UCLA's MBA program.

It was the summer of 1984 and Los Angeles was hosting the Olympic Games. Allan lived near the UCLA campus and it was convenient to many sporting events. He got to see his idol in diving,

Greg Louganis, win two gold medals. At the games, Allan collected and traded Olympic pins he later mounted and framed along with his ticket stubs. That 1984 collection is hanging on the wall in his den, along with his souvenirs from attending subsequent Summer Olympics: Seoul, Korea in 1988; Barcelona, Spain in 1992; Atlanta in 1996; Sydney, Australia in 2000, and even the 2002 Winter Olympics in Salt Lake City. He has his tickets to Athens for the upcoming Olympics. To complete his set, I gave him my own small collection of pins from our trip to the Montreal Olympics in 1976. I went to Atlanta with him in 1996 and spent three fun days at some great track and field events.

Allan has a good career in the computer and software business. After working for Arthur Andersen & Company, he and four partners formed their own specialty company called i-Cube. It went public and was sold before the silicon bubble burst. He married Beth Cowan, a speech therapist in the Los Angeles school system. Austin and Julia are the two terrific grandchildren they gave me. They lived in a large house in Redondo Beach, California. Unfortunately the marriage fell apart, but Allan is extremely close and devoted to his children. He is now in the process of developing and marketing a new software company called Charity Finders of which he is the CEO.

I am just as proud of David. After receiving his undergraduate degree in Biomedical Engineering at Johns Hopkins University in Baltimore, Maryland, David moved to St. Louis for medical school and graduate school. He studied the mechanisms of insulin secretion and earned a PhD in neuroscience as well as an MD degree from Washington University. He completed his postgraduate residency training in pediatrics at St. Louis Children's Hospital. David is currently an attending physician for the Nemours Foundation at A.I. duPont Hospital for Children and Bryn Mawr Hospital and is faculty at Thomas Jefferson School of Medicine. He lives with his wife Karen, a former Contracts Manager, and two terrific boys, Robbie and Adam, outside of Philadelphia.

A highlight of both of their weddings for me was dancing the *Kazatzky,* the Cossak dance, where you squat with your arms crossed against your chest and kick each leg out alternately. It's a great way to pull out your back and bruise your butt, but it's so much fun and makes for lots of laughs.

Linda went to the University of Pennsylvania in Philadelphia and graduated Magna Cum Laude from the Wharton School of Business, majoring in marketing. She spent the last half of her junior year studying at the University of Barcelona, where she immersed herself in the local culture, became fluent in Spanish, and then traveled extensively throughout Europe.

As soon as she finished school, she started a marketing management training program with Nestle USA, where she gained valuable experience in training rotations in different aspects of company operations. Finally, there came a position as a marketing assistant on Nestle Milk Chocolate in the California headquarters, fulfilling her dream of living out West.

She worked for Hunt Wesson, Red Bull, and now markets products for Specialty Brands. She eventually met the love of her life, Lenny Rosenberg. They dated for two and a half years and married in May 2002. They live in Culver City, California. Lenny manages a store specializing in snow and water sports equipment such as skis and wakeboards. He is also a pilot, doing some charter work and flight instruction part-time.

I don't know why I've been so blessed, but all three of my children have given my mother, and the rest of our extended family lots of *nachas*, pleasure and grace, as well as hope. When we see the grandchildren, they are our future. I wish that my father could have known them, and that they could have known him. That would have been great for everyone.

During summers and some school vacations Pat and I traveled to various destinations in the United States, Europe, Asia, or Africa. On trips to Europe we visited Asnieres, a suburb of Paris, Lyon, Vourles, and Marseille to see the places I lived in during the war. We saw the house at 24 Quai Fulcheron in Lyon. It had been greatly upgraded and looked much better than I remembered it. The lot next to it was now a park. It had been the site of the building that was bombed and apparently nothing was rebuilt on the lot. Vourles appeared very much like I remembered it during the war. The town hall and the church on the square hadn't changed in centuries, and the last fifty years made no difference at all.

We tried to find out what happened to the Sabathiers, and even visited the local cemetery hoping that we would not find any evidence of untimely deaths. We didn't. We asked about them at the town hall, but there was no information at all.

In Marseille, I took Pat to see the first apartment that we lived in. It was still in the red light district at 55 Rue des Petites Maries. Now, immigrants mostly from Northern Africa and the Middle-East inhabit the neighborhood. There were wagons full of fruits and vegetables and street vendors hawking cheap goods. The street had no sidewalks and was still cobblestone. It was not clean and seemed unsafe. We also went to see the apartment house at 18 Rue Elemir Bourges. The main entrance looked familiar, but we couldn't gain access to the interior.

In Antwerp, Belgium, we found Lange Leemstraat where my mother's family had lived and saw the house at #328. It was still intact except the ground floor had been converted to a business. The house at #303, where I remembered staying after the war, was leveled and there was just an empty lot where it once stood, leaving me with a hollow feeling.

The only family home that I had known in Belgium was gone. We also went to the last known address of my Uncle Jules, at #85 Isabellelei Straat, but he was gone, another family in his place. I was anxious for some news as to his whereabouts, so we went to the Antwerp civil records department where a clerk looked for my uncle on the computer, and read off the following: "Jules Pressel died in a nursing home on September 28, 1984 in Antwerp. No further information available."

I was quite upset, and though I had not been in touch with him for many years, tears came to my eyes because he'd been the last senior Pressel relative left.

Pat and I also visited the nearby La Moriniere Straat where my mother and her sisters had attended the *College Marie Jose High School*. The front entrance, which was over eight feet wide, had a flagpole and two heavy wooden doors. There was an approximately fifty-foot long walkway through an enclosed alley, leading to a large courtyard where the students, who wore dark green uniforms, played during recess. Once through the courtyard, there stood a large red brick administration building with several floors of classrooms. We went inside and toured around. One of the directors of the school brought us to the basement archives, conducted a search on our behalf, and found information on some of my mother's sisters.

Visiting these places brought back memories, created new mental images and helped me a great deal in discovering information about my youth. I did not regret coming to the United States in the least. I fit in at last, I am who I am, totally Americanized, as Jewish as I need to be, and happy about it. Occasionally I do wonder what would have become of us had we remained in France.

On one trip, Pat and I spent some time in Israel with my Aunt Alice and her sons and families in Rehovot. We passed the days walking and wandering all over Jerusalem, especially in the Old City's Arab, Christian, Armenian and Jewish quarters. It was a thrill for me to be at the Western Wall, which Papa had wanted to visit in 1951.

We spent three weeks in South Africa and Zimbabwe, and went on an exciting safari at a game reserve near Krueger National Park. We got to see lions close enough to touch. Elephants, buffalos, rhinos, a leopard, and many other animals and birds all in the wild roamed free for us to look at. In Zimbabwe, we saw the magnificent Victoria Falls and went by seaplane to another safari on the shore of Lake Kariba. In South Africa, we traveled by car along most of the southern coast from Port Elizabeth to Capetown. South Africa is a beautiful country and one of our most memorable vacations places. I am a hat collector, and gathered hats wherever we traveled, then hung them on the walls and from the ceiling of the den in Bethel.

We've not neglected the United States in our travels. Pat and I took trips to the Rocky Mountain States, Arizona, California, New Mexico, Utah, the Canadian Rockies, New England, Florida, the Carolinas, and Georgia. We spent many summer weeks in San Diego, where I often went to engineering conferences. Each of those trips was part vacation and we grew to love San Diego, its great weather, the beautiful beaches, and the environment.

We spent almost every Christmas holiday with Pat's family in Virginia, going from one party or family dinner to another. It was something of a change for me, an only child of Jewish Holocaust survivors in hiding, to experience such an American Christmas. At every gathering there were so many kids, babies, dogs, and cats tripping all over each other. It was sometimes loud, sometimes controlled-pandemonium, but it was always pleasant and different.

It was also pleasant for us to spend time with Pat's parents, Roland and Estelle Trudel, at their warm and friendly house in Stamford, Connecticut. Roland was the long-time manager of various Sears stores, including the one in Stamford. He became a successful real estate man. His passion was to collect stamps and was very proud of his collection that lined the walls of his den. From floor to ceiling, Roland had volumes containing stamps from every country in the world, past and present. I believed he had virtually every stamp ever printed in the United States. The stamps were perfectly mounted and each volume was beautiful.

Estelle raised her children and was in charge of the house, food, and entertainment. She also worked in their real estate office. They enjoyed playing cards, particularly with Estelle's identical twin sister, Jeannette Langelier, and her husband, also Roland. Both were retired civil servants, who lived in Virginia, but visited quite often. The sisters dressed alike even in their older years. The ladies became very modern. After they were both widowed, Estelle moved to Alexandria, Virginia to live with Jeannette. They got a computer, e-mail addresses, and had their ears pierced at age 88. Pat's mother and her aunt took a cruise to Alaska at age 91.

Our day-to-day life in Bethel was a good and calm one. We had some nice friends, the best of whom were Pat Cody and Jim Miller, our neighbors. They eventually married and now share a nice home in Danbury. For years we went out to dinner on weekends and then played cards at their home or at ours. We also socialized with some of my colleagues from work or Pat's fellow teachers.

Starting around 1987, when I was 50, we decided to jog for additional exercise. After several months of jogging we joined the New York Road Runners Club, so we could participate in some of the fun runs in Central Park, such as the Trevira Twosome, a five-kilometer race for couples, one male, one female.

During the winter of 1981, one evening just after a snowstorm dumped ten inches of snow on us, a next-door neighbor knocked on our door. He had just received a telephone call from another neighbor's wife, frantic because her husband had collapsed on a stairwell. He knew that Pat had been trained to do CPR. So we ran through the snow to their condo. The victim, who was in his fifties, looked blue-gray to me and I thought that he was dead. His wife had already called 911. Pat started to do CPR on him. Seconds later a paramedic arrived and he and Pat worked on the man together, but to no avail. There was no response. He was taken away by ambulance, but we knew he was dead. At least we tried to help.

In the spring of 1982, a CPR course was being given in Bethel. I enrolled and was certified. Two weeks later, we were returning home from Stamford when we arrived at an intersection where a fellow on a motorcycle was crossing. We followed him into a right turn, and then he disappeared around the next bend in the road. When we took the bend, we saw him lying face up in the middle of the road with his motorcycle on its side nearby. He had slipped on some sand in the road and flipped off his motorcycle. I immediately stopped the car in front of him to prevent any cars from running him over and checked him out, while Pat went to the nearest house to call for an ambulance. He wasn't wearing a helmet and appeared badly hurt. He had no pulse and was not breathing. I immediately used the CPR techniques I had been taught just two weeks earlier. After several minutes, he started to gurgle. An ambulance arrived; the medics took over and brought him to Norwalk Hospital. I found out that cyclist's name was Tom Barry.

The next day I called the hospital to find out his condition. He was in a coma and they did not have a prognosis. I spoke to his wife Kathy and told her what had happened. I also asked her to call me to fill me in from time to time. Several weeks later she called and told me Tom had come out of his coma after about two weeks, that he would make a slow recovery and that they hoped there would be minimal brain damage. We stayed in touch and some months later we visited them in their home in Ridgefield, Connecticut. They were very grateful for our help and we became friends. Tom recovered well enough to resume his life, and we wound up occasionally playing cards with them, and following Kathy's running career, as she was an ardent and excellent long distance runner who placed high in many road races.

After several years of jogging, my knees started to hurt from the pounding, and Pat sustained a foot fracture. So we decided to stop and resume our walks. In the spring of 1992 I found out about the Senior Olympics for people 55 years plus. I investigated further and discovered that swimming was one of the sports. I was then close to being 55 and although I had stopped competing in swimming after college, I decided to compete in the 50 and 100 yards sprints in the freestyle and breaststroke. The first regional Senior Olympic competition was going to be in Portland, Maine in September, so in April I joined the Danbury, Connecticut YMCA and started training.

We went to Portland on the designated weekend in September. I had only entered the 50-yard freestyle and 50-yard breaststroke races, not knowing yet if I was in good enough shape to really compete. In the 55- to 59-year-old age group, I was thrilled to win both of my events and have gold medals placed around my neck. The camaraderie with the other athletes was also a lot of fun and encouraged me to continue my new "athletic" career. I joined US Masters Swimming and started entering other sanctioned Masters competitions in Connecticut and New York.

In the fall of 1993, at Vassar College, I entered the Duchess County Masters Championships and took second in both the 50 yards freestyle and breaststroke. I was proud to take a third in the 100-yard individual medley, a difficult event. I continued training and competing in the Connecticut Senior Olympics every year and did quite well winning first, second, and third place medals each year. I also qualified for the National Senior Olympics which were held every other year, but I never went because it either interfered with other plans we had, or was held in the summer in a very warm location such as Baton Rouge, Louisiana. Linda was the only one of my kids who saw me race at any swim meets. Pat, of course, saw them all.

Pat and I had discussed our eventual retirement and after so many trips to San Diego, we decided that was the place where we would feel most comfortable. In the summer of 1992, on a whim, on a rare rainy day at the start of our vacation, we went looking at houses instead of going to the beach and found our dream house. We put out a bid and it was accepted. During the next two weeks, we were very efficient. We got a mortgage, the house was inspected, we took out an insurance policy, and very importantly, found a reliable renter who wound up staying there for years until our retirement. Almost every year we visited San Diego for our vacation and to check on the house.

The financial success and the excellent human assets at Perkin-Elmer resulted in its being sold to Hughes Aircraft in 1989, but the work remained essentially the same. The paycheck signature was all that changed. Ninety percent of my work and the associated programs are still classified at very high levels, and for some programs I had to take lie detector tests in order to get security clearance. I am happy to report I had no problems with the test.

I am very proud of my significant contributions to the design of essential, extremely valuable, and highly important programs for national security. Many of us at Perkin-Elmer were cited and complimented for our achievements by the President, the heads of the Defense Department, the Air Force, and other branches of the government.

Six years later, in spring 1995, there were rumors of significant layoffs to come and the possible loss of really good retirement packages. I wanted to continue working for another few years, so in order to protect myself, I went job hunting. Through one of my friends, Kevin Thompson, I took a position with a company in Cambridge, Massachusetts, which meant I needed a place to stay during the week and would commute home on weekends. I found a one-bedroom apartment in Woburn, Massachusetts. After thirty years, I left Perkin-Elmer (my division had been purchased by Hughes by then; it was then owned by Raytheon, and is now Goodrich).

I furnished the apartment with odds and ends, new and old. The idea was to use this job as a temporary situation while I looked for something closer to home in Connecticut. Things started out fine when I began working in Cambridge in May 1995. But then, in late June, Pat's father, at age 85, was diagnosed with brain cancer and given three months to live. We were stunned, and it was a difficult summer for us as Pat spent time in Stamford with him. Roland died on September 30, 1995. He was involved in Stamford community, in charitable, church, and real estate activities, as well as well-loved and respected by everyone.

That fall I went for a general physical at the Lahey Clinic in Burlington, Massachusetts. My physician decided to have my kidneys checked. An MRI showed a suspicious dark mass on my right kidney and the doctor said that I could possibly have kidney cancer. If it was cancer, it was a slow growing one and could be watched and retested in six months, or I could have exploratory surgery. Soon after that diagnosis my work in the Boston area was completed.

Since I now had free time, I decided to have the surgery done as soon as possible in order to get it out of the way. Dr. Robert Roth, a urologist, did the surgery on Monday, December 26, 1995 at the Lahey Clinic. I woke up in the recovery room and told my right kidney had been removed because it was infiltrated with cancer, but that my prognosis was good and I would not need any chemotherapy or radiation. Luckily, the cancer had been contained in my kidney and had all been removed. The care I received was outstanding. My biggest supporter and caregiver was Pat. I made a quick recovery and was released from the hospital to Pat after only five days. We returned to Connecticut.

I was told to wait six or seven weeks before doing anything strenuous or looking for a new job closer to home. I walked to gain my strength back, update my resume, and start networking. Three weeks after coming home, I did some part-time consulting for a company in Westchester through the kind recommendation of Paul Yoder, an associate from Perkin-Elmer. I could drive by then and felt pretty good. Approximately six weeks later, I found a permanent job at Barnes Engineering, in Shelton, Connecticut. Barnes designed and built attitude control earth sensors for sixty percent of America's orbiting satellites. These include military and commercial communication satellites and those controlling GPS (Global Positioning Systems) systems.

The work was interesting and in my field of optics. I started as a mechanical engineer on a brand new sensor design. One of the important tasks was to interface with the department that tested all the sensors in thermal-vacuum chambers, which simulated conditions in outer space. We did lots of trouble shooting on the sensors being tested, and on the test equipment itself. All of my previous experience came in very handy. Several months later, when the department manager left, I was promoted. Our main task was to design an optical test system for the new sensor.

A year later, when their Director of Engineering left, I was asked to fill his position. I was reluctant to take it because it would mean much more responsibility, more time spent at work, and being in charge of close to one hundred people in a number of departments. It would also mean that I would be doing a lot less of my favorite thing, which was design and analysis. Against my own advice, I took the job and found I devoted so much more time to management and meetings that my time spent in actual design diminished drastically.

By the fall of 1998, Pat and I decided that we'd had enough. We were both stressed out by our respective jobs, and we decided to retire at the end of the 98/99 school year. By then, I would have been at Barnes for three years. Our plan was to put the Bethel condo up for sale and in June to move to our house in San Diego.

The moving company packed the fragile things and we packed the rest in boxes. Our downstairs looked like a warehouse, but there was one benefit: we got rid of a lot of unnecessary household items and furniture. I have always been a pack rat, probably because I didn't have anything as a youngster, and so I treasured anything that was mine. Still, it was time to cut loose.

We easily found a buyer for the condo. I left for San Diego two weeks before Pat as she was to finish her school semester and I was needed for the house preparations. I flew to California with our cat, Charlie. The house interior had a clean fresh smell. I kept busy taking delivery of some new furniture, having new rugs installed, and having cable TV, phones, and a water filtration system installed. When our furniture van arrived, I spent the whole day checking off all the items and telling the movers where to put them. The boxes that we had packed wound up completely filling up the kitchen, dining room, and the upstairs hallway. There were boxes piled halfway up to the ceiling. The movers had done all of the heavy work, but I was exhausted. I spent the next two days unpacking the most essential boxes until Pat arrived.

I had been looking forward to Pat's arrival at the airport that I wanted to make it a special memorable experience. I arranged for a white stretch limo to pick her up at the airport. I met her at the gate and gave her a bouquet of yellow roses and we hugged a lot. I then surprised her as we exited through the outer gate when I introduced her to our chauffeur, Alva. She was very happily surprised. Pat was tired but when we got home I brought her to our outside deck where I had set up wine glasses. We enjoyed a welcome home glass of wine. This would be our first night together in our new home in San Diego.

# 13

# RETIREMENT & RETURN TO VOURLES

After our house was all fixed up we found that living in retirement has been busier than when we were working full time. We enjoy the outdoors a great deal. San Diego is right on the Pacific Coast, and is a beautiful city with nice weather all year round. This means beach weather almost daily and the kind of weather that lends itself to nice long walks, bike riding, and a leisurely pace that encourages visits to all the local attractions, including the zoo and wild animal park.

One of the things we love to do most is visit the Cove area in La Jolla, a handsome residential part of the city that is directly on the coast. At the Cove, you look north over a magnificent seascape, with the stunning shore, the beach, Scripps Oceanographic Institute pier, all the way to the famous Torrey Pines Golf Course above the high cliffs. From the pier north, there is only sandy beach and the largest hang glider port in the country. We often have a picnic lunch right at the glider port and as we eat, we watch daredevils jump off the cliff and fly into the wind. It's a little crazy, we know, but we love it. We take walks north or south and see all sorts of life enjoying the water, from harbor seals sunning themselves on a beach, to body and board surfers riding the waves. Kyackers paddle around in the surf and fishing boats can be seen trolling for fish way off shore.

The local community center near where we live, with its tennis courts and large pool, is where we go to keep fit and trim, with Pat doing water aerobics and I swim laps. This gave me the chance to continue competing in Masters swimming races. A new sport that I have started to learn is golf. I have an excellent instructor, Justin Hicks, and I play a short course once a week with other retirees.

Several times a year we visit our respective families on the East coast. We have also both kept somewhat active in our professions. Pat has done some part time substitute teaching and I have been doing some engineering consulting for a terrific local mechanical engineering company, called Quartus Engineering. With my skills in design and stress analysis and many years of experience, I fit in well with their needs and have enjoyed it. It provides me with mental stimulation in my field of engineering.

Because sports have always been my real hobby and because there are many opportunities to participate in or watch different sports in San Diego, I discovered I could be involved in track and field, not as a participant or spectator, but as an official. I attended a training class in January of 2000, took a test, was certified and became a member of the national track and field officiating organization. I wear a USA Track & Field uniform. During the spring and summer season weekends, it's always a thrill for me to officiate at track meets at high schools, colleges, and even at the Olympic training site. My favorite events to officiate are the field events, and by now I have officiated for them all. These include the high jump, pole vault, long jump, triple jump, shot put, discus, hammer and javelin throw and the decathlon. The most fun times I had were at the Olympic training site in 2000 and 2004, prior to the Sydney and Athens Olympics. I got to see athletes "up-close and personal" and met many of the participants and eventual medallist winners on the US team.

High school and college meets are terrific because the kids are cooperative and I have the opportunity to visit the college and high school campuses in the San Diego area. I also officiated at another tremendous event, the San Diego Suzuki Rock and Roll Marathon. I once rode in the lead press truck, feeling like the kid who got picked to be a batboy in Yankee Stadium. At every mile marker, for twenty-six miles, there was a different rock 'n roll band urging the runners on, and so I got to see them all. That's what I call "cool!"

The year, 2001, started off very badly when I developed serious intestinal problems. In the middle of one January night, I was rushed by ambulance to Sharp Memorial Hospital for emergency surgery and then I developed sepsis landing me in ICU on a respirator, on the critical list— for five days. Pat even called my children to tell them they'd better come to my bedside because no one was certain I would survive. Somehow due to perseverance and determination by me and by Pat and her constant presence, and as a result of excellent care by the doctors and nurses, I recovered, and after twelve days in the hospital, I was released.

The doctors who saved my life were Dr. Gary Bench, the surgeon, Dr. Michael Bennett, a gastroenterologist, Dr. Wilms, a pulmonary specialist; Dr. Steven Mosher, an infectious disease specialist; and Dr. Steven Steinberg—a Nephrologist called in when I went into kidney failure. A specialty nurse, Peggy Long, was also very helpful to me. Pat was at my bedside at least eighteen hours a day, and in some ways, I am sure that the whole ordeal was harder on her than it was on me. The two doctors who continue to periodically care for me and help keep me well are Dr. Steinberg and his fantastic nurse, Kristin, and Dr. Bennett.

I came home weighing twenty-five pounds less than when I went in and it took a year and a half to recover. On April 3, 2001 the day after I came home, from the hospital after follow up surgery, Pat's mother died from a stroke. Pat flew to Virginia for the funeral—and she was gone only forty-three hours. This ordeal had to be really hard on her, but she says she did what she had to do and what she wanted to do. I am not given to public declarations of love, but to me Pat is an angel, and through her support I have been able to resume my life. All I can do is give her my love and stick to my determination to stay well. I am doing o.k. although there is a possibility that sometime in the future my remaining kidney, which is diseased, may fail. In that case, I will owe Pat even more, because she wants to donate one of her kidneys to me. What love!!!

**Pat and Phil Pressel, 2002**

Linda's wedding, May 2002. Allan, Austin (Allan's son),
Phil, Miriam, Julia (Allans daughter), Linda, Len,
Pat, Karen (David's wife), Adam and Robbie
(David's children), and David.

Then in June 2001, Harry, Ma's devoted husband, was diagnosed with brain cancer. He was 94 when his health badly deteriorated in the middle of July; Ma hired a wonderful woman, a "nurse/companion", Marie Sookram, to help. Harry died on the last day of July, and Marie has remained on as Ma's caretaker and companion.

Harry and my mother were married for thirty-five years, and I know that those were the happiest years of Ma's life. As much as she loved Papa, life was so difficult for them during the war. Then Papa was ill, and I know that their love was deep, but it was so sad for her to lose him having survived so many hardships. Just as deep as my love was for Papa, as much as I adored and admired him, I also loved Harry as a father. He was there for me with advice and caring respect. And he made Ma happy, which was so important for me. After all she had been through to keep me alive, I was glad for the blessing in her life that was Harry. I loved him because he loved her and was a wonderful man. Ma and Harry were involved in so many things together—art and music, and the art of conversation.

After I recuperated, I eventually started swimming again. I have gotten help from Alan Voisard, a talented Masters swim coach and a former national champion. We became friends and he's given me pointers on my swimming stroke and training methods. He inspires me to improve and to do better. My goal is to stay healthy, and my determination to do so is primarily motivated by my love for Pat and my desire for us to enjoy our lives together for as long as we possibly can. I follow doctor's orders to stay active and try to accomplish something good each and every day.

I had decided that when I retired I would attempt to write about the things that happened to my parents and me during the war. For several years, I have spent several hours a day writing this book, putting down my thoughts, and re-reading those letters Papa wrote during the war. Upon the advice of my editor, I expanded the writing to include my life after the war.

Over the years I made notes about my youth and the war, about memories that floated to the surface. I also made recordings with Ma, wherein she discussed her life before the war, her family, and some episodes from the war. I translated Papa's letters from the original French. Their words have been seasoned with the salt of my tears.

Talking and writing about the wartime events has been a cathartic experience for me, and the experience of writing this book has brought me closure.

For a long time Pat urged me to locate the Sabathier family who sheltered me during the war. On our previous visit to France we weren't able to find them because there were no records at the Vourles town hall or cemetery. I was skeptical, but on a hunch, on the Internet, Pat looked up the name Sabathier in the area around Lyon There were quite a few of them, so I wrote a general letter asking them if they were the people with whom I'd stayed with during the war, and I included copies of some wartime pictures. In spring 2001, we received several letters from France, each one filled with regrets. Whenever I went to the mailbox and saw an envelope with French stamps, my heart jumped into my throat. At last a letter arrived from a Jean Sabathier, who turned out to be my wartime playmate. One of the people we'd written to had forwarded my letter to the town hall in Vourles and someone there knew Jean and forwarded it to him.

It was amazing. After all the intervening years, after all the differences in our lives, it was as if the past disappeared in a flash. Jean's letter talked about his family, his two daughters and four grandchildren. His father had died in 2000, but his mother was 91 and living in Boyer, the village of her birth, near Lyon. Jean and his wife live near Avignon, in the south of France, and are retired. Photos of his family were included.

I cried with joy at finally being in contact with the Sabathiers. I wrote back about us and included pictures. I asked for his telephone number, received it soon thereafter and made an all-important and emotional telephone call. We spoke for almost an hour. Although my French is a bit rusty the conversation went extremely well, and we've been in constant touch ever since.

One very important question had remained in my and my mother's minds. Did the Sabathiers know I was Jewish when they sheltered me? I asked Jean and his answer was "Non." But he also said his father told him many years later that he suspected that we might be, but did not want to say anything for fear of being found out. When Mr. Sabathier finished his military career he became the superintendent of a private school until his retirement. I realized I very much wanted to see the Sabathiers, so in fall 2002, Pat and I prepared to take a trip to France and discussed it with Jean, who planned a four-day visit for us. He would meet us in Lyon, we'd spend the day with him and his mother and visit Vourles.

On May 17, 2003 we flew from San Diego to Paris. Two days later, we boarded the TGV (Train Grande Vitesse—very fast train; it averages close to 200 miles per hour) to Lyon in central France. We booked a room at the Mercure Chateau Perrache Hotel right next door to the train station, where Jean was to meet us with his good friend Henri Viallon, who was to record the day with his VCR camera.

As we walked from the train to the hotel, pulling our suitcases behind us, we spotted Henri filming us. As soon as I saw Jean standing at the lobby door, I recognized him. He had sent me pictures of himself and his family, but he also looked lots like the kid I'd known in 1944. I put my suitcase down and greeted him with a huge hug, my heart pounding with excitement. We spoke for a few minutes before entering the hotel. Unfortunately Jean's wife Janette was convalescing from chemotherapy and breast cancer surgery and could not join us.

After we checked in, we spent the next hour talking in the lobby as we waited for Jean's mother, Mrs. Sabathier, to arrive from her home in Boyer, about sixty miles away. She was coming with her companion, Marie-France Lagoutte. This time I was the one waiting in front of the hotel. Jean escorted his mother from the station and when she arrived, we embraced and kissed in the traditional French way; that is on both cheeks. Again my heart was filled with emotion and my eyes moistened. I told her that I was happy to see her, and gave her a big thank you for sheltering me during the war in 1944. We hadn't seen each other in fifty-nine years, and other than gray hair, a few wrinkles and a slightly stooped walk, she looked exactly the same.

We spent several hours talking in the hotel dining room during lunch. I read aloud parts of the chapter about Vourles during the war. She remembered and confirmed everything, but hadn't been back to Vourles in many years. She said that the decision to take me in during 1944 was natural and spontaneous, and she would have done so even if she had known at that time that we were Jewish. She never thought that she was risking her life. Jean remembered only some of the events, as he was about one year younger than I.

After lunch we climbed into Jean's car and rode to our apartment house at #24 Quai Fulcheron, right next to the Rhone River. It had been renovated again, with a new façade and front door. Our old balcony on the second floor was now totally enclosed by windows. A concrete balustrade replaced the original black metal grillwork on the balcony. The park that replaced the building next door was still there.

Then we headed for Vourles. I was totally unprepared for what came next. We arrived at the main square of Vourles, which, it seemed, still hadn't changed and, we parked right in front of the church. The old town hall building where I had lived with the Sabathiers was still standing there. As I got out of the car, I broke down and cried. Jean, his mother and I then clustered together and spoke of the old days, pointing to the four second-story windows on the right side which were those of the our old apartment. But it was not the town hall anymore. The word "Mairie" that had been inscribed above the front door was gone. It was now the town library. The outside façade of the front of the building was renovated and painted a pink/red color. It had originally been light brown. All of the window and door trimmings had been painted white. Meanwhile, Pat and Henri were filming. Also filming was a French television cameraman, who had been given a heads up by Jean. We walked to the back of the building and pointed to the window where a bullet had entered during a battle between the Allies, Germans and the Maquis.

We walked over to the two-room schoolhouse that had been run by Mrs. Sabathier and where Jean and I attended classes. We also entered the church, where I sometimes had attended Mass with the family. The spiral staircase and elevated pulpit where the priest spoke in those days was gone, and we were told it now was housed in a museum.

When we came out of the church, the TV cameraman and a reporter from Television Lyon Metropole interviewed the three of us in front of the building. They asked about events during the war and how I felt about coming back. I said it was extremely emotional to return and re-live that time, and that I was grateful to have survived, thanks in part to the heroism of the Sabathier family. Mrs. Sabathier stated that she volunteered to shelter me, never thinking of the danger, since they had no proof of who I was and where I came from. Jean also spoke of the days he and I played outside, and of surviving the war. He said in French "We survived our youth."

Jean suggested that we visit the new town hall, and so we climbed back into his car and drove through the old and new parts of Vourles. The old part was the same as I remembered it; narrow cobblestone streets and old cement-faced two story buildings. In 1944 there were about 500 inhabitants. Now there were 2900 residents of Vourles and many beautiful new homes, gardens and apartment buildings surrounded the old section.

We parked the car and walked slowly to the entrance to the new Mairie. We came in through the main door and were led to a large room on the left. As we entered the room, cheering and applause greeted us. It arose from approximately forty people. They were waiting for us, including the TV cameraman, who was still filming.

**Phil, Mrs. Sabathier and Jean in Lyon, 2003**

**Jean, Mrs. Sabathier and Phil in front of Vourles Town Hall. Their apartment was on the second floor of this building. 2003**

Apparently, Jean and Mr. Pierre Neyroud, the mayor of Vourles and some of his staff including his assistant, Mrs. Martinet, had organized a celebration to honor my return to Vourles after 59 years, and to honor Mrs. Sabathier's return to the town where she had been director of the school and the girls' teacher. They had invited all of her students from 1943, 1944 and 1945 that they could find. Sixteen of them were there. I was overwhelmed with surprise and emotion, and I am sure Mrs. Sabathier was also. My attention was focused on Mrs. Sabathier who was surrounded by her students. They were kissing and hugging her and calling her "maitresse" (instructor). The joy on her face and in her eyes was heart-warming.

Jean introduced me to Raymond Marcel, the son of our teacher, Mr. Marcel. He also introduced me to the mayor and his staff and to a Mr. Jean Sabatier (notice no h in his name), who was one of the recipients of the letters we had sent out in search of the family. He'd forwarded my letter to the Vourles town hall, where it was read by a secretary, then by Mr. Jean Morel, the town counsel. He recognized the names Sabathier and Pressel and sent the letter on to Jean, who contacted me. Jean Morel knew us because his wife Josette and her brother Raymond were Mr. Marcel's (my old teacher) children. Unfortunately Jean and Josette were on vacation and weren't there that day.

We were served champagne and pastries. I was so overcome, all I had was water or I might have collapsed. There was a table display dedicated to Franco-American friendship and large American and French flags on either side of a large poster board with photos of Jean and me and our parents in Vourles during the war. It also had photos of our present families and newspapers printed immediately after the Liberation of the area.

Jean then made a beautiful speech that recapped our adventures. Part of it said:

> "Mr. Mayor, Ladies and Gentlemen of the town council, Ladies and Gentleman,
>
> First of all, thank you Mr. Mayor for inviting us to attend this emotional reunion in one of your Town Hall chambers. This morning Philip Pressel, American citizen, and I were reunited after 59 years of separation on the quai of the Perrache railroad station in Lyon.

It was an emotional moment as you no doubt realize.

But, if you please, we will start this long history, which could also have ended tragically in 1944 for both of our families. In 1942 in the village of St. Foy near Lyon, there was a school teacher who taught school in that community. She is here near us this afternoon. She had come from her native Bourgogne in order to be near her husband who was in the military in Lyon.

By chance she met Philip's mother at a commercial store in Vourles, and thus a friendship started. Mrs. Miriam Pressel was a dressmaker. She offered her services not for money but for food. Food was scarce in Lyon where the Pressel family lived at 24 Quai Fulcheron at the side of the Saone River"

....and then Jean recounted the story as I have put it forth before you. And then he concluded,

"My dear Philip and Patricia, you took a trip to France in 1993 and you tried to find us, unfortunately without success despite your visit to the Mairie in Vourles and to the cemetery. In February 2001 you sent 16 letters to the Jean Sabatiers in the vicinity of Lyon, and one of those gentlemen had the thoughtfulness and kindness to send the letter to the Mairie of Vourles. The letter came into the hands of the Morel family who then contacted me in Avignon. Regretfully they are on a trip this week and are unable to be with us today.

On my side, in July 1969, during a trip to New York I tried to find you in the New York telephone book but there was no Pressel there who had lived in Vourles!!

....Tomorrow you will get to know another village next to Avignon in the Provence where I have lived since 1977, and I will introduce you to my 2 daughters, Catherine and Laurence and my four grandchildren, Camille, Juliette, Antoine and Elodie. Then it will be in Nice where we will separate again, but I presume that there will be an invitation to visit you soon in San Diego.

Now, when you return to the USA tell your fellow citizens that if our respective presidents and governments have had divergent opinions on how to handle the conflict in Iraq and create a cold barrier between our two countries, know that the French people consider the American people friends and allies.

Encourage your friends to discover "the old Europe" specifically France, the land which is the most visited in the world, with 70 million tourists in 2002. You will always be welcome by Frenchmen and Frenchwomen.

Before ending and passing the floor to the mayor, I would like to thank all the people who made this moving reunion possible."

The mayor graciously welcomed everyone, Mrs. Sabathier and I were presented with lovely certificates proclaiming us honorary citizens of Vourles and I was also given four beautiful books about Vourles and the area surrounding Lyon. They were written by Mr. Michel Regnier an author and historian who resides in Vourles and was in attendance that day. I made a short speech thanking them for the great honor they had bestowed upon me. I was so surprised by the whole thing and so caught up in the emotion of the moment that I did not do justice to my emotions in my words, yet everyone was aware of how touched I was.

After many personal greetings and thanks, we left and returned to our hotel in Lyon. Then we all came up to our hotel room and turned on the television, and to our delight, watched our reunion and interviews in the town square. Isn't technology great! When the show was over, Jean, Pat and I walked Mrs. Sabathier and her companion to the train station, where I bade her a fond farewell with tender hugs and kisses. She is an absolutely lovely, charming and vivacious lady who reminds me very much of Ma.

Jean then brought Pat and me to Henri's house, where we capped the evening with a delicious dinner prepared by Henri's wife, Jacqueline. They were gracious hosts and certainly dedicated a lot of effort to us and to their good friend Jean. They also gave us a cassette with all of the days' events, including the program that was on French television that evening that I have enjoyed showing repeatedly to family and friends. It was not easy to fall asleep later, as we relived all of the events of the day, one of the most memorable days of my life.

After breakfast the next day, we were on our way to Jean's home in Jonquerettes, a small town just seven kilometers from Avignon. We greeted his wife Janette and two of his grandchildren, Camille and Antoine, children of his daughter Catherine and her husband Maxence, with hugs and kisses. The children live about a mile away in the same town. Jean's house is beautiful. It is on a large plot of land with a garden, a manicured lawn, and an in-ground swimming pool. After checking into a lovely Pension called Le Clos Des Saumanes, and resting a bit, we walked back to his house.

We talked a great deal about the previous days' events, the war, and our childhood. Jean's first occupation was as goalie for a French professional soccer team based in Lyon. He showed us plaques and articles about him and the team, including good photos of him in action as goalie. Prior to arriving in Jonquerrettes, he'd shown us his sports club and the Sports Palace stadium. At the sports club called "Olympic Lyon," he introduced us to his friend and former center forward for the French national championship team, Mr. Bernard Lacombe.

Eventually Jean became involved in the auto parts business, and then Jean and Janette owned an English Tea House called "Simple Simon" in Avignon, with another partner. Jean took care of the purchasing of food and supplies for the restaurant. Among other responsibilities, Janette cooked the desserts. We were the beneficiaries of her culinary skills that day—the meals she prepared were superb.

The next day was another beautiful sunny day. Jean and Janette took us on a sightseeing tour of Avignon that is famous for its bridge and the song named after it. We ate lunch at Simple Simon, now under new ownership. We had a delicious lunch and dessert and were treated as special guests. In the late afternoon we visited Jean's daughter Catherine and her family and were treated to another wonderful dinner. We also watched all of Henri's cassette tapes to share the joys of the reunion with everyone.

The next day was the last full day with Jean and Janette. We visited Nice on the Mediterranean coast with a stop in the small coastal town of St. Raphael, where they keep a summer cottage, a small place with one bedroom used occasionally as a vacation hideaway. Friends of his late father were playing *boule* in a small park across the street. After watching I asked if I could play one game. I'd never played it before, and I did not disgrace myself.

After checking into our hotel in Nice, Jean drove us to see Laurance, his other daughter, and her husband Marc, who live up in the hills overlooking Nice. Their two daughters Juliette and Elodie were playing in their swimming pool. We had another wonderful dinner, followed by a showing of the tape. This was Pat's first chance to speak English as both Laurance and Marc were fluent. Pat had done really well with French. She understood most of the conversations, and made a terrific effort to speak French—she was a lively participant and everyone appreciated her efforts.

Jean and Janette were staying in Nice for several days and so we said our goodbyes to all. Janette was such a gracious hostess during our four-day stay you would never know that she was still weak. She still had some post-surgery treatments to undergo and her prognosis appeared good, but it was still difficult to say goodbye. She is an absolutely wonderful, kind and loving lady. They treated us like well-loved family, not new acquaintances. We have never been so welcomed, and treated so generously. We hope that in the near future they will visit us, and we will try to reciprocate.

When Jean and I hugged goodbye, I thought of our childhood during the war, and of the fantastic reunion that he organized. I thought of his family and all of the other charming people that we had met. We stay in close touch now and I hope that we see them soon. Having shared part of our youth, I want Jean and our families to share our later years.

When I ask myself, "Why did you survive?" my answer is that I did so because of the courage and love Papa and Ma had for me and for life itself. Other than that, I believe it was just plain luck.

I decided a long time ago to write my memoirs so that my children would have an accounting of our family during World War II. My children, born as Jews in America, through me, and their grandmother, still have a special connection to an event that occurred years before they were born, but had a direct impact on their lives.

Until now, my children will have heard a story here, a story there, but will never have gotten a comprehensive vision of what their father and grandparents had gone through in Belgium and France. And despite our terror and suffering, they need to understand there were millions more who went through infinitely worse hells than ours.

I also wanted this to be a personal catharsis. And finally, I wanted to add one more document to the existing literature, to add my voice to the litany of those reminding humanity not to forget what happened during those dark years, in the hope of preventing it from happening again. This is the toughest thing we have to do, because since the war mankind seems to have found other peoples to wipe off the face of the planet. This is definitely a millennium of genocides, and genocide and racism must stop.

Ma always said, as hard as it was for her to talk about the war, she would never forget or want to forget. She was always very strong during the war and after, and said to me "I didn't have time to be weak." I, also, can never forget or want to forget those war years. Every day I spend on this Earth, I fill it with appreciation of what is good, kind and compassionate, and trying to make it a better place.

Though Ma and I are not at all religiously observant, it is important to her and to me, and was important to Papa, that we have the basic Jewish morals and true sense of ethics. They taught me that it is important to be proud of our Jewish heritage. I am far from perfect, but I have drawn courage, sensitivity, caring and my work ethic from my parents.

As far as God and religion were concerned, starting at age 8 I learned about being Jewish. Later I observed others, including my mother's family, go through the rituals in the synagogue and prayers for various occasions. I could never get used to any of it. As I matured I could not understand why so many prayers were read or recited in a language (Hebrew) I could not understand. My parents never told me absolutely that there was a God. My parents did not actively practice religion but still wanted me to learn and be proud of my heritage. My father rarely went to synagogue, but he was a secular Zionist of the highest order. We were cultural Jews, not religious Jews. Until well into my adulthood I thought that there might be a God, and so to play it safe, I did some "religious things" like going to synagogue on holidays, and saying Kaddish.

I am so grateful that my parents and I survived the terrible war. I am grateful that I am alive today and for all of the good things that I have. I appreciate the material things that I have, though I often find I take many of them for granted now. As a youngster in peacetime America it was easy for me to adjust to a new life and have easy relationships with other children.

I was brought up to be obedient and so I did what my mother told me to do. As I matured, I kept saying to myself " If there really was a God, why did he let the Holocaust happen? And much later "Why did God let my son die? Or, why did God let my father die so young? The more of life that went on, the less I believed in a God. Today in my second marriage to a wonderful woman Patricia Trudel, a Catholic, I feel the same way. She knows of my disbelief. When I have attended church with her, I felt the same way–to me it's a lot of hocus pocus. I realize that all of these things are meant well, so I just follow the service and try not to say anything stupid or be critical. What I enjoy the most is the traditional music during the Jewish service. My basic belief is that man created God, not the other way around, in order for people "in power" to help control populations, whoever and wherever they were.

As a kid it was hard for me to be close and totally trusting with anyone in particular. I did not know how to confide in anyone. I was shy and reclusive. I certainly couldn't learn independence as a child during the war, so I was not independent nor did I even try to be independent in my teen years. It was hard for me to try new things. I certainly did not want to go shopping for myself, or travel alone. I stayed close to home during my college years—all as a result of my formative years and the relationship I had with my parents as they tried to save our lives.

My experiences during the war, my health problems, my relationship with my parents, their nurturing and love, and the forced separation from them, molded me into the person I am today. I am highly sensitive to the feelings of others and to their opinion of me. I have always had a great respect for authority figures such as parents, teachers and bosses. I still respect authority in general, though now, like others, I have earned the right to be occasionally cynical about them. I want my opinions to be accepted by others but I do not like to be confrontational or pushed into defending myself. I can take criticism and am not too proud to admit errors. I work to avoid disagreements.

I do not like to be alone because then I feel abandoned and my self-confidence goes down the tubes, and I wonder if I can take care of myself, even though I *know* that I can. I think I have learned to cope fairly well with difficult situations, although I try to distance myself from some of them. It took me many years to learn how to argue in a calm and quiet manner. I also learned that relationships work better if you compromise and bend with the force of the other's opinions and wills and by accepting or absorbing instead of instinctively fighting back. Pat taught me that.

Though I was never interned in a concentration camp and have no tattoo on my arm, there is a tattoo in my memory. Not surprisingly one of my idiosyncrasies is that I dislike anything German. I will never go to Germany and I do not buy German products. I admire the quality of German cars, but would never own one. When buying items I look at the mark "made in" before I buy it. I have trouble being comfortable in the company of people speaking in German.

I was a packrat—I saved everything, though in my later years I have been ruthless in getting rid of some stuff for practical reasons. Some of the things I save are old books, report cards, driver's licenses, my draft registration card, newspapers with major headlines, and miscellaneous paperwork. And there's one habit I've never broken, doing simple arithmetic—like when I balance a checkbook—in French. I do my engineering and higher math in English.

Now the only "old" relative I have left is Ma. Her sisters and their husbands all have passed on. I have numerous cousins in the United States, England and Israel, but I am close to only four of them: Jeanine Klein, who found my father's wartime letters to her father Elie Schwerner; she is a family counselor on Long Island, and is the liveliest and youngest senior that you can imagine. I stay in touch with Suzi Pantzer's daughters, my cousins, Helen Fogel and Carol Samet, who live near London. And I am still close to my cousin Sylvan Suskin and his wife, Malou. Sylvan was a professor of musicology at Oberlin College in Ohio. He and Malou have two children—Karine, a clinical psychologist and Marc, a law student.

When I visit close relatives, especially senior ones, I often wonder, "Is this the last time that I will ever see this person?" This is true with elderly relatives, like Ma and with others who are dear to me. I become so nostalgic that it hurts to leave them. I cherish my health, and the health of my loved ones. I also treasure many events I attend and places that I visit. I inhale every moment and try to capture it so that I can continue to savor it. This includes my appreciation of the classical and Jewish music that helps nourish my soul. I feel I am truly blessed. I understand how lucky we were to survive and live to love again.

Down deep, I believe I coped as well as any survivor in America has. I had good experiences in school, picked a good profession, earned a good living, and raised a good family. In my work career I helped in maintaining the security of my nation. How lucky that my children never faced the sacrifices of war, or were never threatened by bombings.

Soon there will come a time when there will no longer be survivors of the Holocaust in the world. The living persons connected to the events that testify to the atrocities of places like Auschwitz will all be gone. As one who survived, albeit under circumstances that were very different from those who were deported, I feel it is necessary to pass on to future generations all the happenings, all the different parts of the story, the varying chapters of what happened to the Jews in those years—whether we were old or young, in hiding, in the camps, in the forests, in the underground. We must continue to tell the story of our lives after the war, to show how we survived, how we kept on living, on creating families, and being people. We each have our own personal testimony, and we must share it, as long as we are able to do so coherently. Each succeeding generation will need to continue telling the saga, to read about it and to honor it, by living righteously and enjoying the gift of life that comes from knowing who they are and where they come from.

In 1949 my parents wrote these quotes to me and I think they are worthwhile thoughts to consider when we decide how to live our lives and they certainly are appropriate in today's world:

From my mother:

*"The greatest happiness is that which one gives."*

From my father:

*"Patience and time do more than force or rage."*

# APPENDIX I

# JOSEPH PRESSEL LETTERS TO ELIE SCHWERNER

The following are copies of letters written by my father, mostly in French, to Uncle Elie Schwerner in New York during the war. I have not edited the letters he wrote in English. I have translated and edited the French ones. There is one letter written by Elie to us. The letters show the progressive desperation we felt as the war continued. Elie was my mother's Uncle who was head of the family hair processing business in New York. The letters are in chronological order.

Marseille,
August 5, 1940

My dears,

We received your telegram from the 3rd and we thank you for doing something to help us to get out of this scrape. At the time we sent you the telegram we were at the end of a series of marches on foot, which exhausted us physically and financially. We had been able these past few years to manage our affairs, but now we have to start all over again, without knowing how or where. In Marseille employment is unavailable to non-French citizens.

Happily a few days ago by unexpected luck we received the first signs of life of the family: Miryam's parents, Ruth and her 2 children, Norbert and Ella are in Antwerp. Ruth's husband and 2 of our Uncles, brothers of Mama, Hartwig and Evan, as well as Erwin, son of Evan and Gunther, son of Uncle Hermann are still interned in a camp in the Midi section of France. We will do all we can to obtain their freedom.

Uncle Hermann and Aunt Miryam are in Antwerp.

Since Uncle Maurice in New York must be worried about his family please apprise him of the above news.

After having feared the worst for everybody, considering the danger to which we have been exposed to from the beginning and for many weeks, you will understand our relief to know that even part of the family is alive. I still do not know where my parents are but hope to get some news soon.

We do not get any mail or telegrams from Belgium since those services are not working.

When the bombs came unexpectedly on the 10th of May (two three-story houses were demolished right next to our dwelling) we decided to be prudent and to move away. After several days most of the family was reunited in LaPanne. We entered France on the 18th of May. After a trip partly on foot, partly luckily by rail, we were in the middle of endless convoys of refugees, many of whom unfortunately died on route. We got to Paris on the 21st of May with our 3 year old child.

I served in the Polish army in France until June 18. On the 23rd after I made a non-stop march of 2 days and 2 nights with many unpleasant circumstances, I reached Miryam and our child who had traveled for 3 days and 3 nights in a wagon packed with refugees and wounded, some who were barely alive.

It is regrettable that these are precisely the actual events and difficulties that we found ourselves in, which made it necessary for us to make contact with you. We would be happy to hear how you are as well as your 3 children who must be quite Americanized by now.

Do you think that you could do something over there to help us to emigrate either to the USA or to another country in the Americas? I suppose that entry into North or South America will be possible due to the war in Europe; could you enquire with organizations or the authorities over there? By what I have learned here, it is possible to obtain a visa for South America as long as it can be proven that a job has been found in that country. We are not afraid of any work no matter how hard it is, and anything is preferable to waiting here for a future, which promises nothing good. The war is not over and its effects will undoubtedly be felt for many harsh days.

We both have Polish passports. What follows the letter are some essential details in case you need them. I also send you a copy of testimony, which should be attached to my dossier of naturalization.

We ask you to take our requests seriously and we hope and expect one day to show our appreciation. We hope to get encouraging news soon.

With our heartiest thanks, our best wishes,

Many kisses,
Jos and Miryam

Pressel, Joseph

Born in Cracow, July 12, 1901
High speed stenographer - typewriter
Proficient in four languages: English, French, German, Dutch.
Knowledge of Spanish
Secretary - translator - professor and diplomat of stenographie
From 1932-1939 secretary of European Consortium of Steariniers
(stearine and oleine -red oil- producers)
Miryam
Born in Fulda, Germany August 1, 1906

Philippe
Born in Berchem - Antwerp, June 22, 1937

**Sarette and Elie Schwerner**

Marseille
September 2, 1940

My dears,

We sent you a letter by airmail 3 weeks ago and we hope that you have received it. So far we have not received the information included in the telegram of August 3. Luckily for the first 15 days of August we qualified (for the first time) for refugee funding. We do not know for how long we will receive this funding or what we will happen to us if we are not given the opportunity to earn a living.

Again we ask you to do everything you can to help us to emigrate. It is impossible here to know what the large emigration organizations are doing and what to do to get in touch with them. Could you please urgently inquire and sign us up so that we may make the quota. If we are allowed to earn an honest living anywhere, we have no doubt that we could manage. We would be more than happy to reimburse you one day for the expenses that you incur to help us. Please do your best. We still haven't heard any direct news from Antwerp. Mail and telegraph service with Belgium is still interrupted.

The latest news is that the situation for us here grows worse. Return to Belgium is not authorized. We are told there are camps where the Poles are interned. It will be an untenable situation if the war continues for much longer. The news that we get from the camp where Maurice and the Uncles are is very bad; the hygiene situation is deplorable, there are several cases of typhus with death inevitable. Luckily our family has not caught it yet. We are trying to get them liberated but so far with no success. In case our previous letter has not arrived, I repeat that according to information here most of the countries of South and Central America are granting visas to those who can show that they have a job there. Perhaps you know of a company there who could get me a contract for a job. It is only under these conditions that the Consulate here will deliver a visa. We also will have to obtain the money to pay for the trip. It is a lot to ask of you or at least to ask you to have the HICEM or another organization intervene for us. As far as we know you are the only source of help for us.

Hoping that this letter finds you in good health, and while we wait for news from you, we send you dear Uncle and Aunt our thanks for everything that you are doing for us.

Our kisses to you,
Jos

Dear Uncle and Aunt,

Do everything you can to get us out of this misery and to give us the chance to resume a normal existence. Thank you in advance. Forgive all the bother. Many kisses to you all.

Miryam

Marseille
October 10, 1940

My dear Aunt and Uncle,

We were so happy to receive your letter of September 21; it gave us a great deal of emotional comfort; not that we lack courage, far from it, but in the circumstances we live in and the upheaval and confusion, we get revived when we get such a nice letter as yours from the land of Stars and Stripes. We are happy that you are thinking of us and that you are trying to get us over there. I will come back later about traveling abroad but first will tell you some news of the family.

We were so happy to see Ella while she was in Marseille for one day. She told us how the family was. She was here on September 28. Papa has a little work in Broechem (the hair factory), as does Uncle Hirsch. Norbert also manages his affairs and has work. Harry as you probably know is safe and sound in Antwerp. Ruth and the two children are fine. The daughter of Norbert is supposed to be a beauty. In a word, everybody over there is fine for as long as the circumstances permit.

We don't sleep very much because we pass part of the night in caves or shelters.

Ella went to see Maurice who is still interned, as well as the Uncles and the two cousins. It is impossible to get their freedom. Perhaps Maurice will get himself expatriated if he can obtain the necessary visas. The whole family passed many days and nights in danger and anguish during the exodus into France. Finally they were all blocked and they returned to Antwerp.

In between the bomb blasts, Ella met an engineer from Antwerp;(Mr. Landenberg) with whom she is engaged to be married! She told us that her marriage would be soon. Her fiancé still has work in Antwerp; she is crazy about him and so is he about her. The stories she told us merit a Hollywood scenario as you can well imagine.

Three weeks ago I received the first signs of life from my parents as well as my sister and my brother-in-law. Happily they are all in good health and are in Antwerp. Unfortunately the mail and telegraph service with Belgium is still suspended. It is sometimes possible to obtain a letter by the intervention of the Red Cross. Many Belgium refugees in France returned, but lately, following the advice published by the press, foreigners and Jews (also Negroes), cannot pass regularly through and are turned back. In order to get papers and visas here you must declare if you are an Israelite; in that case you do not get the necessary papers to return to Belgium. On the other hand foreign men, from 18 to 55, who find it impossible to return to their homeland, are assembled in groups and must work for the French economy. They do not have normal rights and privileges of citizenship, but maintain the right to emigrate.

Now I shall write to you concerning our immigration. In essence I speak and write Spanish fluently and I am planning to perfect my knowledge of this language. As I told you previously it has been confirmed to me that if I obtain a position with a Central or South American company that is recognized by the minister of labor and who would notify the consulate in Marseille, the latter would grant the necessary visa.

Having learned that the Zionist Organization in the United States has the opportunity to grant visitors' visas to deserving persons whom they recommend, I have just requested such visas for Louis and me; these visas are valid for the titleholder and their families (spouse, children). My request was sent to Mr. J. Blumberg, Hotel Metropole, Lisbon, whom I asked to intervene for me to the appropriate Zionist groups in the USA. I added that if personal references in the US are useful they could contact you. I requested an answer by cable and I suppose that in a week I will know something about my request.

Your latest telegram still has not come. I thank you Aunt Sarette for my Aunt Louise's address (Mrs. M. Pressel) and for your note. She is as you say a very good and charitable person, but happily until now we have been able to fend for ourselves in order not to starve to death. When we sent you the last telegram we spent our next to last 100-franc bill, and were happy to find some charities that advanced us some money, which we have already paid back. Concerning the son of my Aunt who also lives in New York, I tell you the following in strictest confidence, I cannot write to him for help or for money because he ignored us since the day that my soap factory went bankrupt, in which he had invested some money. If I were to contact that family over there it would have to be by an intermediary, because then and only then, could they not ignore us or treat us like beggars. Excuse me for exposing you so cruelly to this situation but in all frankness, Aunt Sarette, I felt obliged to tell you this following your suggestion made in all good faith to me. Again please keep what I have just told you to yourself. Perhaps one-day feelings will change, and the contact that was broken in time of joy will be resumed in times of distress.

If we leave for America we will be able to pay for part of the trip providing that we receive an advance on the balance; we will gladly reimburse after we find work over there.

I shall end this letter, already very long; we understand that you also now live in hours of excitement such as those that precede great decisions that a country must make for it's future.

How are you and how is the family over there? We wish you good health and send you our best wishes and affectionate kisses.

Jos

My dears,

Thank you for your nice letter. It did us a lot of good. Jos wrote you a lot and there is not much more for me to tell. We live here the 6 of us in two tiny rooms in primitive ways. There is no gas; we cook on 2 alcohol burners (modern comforts). Happily the kids are well and are well behaved.

We are waiting for an answer to our letter soon and send you our love and kisses.

Your
Myr

55 Rue des Petites-Maries
Marseille
November 14, 1940

My dear Uncle and Aunt,

We assume that our letter of October 10, in answer to your letter of September 24 arrived. Meanwhile, we received the money that you had the kindness to send us; the American Express Company of Marseille paid me 1072 francs on October 14 against your funds. We also learned from Sam Heilpern's letter to his sisters in Marseille that we can collect $20 from them on your behalf. You cannot imagine how welcome this money is, for at this time we have no other source of money other than what Myriam earns as a dressmaker. We have not yet been able to get the $20 from that family for they are having financial difficulties; we will probably receive the money from Mr. Fajnberg who is leaving momentarily for New York and who will arrange this over there. Since September we have not received any allocations as refugees. We therefore thank you doubly for your kind financial help.

We still have not received any letters from our parents, other than the one letter from my parents that I told you about previously. We assume that everything is all right. Concerning Ruth's husband and the Uncles, they are still interned and have just been transferred to another camp. We send them packages of food to supplement their meager nourishment.

Yesterday I sent a telegram to your company concerning a new request for a visa to the USA. This is for a special visa, which is accorded to intellectuals who need to be saved for reasons that I do not need to tell you. If I am well informed, it is the American Rescue Committee who decides who gets authorized these visas. I gave my references here as well as to Leon Kubowitzki who is in New York and is aware of my activities as a journalist and stenographer. I hope that you (rest of letter is missing)

(This letter was written in English and is reproduced here unaltered)

18 Rue Elemir Bourges
Marseille
May 30, 1941

Dear Uncle Elie, dear Aunt Rose and dear Cousin Nat,

I wish to express to you our best thanks for your affidavits. It is only a pity that we did not receive them earlier, when we could have availed ourselves of them immediately. Now we shall have to wait till the quota is open again, which we are told will be the case towards the beginning of July next. On the other hand, conditions are growing worse and worse. Most of the refugees have been transferred to small villages or to camps, and in most cases husbands are separated from their wives and children.

We are lucky enough at least to be still together for the moment, but what will be tomorrow? In any case there seems to be no alternative for us; we want to hasten the formalities necessary for our emigration and only hope that it will not be too late to find an opportunity to leave.

Some days ago, I had a talk at the American consulate with one of the Secretaries who examines the papers before submitting the same to the Vice Consul. I could, of course, only show him the copies of affidavits and the personal letter which you sent to us. The documents which you directed to the Consulate only, are not yet filed; they receive heaps of papers every day and it takes some weeks until the papers can be considered by the Vice Consul who gives his final advice and grants or refuses the visa. According to the advice of the Secretary, your affidavits appear to be sufficient but he required a proof of the corrections to the earnings declared.

The Consulate requires a copy (or photocopy) of the Federal Income Tax paid for 1939 and 1940, certified by the Collector of Internal Revenue- to be added to the affidavit of each of you. We have cabled you to let us have these papers which we suppose will be in accordance with the declarations on the affidavits and what is stated in the report of the Public Accountant whose statement you addressed to the Consulate.

There is another document which you did not send us and which is indispensable, namely, a moral and political guarantee respecting us. The moral and political guarantee is to be made up in the same way as the financial affidavit (before a Notary Public) stating that the applicants for immigration (that is to say ourselves) are the agents of no foreign government and that their activities will by no means be contrary to the interest of the American Nation. I have seen a lot of such guarantees which contain a somewhat more extensive wording in which it is said that the people in question are honest, hard working, of a perfect moral and intellectual integrity etc, and that they will prove to be useful citizens etc. No doubt you can easily be shown over there a specimen of such declarations made up for other people. As a general rule, such a moral and political guarantee must be given by an American citizen residing in the United States and preferably by a well known person. In case the person giving this guarantee is not known to the Consulate here, a declaration has to be added made for instance by a judge, a member of the Senate etc., certifying that the said person is honorably known in the United States.

We asked for these papers in our cable of the 28th reading: "Consulate requires evidence of your stated earnings. Airmail us immediately, not to Consulate, Federal Income Tax return 1939, 1940 certified by Collector of Internal Revenue. Also moral political guarantees respecting us". We are now anxiously awaiting same in order to submit them without delay to the Consulate. We thank you for the financial assistance which you are offering us and shall revert to this matter in due course.

For your guidance, I addressed a very urgent appeal to my cousin Louis Birnbaum, on the 20th of May, asking for affidavits. Afterwards, I received a cable dated May 22, from Dr. Kubowitzki, in which I am told that my case has been submitted to the State Department and that a decision is to follow. Should this endeavor fail, then I hope that my cousin Louis Birnbaum will send affidavits because I am not sure whether your own affidavits will suffice for our 6 persons.

I take this opportunity to inform you that my cousin Joseph Pressel must now have arrived in New York and that he will probably call on you. He and his wife were very kind to us; he also gave me the small sum of money which Sam Heilpern asked his relatives here to remit us, but which we could not obtain from them.

Excuse the length of this letter, but I wanted to make the matter quite clear to you.

Sonja is going to add a few lines. We are sending our best greetings to you and the other dear members of your families not addressed to in the top of this letter. We remain, with love,

Your
Jos, Miryam and Philippe

Dear Family,

We thank you very much for sending the affidavits. As Jos wrote above, you can see that we need a lot more before we can leave. But we have much courage and hope all will be arranged. For the time being Louis is in Nice, and also sincerely thanks you.

We are also in correspondence with Jacques Schwerner's family and Kincler, who complain of not getting news from you. You know that we are all here in a very sad situation. If you can send news they will be very pleased. It is a little effort especially since Uncle Isidor is quite sick. Happily the others are well. Licy and Ella got married. The former lives in France, Ella is in Antwerp. Our brother in law Maurice is now in a camp in Milles which is near Marseille; he is trying to get to America.

We hope to continue to correspond with you, and hope to shake your hand soon.

Meanwhile we send our kisses from your
Louis Sonia and Sylvain

(This letter was written in English and is reproduced here unaltered.)

Marseille
June 28, 1941
18 rue Elemir Bourges

Dear Uncle Elie,

You will have received our letter of May 30 in which we expressed our thanks for your affidavits and for those of our dear Aunt Rosa and our Cousin Nat. The additional papers which you mailed us on June 6, also duly arrived. Many thanks! Unfortunately in the meantime, the issue of visas here has been suspended. We were told that the delivery of a visa is now subject to the prior approval of the State Department in Washington.

Therefore I cabled you on June 24 to ask you to obtain from the State Department a visa to be granted to Louis and Sonja and I hope that you will be in a position to find the necessary introduction to the State Department to that end.

As for our visas, these were granted by Washington, according to a cable which I received ten days ago. The Consulate at Marseille received the necessary notification and I was fixed an appointment with the Consul for June 30th. We should have probably received satisfaction at that moment, but for the time being all appointments at the Consulate are cancelled, and it is necessary to have my visa reconfirmed to the Consulate. I cabled New York and hope that Dr. Kubowitski will have done what is necessary at once. Will you please enquire on receipt of this letter how the matter stands? I hope that the question will be in order soon.

In your letter of May 4, you were so kind as to suggest the remittance to us of the money necessary for supplementary expenses. In my cable of June 24, I asked whether you can remit me ten thousand francs which is the sum at which we value our travel expenses to Spain and Portugal, including visas and additional expenses here and en route until the moment of embarkation. Price of the American visa is 400 francs for each of the three of us, except perhaps for our child; travel expenses to Portugal is approximately 1500 francs each.

As to the fare to America, I shall apply to my cousin who spontaneously offered to share into this expenditure.

We have been passing very embarrassing times of late, and in addition we lived under the continual threat of being sent somewhere in "forced residence." On the 17th of June, I acquainted you by cable of these impending difficulties and on the next day we were effectively assigned a small place which we were ordered to go to within four days at three or four hundred miles distance from Marseille. In our present situation as Jewish refugees, a position which is growing worse every day, our stay here and certainly elsewhere in some small village, is all except encouraging, to say the least.

Just "in extremis" on the 19th I received the cable that my visa was granted by the State Dept. and this enabled us to prolong our stay at Marseille in order to accomplish the final emigration formalities.

Sonja and Louis have temporarily avoided these difficulties by moving to Nice.

We are causing you a lot of trouble, taking much of your time for the sake of our emigration. Be assured that we are extremely grateful for anything you have done until now and for all the assistance you will further give us until we are able to leave.

For three months we received no mail from Belgium; Ruth has succeeded in contacting her husband through the International Red Cross and we heard that all the family is in good health but the prevailing condition are rather bad. It is luck for them that the garden at Broochem is helping to overcome to a certain extent the deficient food supply.

Miryam is working hard for the household etc; she apologies for not adding some lines, but sends her best greetings to you all. Please also convey my best regards to Aunt Rose, Aunt Sarette, her mother and all our Schwerner cousins over there.

With my good wishes and best regards to you personally,
I am very cordially yours,
Jos

(This letter was written in English and is reproduced here unaltered.)

Marseille
August 12, 1941
18 Rue Elemis Bourges

Dear Uncle Elie and dear Family,

You will have received my letter of June 28. As you know, we were granted a special visa, but we could not yet obtain it, as the Consulate needs an additional authorization which we hope will now soon be given.

If so, we may shortly be in a position to arrange the final formalities at the American consulate and the purpose of this letter is to convene with you respecting our travel expenses. These, in fact, must be an easy matter to arrange, as we shall be able to refund you on arrival. As soon as we obtain confirmation from the Consulate that the visa is at our disposition, we shall send you a cable asking to place at our disposal a certain amount either in Francs at Marseille, or if you cannot dispose to that extent, to pay in your local currency in New York. Please let us know on receipt of this letter whether we may rely on this arrangement, and be so good as to leave the necessary instructions at your office so that your payment can be made even in your absence, should our cable arrive if you are on a travel.

From the numerous people who arrived in New York recently, it will be easy for you to obtain information as to how the travel expenses are to be settled. If I apply to you for this payment, it is because we suppose that your friends over here will be willing to make the disbursement in French francs, but if this should not be practical, please contact my cousin Birnbaum who is prepared to share in the expenses. Moreover my cousin Joseph will also explain to you how to deal with the fare.

If, against our anticipation and hope, the authorization to be granted by Washington should be refused, then we hope that you will manage to procure us a visa for Cuba, which as we were glad to learn from Sonja and Louis you were trying to get also for us.

Unfortunately, we are still looking for emigration as the only remedy to a desperate situation. The question is as urgent as ever. Let us hope that it will be given to us to get over to the States where we will prove our gratitude to you for all that you are doing for us in these sad times.

With our good wishes to you all
Best kisses,

Jos, Miryam, Philippe
(This letter was written in English and is reproduced here unaltered)

18 Rue Elemir Bourges
Marseille
September 25, 1941

My dear Uncle Elie,

It is now more than three months ago since we were granted a visa by the Department of State, Washington. Owing to the restrictive new regulations, however, the Consulate at Marseille could not yet visa our passports and therefore we are still longing for the new authorization to be given by the State Department. We cabled repeatedly to the Congress, New York: June 24, July 2, July 18, August 21 and August 29.

On July 12 a cable was sent to us saying "Congress tried intervention State Department; result uncertain; await Clipper letter." We never received this letter, and whilst I cabled on July 2 the exact residences of our close relatives I was surprised to receive a cable dated August 25 reading: "Cable exactly the names and present addresses, dates of death of parents, brothers, sisters, children of yours stop trying to intervene."

Thereupon, on Aug. 29 I repeated the data cabled already July 2 and asked our friends to apply to you for the exact names of Miryam's parents, brother and sisters.

We are very impatient, and anxious to know how the matter stands. Perhaps you will be so kind as to ask Dr. A. Tartakower, 275 Seventh Avenue 24th floor, New York City whether everything is in order now with the new application for our visa and ask him whether something can be done to bring up the issue of the authorization from Washington. Since a few weeks several visas are being granted daily at the Consulate at Marseille in consequence of instructions received from Washington. Perhaps something can be done in our case to hasten the matter?

It was suggested I apply to the Marseille's office of the "International Migration Service" New York, whose President, as I was told, is a member of the "President's Advisory Committee" (this committee considers as I understand all the applications for immigration). The Marseille bureau of the above said Migration Service recommended us to the New York office by cable and by letter and asked to contact Dr. Tartakower and cable to Washington to ask whether we can soon expect to receive the authorization necessary on account of our relatives' residence. We thank you for paying additional expenses up to $100 but only $90 were paid. We also thank you for your cable informing us that you will approach our family over there. We hope to receive soon a cable from you or from the Congress informing us that our visa is confirmed and then we shall find out the cheapest way how to pay the fare.

If, from the information gathered by Dr. Tartakower, we may expect a favorable result soon, some words to this effect by cable will be very useful to us; this in connection with the unsteadiness of our stay here. It is only because we are considered as emigrants "ready to leave" that we are tolerated here. If this were not the case, we should be long gone, somewhere in a remote place, locked up in forced internment, or in a camp. We can expect the same trouble even now, if we have no real possibility to emigrate soon.

Should all the endeavors to bring us over to the States meet with such difficulties that a prompt favorable decision can not be anticipated then, we think, that the best for us will be to get to Cuba and await our authorization over there. It would mean a calamity to us to spend another winter here. As matters stand now we shall be in a position to refund the fare to Cuba; so please give this question your best and immediate attention.

This letter turned out very long, but I found it necessary to give you more than a brief report on what we attempted to get our visa. Please, Uncle Elie, do what you can over there, to get us out of this bad situation, and be assured that this in not a mere request but, as we feel it, an absolute necessity; we cannot put it down in clearer words, but nevertheless you will understand us.

On the occasion of Rosh Hashana, we are sending you our most sincere good wishes for good health and prosperity and are extending the same wishes to all the family.

With our best regards and many kisses,

Yours affectionately,
Jos

(This is a letter from Elie.)
Brooklyn, N.Y.
May 25, 1942

Dear Miryam and Jos,

After having worked incessantly during this time and failing to see anything happening, I decided to consult with an influential lawyer in

Washington who was recommended. His fee is $250, and I gave him $50 with the rest to be paid when he obtains the visa. This was done several months ago. I have a stack of correspondence with him and have had many telephone conversations without any results. Last week I went to Washington and I spoke with the appropriate officials as well as with the lawyer. Unfortunately, I was unable to obtain any results. One must wait his turn; they refuse to say what the delay is due to. I am supposed to be called to a hearing in Washington where I will go with the lawyer. Hopefully that will happen fast. I tried to send you as well as to my brother Jacques and to my sister some money, but that was not allowed. I am in correspondence with Schild and Louis. I just received a letter announcing the arrival of Ruth and babies. You never wrote to me whether you received our packages of food; it has been quite a while.

Needless to say I will send you a telegram as soon as I hear anything favorable. I have not heard from Moses, Hirsch and family. Please write to me if you have news of them.

Meanwhile I embrace you all.

Uncle Elie


(Early June 1942.)


Dear Uncle Elie,

At the beginning of this month we finally received a telegram from Louis announcing that all arrived safely. We assume that this telegram was sent to us following the cable which we sent to you on May 5. We have been very worried about our parents whom we also were told have been equally worried. Let us hope that now we will soon receive more complete news by letter. As far as our own immigration is concerned, we are very hard put to stay without any information. What is happening to the efforts in obtaining our exit permits? The last news that we received was in the month of February (a cable from Dr. Kubowitski) that said you have been in touch with a lawyer in Washington and that he would let us know of a favorable decision. But the months pass and we unfortunately do not see anything happening. We have previously explained to you that our situation here is without any hope. Could you make an ultimate emergency effort to accelerate obtaining a favorable decision. Recently, every day there are visas being delivered here, but that will stop soon. Therefore, you can understand that we want to take advantage of the possibility of leaving as long as the possibility exists. We would like no less than to be able to reimburse you all the expenses incurred in our quest for immigration, and if it is a matter of supplementary expenses to obtain rapid satisfaction, we beg you now to do all you can to help us. Eventually wherever we are, with the possibility of work, we will without much effort and with great pleasure, refund you.

In case our request for immigration has not been put under consideration, for reasons that are unknown to us, I hope that you will do your best so that our case will be re-examined, because we are certainly living in sinister and desperate times, and time is running out for us to be finally granted the requested permits. There are people here who have been refused delivery of permits twice and who just now received their visas.

If the visas are finally granted, will you please, as promised, get in touch with the family as far as the question of reimbursement for our travel costs. It will be sufficient for an account to be established with Hias and the freight can be paid here in order to reduce the cost. Mr. and Mrs. Spielman who are aware of the cost of travel and how it is paid will voluntarily give you the necessary explanations, and will tell you how much is necessary for a favorable solution to be found for our departure. Uncle, please do the maximum that you can and keep us informed. It is with great impatience that we await your cable.

The last news that we received from our dear parents was on the 12th of May. Papa was suffering a great deal. At the beginning of May, he had to be operated on for a cyst on his liver. The operation was performed at St. Elizabeth hospital. Mother gave us some reassuring news on this subject; he was well taken care of, and has regained his strength after being very weak. Someone else told us that he subsequently went home and is well on his way to recovery. Let us hope that we will soon receive satisfactory news as far as your health is concerned; as far as the rest of the situation, it leaves much to be desired.

How are you, and you Aunt, and the children? And how is Aunt Rosa? We hope that all is well with you. Are our cousins in school yet?

While waiting to receive news from you soon, we send you dear Uncle Elie, Aunt and the whole family our best wishes and affectionate kisses

from your,
Jos, Miryam, and Philippe

J. Pressel
24 Quai Fulchiron
Lyon, France

September 28, 1944
Mr. E. Schwerner
539 Ocean Parkway
Brooklyn, N.Y.

Dear Uncle Elie,
    "They are still alive!..."
    Yes, we are still alive and we can finally breathe in freedom. We are living in Lyon since the end of 1942. The city was liberated on September 3. We feel like the survivors of a cataclysm. The joy of feeling free is profound, but we have seen too much suffering, and we worry a great deal about all those dear to us whose fate is unknown, for this joy to be complete.
    It is almost a miracle that we were able to survive safe and sound from this torture. For the past two years, human life counted for nothing. Perhaps later we will have the opportunity to tell you in more detail all that we went through. On November 11, 1942, we saw the arrival of the masses of German troops in Marseille, and we had to wait until the month of August 1944 in Lyon, to see the withdrawal of this army, in endless file in front of our house, while being routed and pursued by the allied armies coming up from the south of France. What a relief! We waited for so long, and so fervently hoped for deliverance. Our son was evacuated under mandatory order to the countryside since last May in order to be sheltered from the bombings. We rejoined him on the 28th of August to be together no matter what would happen. The village where we found ourselves was already in the hands of the resistance and all around the French army of the interior were attacking the German troops. Also, in the distance we could see the allied planes diving and strafing the German convoys and releasing their bombs on the enemy trucks. The village was caught in a crossfire and for several days we lived in an agonizing situation. Anyway the essential thing for the moment is that we can announce to you that we three are safe and sound and happy that we were able to save our little Philippe, who is now 7 years old and who never lost hope and who had confidence in everything that we had to do to shelter him from harm.

Now concerning other members of the family. Since the battle of France, postal communications were halted and are still not normal, and we are waiting for news from various quarters. We were therefore very happy to receive news today in the form of a letter, that Jacques and Jeanne Schwerner are in good health. They are still in Argenton sur Creuse. Ady is still in Toulouse and intends to rejoin her parents soon. Edmee is in Switzerland. Harry (Schwerner) as you probably know was arrested in 1942 at the Spanish border just as he was intending to resume his Belgian military service; he was interned for several months in a camp in Drancy (near Paris) and was subsequently deported. We have not heard from him since. Licy, the eldest daughter, and her husband and two children are also safe and sound. We have not heard recently about the Kincler family. You probably don't know it but unfortunately their daughter was deported in August 1942; little Irene stayed during this whole time with her grandparents; Jacques was also arrested but was able to escape in time and went underground; we last heard from him about 2 months ago. We hope that we will learn soon that he too was able to celebrate freedom with his parents.

We have not heard from Belgium for about 6 months. At this time my in-laws as well as Ella were still there and we hope that they are safe and sound. My mother, unfortunately, was deported in 1942 and I have not heard about her fate; my sister and her husband were also taken in 1942 to "a destination unknown." Will I ever see them again? Norbert, his wife and child underwent the same sad fate, as well as Ella's husband, but he and Norbert were able to communicate several times since. My wife's Uncles who were in France were deported... It is an un-ending list. My wife would have liked to go to Belgium immediately to see her parents except that travel by rail is not yet possible, and to go by road is an expense that we cannot afford.

Since I only have your address Uncle Elie, I cannot write to any other members of the family, therefore I ask you to please convey this letter to my family in New York, to Miryam's two sisters, and to all the good friends who have asked about us during these hard war years.

We would like to know how you all passed these last few years, if you are in good health, what you are doing, and what are your plans for the future? Where are Ruth and Sonia, how are the children, etc...

We do not intend to stay long in Lyon, but we do not know yet where we will go. Like before, we do not know how long it takes for correspondence to go from France to the USA and back, so I ask you to please note that all correspondence sent to us should be temporarily sent to: Societe Emile PRAT & FILS, for J. Pressel, 24 Quai Fulchiron, Lyon, France. If we leave here, the Society will forward our mail.

Hoping that we soon receive detailed news from you, we sent you our best wishes and kisses,
Your
Jos, Mir and Philippe

My dear all,
We have returned to life; let us hope that our dear parents are also safe and sound, as well as brother, sister, sister-in-law, brother-in-law, mentioning only the immediate family. You cannot realize the good fortune of all those who did not have to live in Europe for the last two years. As far as the future is concerned, we cannot make any plans, but I want to return to Belgium as fast as possible.
Write to us quickly if possible, it has been so long since we have heard any news from the family that every letter give us a great deal of pleasure.

A thousand kisses to divide among you all
Your
Mir

I would like to see you all again. I send you lots of kisses for both cheeks.

Philippe

Lyon
October 16, 1944

My dear all,
Since our day of liberation at the beginning of September we have tried to give you signs of life and we sent you a letter dated the 28th of September. We assume therefore that you will have learned that we are

safe and sound. We have also had the joy of learning that the Isidore Kincler family is in good health, that is to say the parents, Jacques and Irene. Sala was deported in 1942; there has been no news from her since. Jacques and Jeanne Schwerner, are still in Argenton, and also let us know of their status. On the other hand, we have not gotten any signs of life from Miryam's parents or Ella, who were still in Belgium several months ago. Miryam would have liked to go right away to Belgium but we cannot afford it. We wait impatiently for news from you about you all, and ask you please Uncle Elie to notify my family over there and Miryam's two sisters that we survived all the suffering of these last few years.

Many kisses to you all,
Jos, Mir, Philippe

J. Pressel
Paris
March 21, 1945

Mr. E. Schwerner
924 West End Avenue
New York

My dear all,
Approximately three weeks ago dear Uncle Elie we had the nice surprise and joy to receive your first letter since the liberation; (letter of 1-1-45 to which was attached the letter from the family in Havana). We thank you and regret only that you said absolutely nothing about yourself, nor of your dear children, and we also were happy to read a few words from Aunt Sarette.

How are you? The last time that we saw Armand and Willy was a long time ago, and they must have grown a lot since...What studies have they done, and what profession are they going into? Even though they are of age to serve in the military, it would seem that the war will be finished before they have to put on a uniform. Jeanine was 3 years old I think when you left to go to the United States. Is she still the "Benjamine," or did the family grow since then? (Benjamine is a term used to designate the youngest of a family). We hope that Aunt Rosa and the children are well. Please give our best wishes to everyone. We also received news about you from Mr. Kaplan, and are very touched by the sentiments tended to us. Miryam recently went to Argenton to see the family and while there gave Uncle Jacques your regards. No one in Argenton had yet received news from any of you.

We suppose that you heard of the sad news of the death of Uncle Isidore last January 24. From what we were able to learn, the hardships that he underwent at the hands of the Nazis before the liberation were fatal to him.

Today we received a package from you from the Gray Globe Company of New York, sent the 11th of January and containing cloth from which to make a suit. I heartily thank you for this gift, more precious inasmuch as clothing prices here are extremely expensive, as well as for all the other indispensable and useful things. The rations here are distributed in minute quantities and are of inferior quality. Coffee, tea, cacao are non-existent for years; milk in the cities is only given to children and in limited quantities; (our child is entitled to 1/4 of a liter per day but he doesn't drink it regularly). We received butter today (50 grams per person) for the first time since the month of December. For three weeks we haven't touched a gram of meat , etc... It is like a great penance as you can see, and yet we are happy to be rid of the Boches, for that alone is worth the deprivations, and yet we know that in this murdered Europe there are many others who suffer more than we.

We left Lyon at the end of November and we now live in Asnieres-sur-Seine, near Paris. I am working as an employee of Prat, in Paris, and therefore we have a few resources; but the salary does not permit even the most elementary expenses in addition to the high cost of indispensable things; for example I just paid the sum of 500 Francs to resole my shoes, and everything else is proportionately the same high price. Luckily an Uncle of Miryam had the kindness to give us 10,000 Francs which under these hard times is coming in very handy.

We will be staying in Paris for some time until we return, maybe to Belgium. Again we are without news from my wife's parents for several weeks; Ella let us know that she would be visiting us soon and we are looking forward to it. Miryam intends to go visit her parents during the next month, which will not be soon enough considering that it has been 5 years of cruel events that has marked this long separation.

Otherwise we are happy to be able to tell you that we are in good health. We passed several weeks of a very hard winter, especially since we had absolutely no heat and a meager subsistence of food. Our little Philippe has become a big boy and will be 8 years old in several months.

He goes to school in Asnieres and is one of the best students in his class; due to all the continual moves he is already in his seventh school...

We think of you often and hope that you will soon send us more news. Let's also hope that soon a curtain will fall on this last act of the European tragedy, and that the fighting in the Pacific will also end soon in a complete Allied victory.

We hope that this letter finds you in good health, and while we wait for news from you soon we send you dear Uncle Elie, Aunt and all of you our best wishes and kisses,

from your
Jos, Miryam

J. Pressel
c/o Ets. Emile Prat & Fils
64 rue de Miromesnil
Paris (8e)

We just received your package from January 17 containing a package of tea, coffee, cacao, and can of condensed milk and some soap. After what I told you above, you can understand how much we need and appreciate it. These are things which we forgot existed. A big thank you for the favor you did for us.

Jos

# APPENDIX II

# PRESSEL LETTERS TO SUSI PANTZER

The following are copies of letters written by my father, some in French and some in English, to Susi Pantzer, his niece in London. I have translated and edited the letters in French. Susi was the daughter of my father's sister Charlotte, who with her husband Naphtali Hamel, were deported and killed in Auschwitz. There are letters from my father to my mother and me. The letters are in chronological order.

March 1, 1941
Post Office
Marseille

My dear Susi,

Your letter of December 11, 1940 got to us on February 24. It was in transit for a long time but nevertheless we were happy to receive your good news. We regularly receive letters from your dear parents. The last one was dated February 19. For a while your mother has not received news about you and she was happy to read your lines of December 11, 1940 that we transmitted to her as soon as we got the letter. I can tell you that your parents are well; they are impatiently waiting the moment that they can see you and your dear Joe. Let us hope with all of our heart that this won't be delayed much more. Have patience like we do in our exile in France. Patience and confidence! Remember us to your in-laws with whom we passed such pleasant hours. Since you do not write about your brother in-law, we suppose that he is not with you and that he is courageously serving his time in the service.

As for us, it is almost eight months that we are in Marseille. How time flies. We are well and we get much pleasure from our child who goes proudly each day to kindergarten where he learns to sing, dance, draw, etc. You know that we live in the same house together with Sonia, her husband and their son who is one year older than Philippe; the two children have the same routine and would like to see their grandparents, and besides that they happily have what they need.

Miryam and I have our occupations and for the moment we don't have leisure time to worry. We are transmitting this letter with one of our friends who is traveling temporarily in Portugal and you should give him your response unless he changes his place of residence and he eventually leaves for the United States. Here is his address:

Mr. Maurice Herschkowitz, Hotel Batalha, Porto. You should attach an international coupon of the same value as an international stamp.

We send our best regards to your Uncle Simon, Aunt Frieda and Annie. We are happy to hear that they are well. I hope that we will soon get updated news from you and your dear ones.

Awaiting this, we send you dear Susi affectionate kisses for you and Joe.

Your Uncle and Aunt, Jos, Miryam and Philippe

(The following letter was the first news from us in over 3 years.)

24 Quai Fulchiron
Lyon
September 26, 1944

Dear Susi,

I just learned that postal communications with England have resumed. Therefore I am writing to you immediately and hope that I remember your address correctly and that these lines reach you.

So many events happened since our last correspondence during the first half of 1942! (Note: No letters exist or were received by Susi after the one dated 4-20-41). How are you dear Susi and what did you do during all of this time? We hope that you are in good health, as well as you husband, your in-laws and the whole family, and that you valiantly held up emotionally. Write us quickly because we would like to know if you are safe and sound. You can obviously write to us in English if that is easier for you.

I know quite well how worried you must have been about the fate of your parents from whom you probably haven't heard in two years. Unfortunately we also cannot reassure you of their fate because we ourselves are without news about them since August 26, 1942. During June 1942 I visited them in Nice and we were together for two days. On

August 8, 1942 in the "non occupied zone" of France, thousands of people were taken and interned for several days in camps or buildings and then deported. I was able to learn that your parents were on a list of people who were transferred to a destination unknown. Probably in Germany or Poland. Since then, without stop tens of thousands of people suffered the same fate and despite all efforts to determine the fate of those deported, it is impossible to learn what is going on. Even the Red Cross was not able to get the least bit of information about them. The end of the war is approaching; let us hope that your parents were able to survive the suffering and that you and us will hear that they survived unharmed through the terrible upheaval that shook the continent. My father died at the beginning of 1941 at the hands of the boches; unfortunately my mother was also deported around October or November 1942, and I have not gotten any news about her fate. Will I ever see her again? Thus in all families there are cruel voids that have been formed and we do not know yet the extent of the disaster that the Nazis perpetrated on the world.

I will not write to you now all that we went through for the last two years; perhaps later we will have the occasion to tell you all of that. But it is a miracle that we were able to survive, my wife and child (whose is now seven years old) and me, to come out unharmed from all the innumerable dangers that menaced us day and night. Needless to tell you the relief that we felt, thanks to the advancing Allied armies, when the German troops of occupation started to pack their baggage and then flee. For 15 days, we saw uninterrupted caravans of the German army coming up from the South, withdrawing, and file by our house. This was followed by the joy of finally being able to breath freely. Lyon, where we lived for the last two years was liberated on September 3.

We are waiting anxiously for news of my wife's parents, who approximately six months ago were still in Belgium; however since then we have received no news about them. It is still very hard these days to go to Belgium; otherwise my wife would already have made the trip. I am working here as a secretary/administrator in a company that has affiliates in London. It is La Societe Prat Daniel Ltd, but I do not count on staying with them for long. We will probably leave for Paris or Brussels, but meanwhile you can always write to me at the address at the top of this letter.

For today, I will end this first episode of contact, hoping that this letter finds you in good health, and send you Dear Susi, and all of you dear ones, our best wishes and many kisses.

Jos Pressel and family

**Susi and Joe Pantzer and daughter Helen, 1946**

(This is a condolence letter from my father to a relative of Susi's parents, the Hamels.)

Asnieres (sur Seine)
February 19, 1945

Dear Madam Hamel,
    We learned from Susi of the heavy loss that you sustained. We share with you deep distress and send you our sincere condolences. May the remembrance of all the goodness of your dear husband, who was kind to everybody who approached him, help you to overcome this cruel ordeal.
    We extend our condolences to your daughter and to her husband and wish you all remain  healthy and courageous.
    With all our sympathy and feelings of cordial friendship, we remain Dear Madam Hamel,

    Yours very sincerely,
    J. Pressel and family

Paris
February 20, 1945

My dear Susi,
    We received at infrequent intervals your three letters of December 13, January 21, and February 2. What joy to resume contact after the years of oppression that we lived in; and such happy news that you sent us, that you are the happy mother and Joe is the proud father of your treasured Helen. Belatedly we can now send you our warmest congratulations, as well as to your dear parents who thanks to your dear baby are now young grandparents. Your little girl has now completed her first difficult year, and has developed normally and contributes to your joint happiness.
    Needless to say, that your mother did not know that she became a grandmother, and was not able to share that happy occasion with your father. Under the circumstances it is doubly tragic and we resent the situation that befell us. Let us hope that your parents won't need to delay in celebrating the liberation, and that your grandmother will also soon receive our affectionate wishes. The information that I have obtained in

Paris indicates that it is too early to obtain news of those who were deported.

Since the end of November we left Lyon and went to Paris where I am working in the same company that had temporary offices in Lyon. Since it is practically impossible to live in Paris due to a lack of rooms in apartment buildings or hotels, we are living in a suburb of Paris and here is the address for you to send mail to.

5 rue Waldeck-Rousseau
Asnieres-sur-Seine (France)

It was very nice of you dear Susi to offer to send us a package. Since we lack literally everything here, any little things such as soap, chocolate, cigarettes would be greatly appreciated. We voluntarily share things with a soldier and you can send a package to him as soon as he sends you his address. Thank you in advance and we will compensate you when circumstances permit.

We received good news from my parents-in-law and Ella, who are in Belgium. They are living temporarily in Brussels. My in-laws lost everything during the occupation; they were interned for six months during which time the boches emptied their home completely and ransacked the whole factory of everything. Hopefully they will be recompensed but all that takes time and much effort.

Thank you for contacting my sisters-in-law Sonya and Alice since we did not have their address. We know that your Uncle Simon and his daughter were in London and we ask you to please remember us to them; Also please give our cordial best wishes to our friends there, and particularly to the Lemer brothers whom I always found quite sympathetic; I had the pleasure of collaborating with them and I think very highly of them. Congratulations to your sister-in-law and also to Joe Lemer on the occasion of their engagement. We hope that you will have celebrated his engagement and ask you to please give our sincere congratulations to your parents-in-law. Best wishes also to Simon Lemer.

Several days ago I received a letter from Saul Hirschel in London. Tell him that we are trying to get information about his mother and will notify him directly as soon as we get an answer.

Before ending this already long letter, several words about us. Happily our health is good enough to have permitted us to withstand more easily the difficulties of this later period of the war; we have endured many other difficulties, but the knowledge that we are rid of the boches permits us to live more easily with the inconveniences of today's situation.

We hope dear Susi and Joe that this letter will find you in good health, that your darling is equally well (does she have teeth yet, how much does she weigh, can she say anything, etc.?) and we send you our best wishes for you all and for your dear parents. We send you dear Susi a thousand affectionate thoughts and kisses.

Your Uncle Jos

PS. We just received a letter from America and one from Cuba with our family's address. We will answer them directly from here.

(Note: this next letter is from my mother.)

Dear Susi,

We were very happy to get your nice letters, especially with the news that you had a little daughter. Congratulations and happiness to you and the family. Without this horrible war, our little Philippe who is already 7 1/2 years old would probably have had a little sister. We are happy for the three of us to be together because we escaped many dangers.

We are feeling all right considering how much we suffered from the cold this winter without any coal. Also Uncle Jos' hands and feet suffer from frostbite and he has bronchitis. All will heal with better weather hopefully soon.

Philippe is feeling fairly well. Unfortunately he lacks all the basic ingredients of basic nourishment. Susi you ask if the little one lacks anything. Happily you cannot imagine what we lack in France. So much is lacking, especially for growing children. However we don't complain because we always think of those who were deported whose fate is a thousand times worse. I don't know if we will ever see my brother Norbert and his wife and adorable little daughter who were deported, and so many other young cousins without even speaking of the adults.

About my parents I have good news. Ella, whose husband is also gone, stayed in Belgium, and is planning to visit us soon for which I rejoice in advance. I would like to go to my parents for Easter; we will see what Ella says.

If it is not too much to ask, I would like to have a little bit of condensed milk for Philippe to make up for the lack of milk and butter (there is 1/4 liter of milk per day available on an irregular basis). Thank you in advance.

Best wishes to you and your dear husband, your lovely family and all of our friends. We send you and your dear little one, whom we would love to know, many kisses, from Mir.

J. Pressel
5 Rue Waldeck-Rousseau
Asnieres (Seine)
April 2, 1945

Dear Susi and everyone else,

It is with much joy that we received your latest letter of March 7 accompanied by the picture of your ravishing little Helen; she is a charming child whose good looks and intelligent eyes indicate a strong character. Give her a big hug on our behalf and on behalf of her maternal grandparents who I hope will soon have the joy to learn the good news that they have a granddaughter. In general we are pessimistic about the fate of those who were deported, but we wait patiently and with confidence; the end of the war approaches and we should soon know their fate.

As far as we are concerned, the three of us as in good health; since the cold weather has passed I have been able to resume working as a journalist with more courage and fewer worries; for several weeks we are in the midst of springtime and I am taking advantage of it to take Philippe on walks in the parks and woods of Paris and it's environs; they are beautiful and crowded with people, like your Hyde Park, with the difference being that in several of these parks there are zoos which are very interesting for children, and Philippe loves to see the wild animals (lions, tigers, etc..). Philippe now has two weeks of Easter vacation on the occasion of Easter. He had a good report card; he is 3rd in his class. We hope that you had a good holiday and that your dear Joe had permission to have time off with the family. We understand well that it is very relaxing for him and a great joy for you each time he comes back to the family. Since the day of victory seems closer than ever, I hope that you will soon celebrate with relief his final    return home. Today we had a little prologue of VE Day in Paris: raising the flags of 150 regiments and General De Gaulle raising the Liberation Cross in Paris; a big military parade with many flags and huge crowds, seemingly the whole city was there. You will certainly see a view of the crowds for this celebration in your weekly newsreel movie. Among the hundreds of thousands of people, I am here with Philippe on my shoulders, but don't try to find us among the enormous crowds.

We thank you dear Susi and Joe for trying to send us a package; this would give us great pleasure. Last week we received a real piece of soap from our Uncle in America and this gave us much pleasure, as well as real tea, coffee, cocoa. You cannot imagine what it has been like to only have ersatz (fake) things for years. A can of condensed milk made the difference for our son; thus soon all the children of these liberated countries, weakened by all the deprivations, will resume a more humane and decent life.

I think that I wrote you in a preceding letter that we heard from my wife's two sisters. Ruth and Sonya with their families are still in Havana. For several weeks we are again without news from my in-laws and Ella who are now in Brussels.

For three months now we are living in Asnieres, a quiet little town about 7 minutes from Paris by train. We have a nice little apartment that has a radio and allows us every day to listen to the excellent news from London about the advancing allied armies. We hope that by the time you get this letter we will have heard the news of the definite victory over the remainder of the Nazi army.

We forgot to tell you that we regularly see the grandparents Stolz and their son Isi. They have another son, a young doctor in Liverpool; another son is in America; their son Henry and his wife and children are interned in a camp in the Dutch Indies. Let us also hope that those who suffer at the hands of the Japanese will soon be liberated; the war in the Pacific is happily taking the same course as the war closer for us in Europe.

Here, this letter is already too long. I hope dear Susi that your in-laws are well and that they withstood with calm and courage all of the emotions that were felt in your dear city of London. You have known devastation, victims, funerals, and all of this after the illustrious Churchill's promise to defeat the enemy which I heard on the radio in 1942; I also will always remember those words that he spoke in French in 1940 on the radio which ended with "he who laughs last, laughs best." After five years that has now finally occurred.

I end by sending you, Joe, and your dear Helen our affectionate kisses and all our best wishes to your parents, brother and sister and to all of our good friends there.

Jos, Mir and Philippe

Paris
April 14, 1945

Dear Susi,

Yesterday we received your letter of the 6th that must have crossed our letter that we sent earlier this month. It is nice to see that correspondence between the UK and France is being established more and more rapidly. We were happy to learn that Joe was able to spend Easter time with the family and that it did you all good. Everything that you write to us about dear little Helen interests and pleases us; this is the period of time that is the most fun for you and Joe since your little darling will start to interest herself in everything that is in your closets, and go through all of your utensils, etc.

You ask us for a picture of Philippe; we have several but none are recent. We took several snap shots last Sunday in the park de Versailles, but these photos have not yet been developed; if they are good we will send you some in the next letter. The good weather these past few weeks allowed us to take walks on Sunday in Paris and in some lovely neighborhoods, but I remember that I told you that in my last letter.

We finally received a new letter from my in-laws and Ella; at present they are still in Brussels but they are getting ready to return to Antwerp. Happily they are in good health. Miryam intends to visit them in several weeks. That will be 5 years since the moment of their painful separation.

Dear Susi, would you have the kindness to transmit the attached letter to my wife's sister Alice. From England mail service will certainly be faster to Palestine than if I send it from here. I suppose that the address: Mrs. Alice Abramsohn, Rehovot, Palestine is sufficient, but you could ask Simon or Jos Lemer to eventually complete the address.

It is very nice of you to think of us and to help us replenish our wardrobe, which is almost completely worn out after these 5 years of war, and it is almost impossible to buy anything without having to spend crazy sums of money. Therefore since you ask us which are the most necessary items, I give you a little list, hoping that it will be possible for you to get a permit to send us a package.

-Stockings for Miryam and Philippe; for him preferably in white; size of shoes is: Miryam 36, Philippe 31.
-Handkerchiefs; tablecloth; bath towels; men's shirt size 41.

All of this is enough. If on the other hand you have by any chance an old suit to fit Miryam, she could sure use one, otherwise an old sport jacket.

Thank you in advance for whatever you can send, and be assured that we will refund you when possible.

Yesterday we received the painful and unexpected news of the death of President Roosevelt; we, who were kept in bondage by armies, can appreciate even more than you the importance of his efforts toward the liberation of Europe. Yesterday we heard on the radio, eulogies, better than mine, and a series of special bulletins dedicated to Roosevelt, not including those from London which we hear everyday.

We read with interest all that you wrote to us in your letter: the upcoming marriage of your sister-in-law; the news of your Aunt and her son Jules and all of that is joyful to us; let us hope now that signs of life of those deported from your family will arrive soon.

As soon as we get the package you sent us by way of the military, we will let you know. We just had the great joy of receiving a little package from New York; can you imagine that for years we haven't had a real brick of soap to wash yourself! A brick of real American soap was in the package and it was welcomed like greeting a good old friend whose memory was even a lost souvenir.

I am stopping for today and send you from the three of us for you, Joe, Helen, your dear parents-in-law and the other members of your family many kisses. Please transmit our best regards to all of our good friends there.

Affectionately,
Jos., Mir, Philippe

Paris
V-E Day
May 7, 1945

Dear Susi and dear All,

Here we are finally at the end of this awful nightmare. We congratulate you all on having escaped all of the dangers and remaining safe and sound until this memorable day.

We attended the proclamation of the end of hostilities at the Place de la Concorde, followed by national anthems, a final sounding of sirens, salvoes of artillery, church bells from all the churches of Paris, after which we marched up the Champs Elysees till the Arch of Triumph which has the tomb of the unknown soldier from the other war. It was a sea of humanity emitting great roars, augmented by the noise of innumerable airplanes flying over this well-known main artery of Paris. Jeeps and military trucks were seized and filled by Parisian youths hanging from all sides of the vehicles that were driven up and down the avenue.

Unhappily our thoughts could not be separated from all of those dear ones who were torn from us in this horrible storm, and it is of them that we think, more than the victory that we so much wanted to share with them. No doubt that with you too dear Susi, that these were the same sentiments which dominated; we have the right to rejoice, but this joy however profound that it is, will not be complete.

We heard on the radio of the celebrations that went on in London. This will be a short letter because we are getting ready to leave. Tomorrow morning we are going to visit my parents-in-law in Antwerp where we hope to stay about ten days, and we are in the midst of getting all of our affairs in order for the trip.

We received your two letters of the 14th and 25th of April and thank you. You were nice to send our letter to Alice, and you did well in asking her to send an answering letter to you since we will then get it more rapidly.

We have not yet had the pleasure of receiving one of the packages that you sent. Maybe it will arrive soon.

We are very happy to know that your dear little Helene progresses well. Hug her for us.

We hope that we will soon receive signs of life from our dear deported ones.

We send you dear Susi and dear all, our affectionate thoughts and many kisses.

Jos Miryam and Philippe

(Note: this letter was written in English.)

Asnieres (Seine)
May 25, 1945

My dear Susi,

Since 5 years I did not use this language that you are so skillfully handling in your correspondence. Let me gather what is left of my vanishing knowledge of English and try to write to you in this language.

Well dear Susi, we found your letter of the 12th at the moment when we came home from a ten days' visit which we paid to my dear parents-in-law and Ella. Useless to say how happy we were to see them back in good health-after these dark and long and awful years. They sustained a lot of ordeals of every kind. Ella made fine resistance work all along the occupation period. Her activity deserves the highest eulogy, but she did everything as if it were the most natural thing, never thinking of any reward, but now the government will not leave the activity of some of their best and modest workers, among whom she occupies a prominent place, without consideration. (They will be recognized).

It would take too long to describe what we saw, or better what we unhappily did see no more during our stay over there. It was an uneasy feeling walking through the town once so familiar to us and now realizing that so big a part of its population suffered and is now missing. The town itself, when it was liberated, was intact but later on it has tremendously suffered. You can easily imagine the destruction since London was similarly damaged.

My first visit was to the grave of my father.

Nobody left from our large family, except Maria Broder and her two sons who fortunately escaped from deportation. They are doing well. As you probably know, Herman Broder died from illness some years ago.

Still no news from all our beloved relatives; let us not despair, since there are certainly a lot of people freed who have not yet been able to establish a contact with their family.

Together with your letter, two parcels for us were on the table that certainly were sent to us through your friend that you had entrusted with these parcels. Many thanks! The parcels contained: soap, sardines, milk, chocolate, sweets, tea.

We see that you have sent other parcels too. Please suspend these shipments; let us wait to see whether the things you have sent, arrive.

The situation of foodstuff supplies (we say ravitaillement here), I don't know how you call it over there, is still as bad as ever. In Belgium, on the contrary, one has the impression to live in a pre-war period of abundance.

We are all three ok. Philippe is a fine big boy.

I am resigning my job at the office where I was working since two years in order to improve my situation by the use of my linguistic and other professional abilities. But we are seriously thinking of going to Eretz, which seems to us to be still the best solution.

Please convey our best regards to your dear Joe and your good parents-in-law and kiss your dear Helene for us many times.

I received a letter from our mutual friend (and your future brother-in-law) Joseph Lemer; please thank him in my name for his kind attention. I feel sure he will make a good husband and a son-in-law Mr. and Mrs. Pantzer will be proud of. Send my regards also to his brother Simon and the other members of the family club over there.

Many kisses to you,
Your
Jos Miryam Philippe

(From my mother, translated from French.)

Dear Susi,

Thank you for your affectionate letter and for all the packages you sent us. Each item is important because almost everything is lacking.

I hope that you don't deprive yourself to send us anything. If possible, send a pajama for Philippe, which would be wonderful. We absolutely want you to keep track of all the expenses you incur for us. It is really very nice of you to help us with the packages, especially since with your dear daughter you must not have much free time. She is of the age where she must be constantly supervised.

I thank you very much in advance for the coat that you are sending me; it is the only article of clothing that I am missing as I have what I need for the rest.

Here are Philippe's measurements: chest 70 cm, width of shoulders 32 cm, distance from shoulders to waist 34 cm, pants length 78 cm. As far as socks for Philippe, they are no longer necessary since we found some in Antwerp as well as sandals. Life in Belgium is much easier for different things than in France.

We spent several happy days with my parents and Ella; yet the joy was not complete with so many close family parents who are missing, without speaking of all of the not so close relatives and acquaintances.

Thanks again for your kindness, many kisses for you and little Helene and best wishes to your family.

Mir

Asnieres (Seine)
June 9, 1945

Dear Susi,

Since my last letter, we received seven parcels due to your kindness. They were extremely welcome and arrived all at one time. Our little boy opened eyes of astonishment and joy on seeing so many good things; he asked whether it was "le Pere Noel" that sent us these cadeaux (presents). We told him, of course, that it was neither Xmas nor Hanukah, but that, these gifts were sent by the daughter of his father's sister.

You have really made a good choice among the things which we lack most over here; it is all of immediate use and of very good service. Many, many thanks, dear Susi. Enclosed, for your guidance is a statement of what we received.

Up to now, the number of acquaintances of ours who were liberated after deportation is still very small. We are awaiting further news from Antwerp.

And meanwhile life is going on here as usual. Asnieres, where we are living is a nice and quiet little town. I leave in the morning to go to my work in Paris, come back for lunch, return to Paris and am back home towards 7 or 7:30 PM. The day is occupied by professional duties and we never leave home in the evening. Our only "distraction" is listening to the radio. For the time being I have no possibility of devoting time to social work, as I did before.

By the way, what has become of the Maccabi activity in London throughout the war? Do you know whether Dr. Jacobowitz, the President of Maccabi, and W. Meisl are still in London and if so, perhaps you could let them know that their Maccabi friend Pressel of Belgium is alive and give them my address. I should be very pleased to hear from them, about their well being, and also about the prospects of Maccabi over there.

I see nothing particular to add to these lines. Philippe is a good pupil, has much interest for planes, guns etc. like all boys, of course, but is nevertheless happy that the war, "cette vilaine guerre" (this ugly war) like he called it always, is over.

What about the demobilization of Joe and your brother in law? How is the good little Helene? OK we hope. We also hope that your parents-in-law and yourselves are in good health.

We are sending to you all our very best regards and love and extra kisses for the little darling!

Yours

Jos Miriam and Philippe

(From my mother.)

Dear Susi,

The parcels gave us much pleasure and everything is useful, especially everything that I asked for. If you can get the same or a similar dress again, that would please me. For the moment stop with your kind giving; we will write to you if we need something. I am confused that you are going so much out of the way for us. I hope that one day we can spoil you and your dear Helene for all that you have given us.

I was very happy to see my dear parents and Ella again. My parents are very well and have very good moral, which is astonishing after all that they have endured. Ella is not feeling well; if her husband could come back, that would certainly contribute to a complete recovery. Let us hope that we will soon get good news from all of our dear missing ones.

My sincere wishes to the whole family and many kisses for you and your daughter.

Mir

List of items in package:
1 robe, 1 pajama, 1 pants, 1 woolen shirt, 3 pairs of socks, 2 hand towels, 1 tie, 1 comb, 1 can of condensed milk, 1 pound of cacao, 1 can of soup, 1 can of goulash, 2 cans of sardines, 1 carton of cigarettes and 1 package of cigarettes, 1 double brick of kitchen soap, 2 bars of soap, 1 Lux, 1 Palmolive, 1 jar of Vaseline, 2 toothpastes, 2 bars of chocolate, 2 oranges, 1 fruit pate.

(This letter was in English.)

Asnieres (Seine)
June 24, 1945

My dear Susi and dear all,

We received your two letters of June 4th and June 15th. In the later you wrote   about your cousin Henriette being retained in France, but meanwhile you will have learnt that she is on the way back to Antwerp. I happened to see her in Paris on the 20th. I stepped into the Belgian repatriations office to approach someone going to Belgium in order to transmit our letters to my parents-in-law and had the chance to see Mrs. Henriette Hamel, and her girl. At that moment they received the permit to return to Belgium and told me that they were leaving the same day. Henriette told me that she knew that her husband was in Antwerp but she had no particulars about his well being apart from a telegram she received from Karfiol announcing that he was there. It seems that Charles has had a good deal of luck (of course he must have to survive Auschwitz miseries) and that he did not suffer too much; let us hope that this is true and that he will be fit again before long. From a letter, which was written by my parents-in-law on the3rd of June, we learned that a brother-in-law of my wife's brother also came back from Auschwitz. He was taken in Brussels in 1942 together with his parents and sisters. He is the sole one to have come back so far and gave my parents-in-law very little hope regarding his family. My brother-in-law, his wife and 3 years old girl were also deported.

We have, alas, not many illusions, but cannot give up the hope, how small it may be. There are still thousands of people who could not communicate with their relatives abroad, although we were told that all those rescued could send a wire through the Red Cross. I heard from people liberated that this was not the case as far as they are concerned (they were liberated in a zone freed by the Russian army). So Susi, let us await the future with resignation but let us not despair.

We also heard from Antwerp that Mr. Klein gave my parents-in-law a lot of very useful items, and in the present circumstances, so rare things for which we have to thank you again very heartfully. You are really marvelous. We hope that the family will find a way to get us those things, otherwise if Miryam and Philippe go to Belgium next month or so to spend the holidays there, they can receive them.

I do not yet know what we are going to do in the near or distant future, but meantime in order to improve our income I'll start in my new job on July 2nd as writer (redacteur) and translator in a press agency; it may prove to be interesting for the future, but as I told you we have not yet made up our mind definitely. We need not bother about that since job opportunities will not be lacking with the return of normal productive activities.

Today we attended a gymnastics meeting where our Philippe was among the participants. It was a meeting of all the public schools in the municipal stadium of Asnieres. It was fine weather, an interesting performances and joy for all the children and the numerous attendees. Within some years you will have the same joy with your dear Helene whose athletic performances are promising as we can gather from what you said in your latest letter!

Have you already been able to enjoy the D-Day of your dear Joe? Or will it be soon? And what about your brother-in-law; is he still in the armed forces? Do the Lemers intend to stay in England?

I'll end this rather long letter to have more time to write to write some others because it takes me rather long to write down in English what is so easy to write in French. But nevertheless it is a good training for me and I am not too old to believe that one-day after having written a hundred pages in more or less accurate English it will go more smoothly.

Well, dear Susi, many thanks for the services you have rendered us, and which we hope soon to be able to reciprocate.

Our very best wishes to you all, much love and kisses from your

Jos Miryam and Philippe

Dear Susi,

I wish to add a PS to this letter. Should it be possible for you to send a pair of trousers (preferably gray or beige-not flannel) it would be very useful to me. Prices over here are extraordinarily high (a suit costs 12 to 15 thousand francs for ordinary material, a luxury which we cannot afford).

I am giving the measurements below.

Perhaps you will get a permit to send this but don't do the impossible if it is too difficult to obtain. Much love and best thanks beforehand. Jos

(Note: on the next page my father has a sketch of pants with the waist size, waist to bottom length and inseam length, all in both centimeters and inches.)

Asnieres (Seine)

July 8, 1945

Dear Susi,

Fifteen days ago we received a letter dated June 5 from my parents-in-law. Mail still takes much time between Belgium and France. My parents-in-law are well and happily Ella's health seems better. We also learned from this letter all that Mr. Klein gave them on our behalf. It is marvelous! There are still great shortages of everything here; the most indispensable things are almost impossible to find or have such high prices that the great majority of people can't afford to buy them. Dear Susi, we are infinitely grateful for all that you have done for us. A thousand thanks and we hope that in the future that it will be our turn to be useful to you. From others, we received 2 small parcels with a shirt for Philippe and a pajama that fits him beautifully; he was thrilled with it. We also got some foodstuff. We sent many thanks.

It is possible that Philippe will pass the holidays in Belgium. Last Wednesday my Uncle Jacques Schwerner and Aunt Jeanne returned to Antwerp. They were in France since the beginning of the war. Their son Harry, who served in the Belgian military, is still absent and we are without news from him since the day in 1942 when he was deported from France by the Nazis; he had wanted to rejoin the Belgian army but was seized at the Spanish frontier.

Life rolls on like a little train; for the last week I am working in my new job and it looks like it will be interesting. Six hours of work per day; I start at 6:30 and end at 12:30. I think I told you that it was with a press agency.

We have been able to follow by radio and the press all of the minute details of the recent electoral campaign in Great Britain. We hope that it will end well for everyone in the world.

Tell me Susi, is your anniversary in September? Please send me the exact date because I must update my calendar, which was destroyed during the war.

How are you dear Susi and Joe? Is Joe being demobilized? And is your dear Helen continuing to grow like a beautiful flower? We send you all and to your dear parents, our affectionate thoughts.

Jos Miryam and Philippe

Asnieres (Seine)
August 18, 1945

Dear Susi,

I have before me several letters that you sent us in July, as well as one dated August 6 and it seems to me that I haven't yet acknowledged their receipt. We were very happy to have received the lovely little picture of your dear little Helen taken at the age of 16 months; she already has very characteristic traits and seems to be an energetic headstrong little Hamel. I promised you some time back to send you a recent photo of our little Philippe but none of them came out; I don't know if the camera is working well (someone lent it to us) or if we used it wrong. There is one photo which is good but you must use a magnifying glass to distinguish any traits; I took it last July and enclose it here; needless to say that it is Miryam and Philippe.

Dear Susi, your package arrived 10 days ago and we thank you very much. The pants fit me; it is not ideal, but I suppose that over there one does not have much choice.

In your letter of August 6 you said that the soldier Klein, wrote to his wife that he had seen Miryam in Antwerp. That evidently concerns his visit to my parents-in-law during the month of May. But meanwhile Miryam and Philippe went back to Antwerp and arrived there on August 11. Philippe will spend part of his vacation, which lasts until October, in Antwerp, and Miryam will probably stay there till the end of the month; as for myself, I can't be absent from my work.

For several days now there has been the complete end to this terrible, second world war; the capitulation of Japan did not raise the same enthusiasm here which was provoked in England, whose sounds came to us by radio, and English newspapers, with pictures of the mobs in Piccadilly Circus, etc. Last year during this epoch, we were in Lyon and started to breath more freely at the sight of the boches, who were starting to flee. At that moment we had more hope than now, to see our dear deported ones, and yet we must not abandon all hope. I went to speak to two committees in Paris who are charged with doing research on the deportees. In one of the offices I was told, that according to information obtained from deportees who were freed and returned to Paris, that there remains a number of deportees in Siberia who are deprived of all means of communication: postal and telegraphic. In the second office I was told that it is impossible to receive any information on the deportees who are in the eastern part of Europe, in the zone occupied by the Russian forces; it is impossible for these people to send any sign of life to their families because neither letters or telegrams are allowed to pass through. One boat with freed deportees should be leaving Odessa soon, going to a French port, probably Marseille.

One must think that this information should allow us to hope that many deportees, from whom we have no news, are still alive, and let us hope that ours are among those numbers, although unfortunately we cannot have any illusions. In the same train of thought it is important to know that hundreds of thousands of French prisoners and slave workers sent to Germany, who are in the Russian zone, still have not come back. Yesterday I heard on the French radio complaints that all of those prisoners and French deportees, have no opportunity to get in contact with their families; thousands of women and children in France are therefore in the painful position of waiting for news of their fathers, sons, brothers, etc and not knowing if they are alive or not. The concern here is that if what the second office told me is true about Frenchmen, without any distinction of origin, that in all probability, the percentage of Jewish deportees who are still alive must be minimal.

I went to the Ministry of Prisoners and Deportees in Paris and asked for a deportation certificate for your dear parents. I received this official document that I will make a photocopy of and send you. The certificate says that your dear parents were deported from Drancy on September 7, 1942. I took the names of several other people who were deported on the same date and on the same convoy, and who came back. Perhaps I may be able to get some information if by chance these people were in contact at any time with your dear parents. If on your part you have been able to obtain any useful information, let me know.

No doubt it is now time for you to make great preparations for the upcoming marriage of your sister-in-law. And what must also be approaching is the demobilization of Joe. Hopefully he will be one of hundreds who will be freed before Xmas.

I end this for today and send you dear Susi for the three of you and your dear ones my kisses.

Your Uncle Jos

Asnieres
September 13, 1945

Dear Susi,

Your letter of 8-31 arrived on the 3$^{rd}$ and I have waited to answer you until Miryam and Philippe came back. She came back from Antwerp at the end of last week. Philippe stayed with my parents-in-law and we hope that at the end of this month he will again be with us. Miryam will tell you about her stay in Antwerp.

Susi, you are excessively generous with one package after another. Three weeks ago I received two packages with condensed milk, sardines, hand towels, handkerchiefs, etc. A great big thank you. A week ago I also obtained from the French Red Cross a package that you addressed to us; the contents matched the list that was in the package. The clothes and linens that you sent are excellent and are being well used. In Antwerp Miryam received the beautiful things that arrived in May. How do we thank you for all of this kindness. I know that if by chance we were in your place we would have done the same. Be certain dear Susi that we appreciate the goodness of your character and we hope that the future will permit us to reciprocate.

There you go again, in your last letter you said that you are sending us another package. You have done more than necessary and really dear Susi, as Miryam will write to you, it no longer necessary now for you to send us packages. The situation is gradually getting better and if in the future we think that you could send us something useful from there we will not hesitate to tell you.

For the New Year we send you, your dear Joe and Helen and your dear family, our best wishes. Let the New Year be favorable to you in all respects. I wanted so much to add words of hope about the return of your dear parents, but alas, hope is faint and I think more and more that we must resign ourselves to the inevitable, and for you, happily, life continues. I hope that you will not suffer too much for what seems, waiting in vain.

I received from your sister-in-law Mrs. Lemer and Jefke, nice words from Torquay along with photos from that beautiful coastal area. I thanked them and would be obliged to you to send them our best wishes. I hope that meanwhile they returned safely to London and that the happy period of a honeymoon will continue to at least their silver wedding anniversary.

Everything with us is fine and we wish the same for you. I pass the pen to Miryam and send you dear Susi, Joe and your shining Helen many kisses,

Jos

(From my mother.)

Dear Susi,

I am back a week now. I spent some pleasant days with my parents and Ella. Unfortunately the joy is not complete as we speak or remember the missing, about whom the hope of returning diminishes day by day. My dear parents and Ella are very courageous.

The two pieces of cloth that you gave us several months ago through Mr. Klein are marvelous; in Antwerp I made a suit out of one of them for Philippe and he will wear it on Rosh Hashana for the first time. The other piece of cloth is really magnificent and I will have a wonderful coat out of it, and I am very happy with the suit and other than a few minor repairs, it fits like a glove. I thank you an infinite amount for all of the nice and good things that you sent us, and as Jos wrote to you, it is not necessary for the moment for you to send anything else; if there is something that we really need we will let you know.

The picture of Helene that Mr. Klein gave us is ravishing and she is a real doll; she is certainly the most spoiled person in the family. I have visited the Katzengolds several times; they all look good; little Georgette is big and roguish. They had good luck to find their belongings. I also saw Henriette Polakof with whom I only spoke a short while. If you see Mr. Klein's wife tell her that we appreciate his efforts in pleasing everybody. The day before yesterday we received a letter from Alice.

She is happy because her husband, who is "chief instructor", is now in Rehovot and can therefore be home each evening.

At this time there are many Jewish soldiers, from the Jewish Brigade, in Antwerp. For Yontov my parents invited several soldiers for each meal. Dear Susi my best wishes for the New Year for you and the whole family, and thank you again for all the nice things.

Many kisses,
Mir

Asnieres (Seine)
September 21, 1945

Dear Susi,

You will have received the letter which I sent you several days ago. I still have to send you the deportation certificate of your dear parents. Attached is a photocopy of this certificate; the original is in my possession.

I also send you a copy of a note from Benjamin Freifeld, dated June 26, 1945, which was given to Miryam during her last trip to Antwerp. I suppose that it is a copy of an inquiry made in Nice, but I don't know to whom, nor if he used a lawyer or if a committee created the document. Perhaps you will know.

Miryam was able to find out in Antwerp that there may be some news about your parents. I don't know if it was communicated to you, but I think that no matter what, you should hold on, just as I do; I have told you all that I know.

Charles Katzengold saw your dear father in Auschwitz in 1944. Charles does not know what happened to your father after that. On all sides that we turn to in order to obtain information we are left without much hope because during the last part of the war many of our people succumbed, and I think that we must face reality and resign ourselves to the worst.

As far as your dear mother is concerned, Charles also knew a Mrs. Hamel in Antwerp who came back from Auschwitz. It is only at the last moment before her departure from Antwerp that Miryam learned of this, and she then went to see this Mrs. Hamel who lived on Steenbokstraat, but she was not there. This woman should have seen your mother in 1942.

There is no certainty about the fate of your dear parents, but it seems to me that the options leave us very little hope.

We also have not received any more news about the large number of members of our family who were deported.

Dear Susi, I regret that I cannot give you more encouraging news but I suppose that you are sufficiently courageous to overcome your pain and to look to the future. We have just been through, the most cruel epoch that humanity has probably ever known, and in all families we deplore many cruel voids.

I also regret just as much not to be able to tell you any joyful things, especially as this letter will probably reach you on the day of your anniversary. Nevertheless dear Susi, celebrate the day with your dear ones and from the three of us we send you our sincere congratulations and all of our good wishes, good health, and happiness with your dear Joe and your beloved Helen.

All the best,
Jos Miryam and Philippe

Asnieres
October 3, 1945

My dear Susi,

We received your two letters of the 23$^{rd}$ and the 30$^{th}$ and we have much compassion with your pain and sadness and we share that with you. However we beg you dear Susi, not to let yourself despair, and to be resigned to wait. We are victims of a bad situation; it does no good to be tormented; we cannot change anything. I think it is my duty to tell you what was reported to me about your dear Maman and your dear Papa, for what good is it to continue to have illusions as for all appearances we cannot count on a miracle, or where it concerns your Papa, that he might have been liberated by the Russians and finds himself somewhere in the zone occupied by the Soviets, and that he has not been able to send news. But that too seems to be a very meager chance.

Since you lived the whole war in England and even though you were also exposed to risks, you probably have no idea or realize how little human life meant on the whole continent, which was invaded by bands of Nazis helped by the miserable ones who sold out in many countries. We saw and learned so much about the animosity that pursued us during the war that we were ourselves resigned for the worst in case we were not to be spared.

Since the end of the war, day after day, we learned not to count on the return of many of our parents, alas, among the <u>millions </u>who perished during the last few years. Despite everything we maintain a ray of hope but it grows more and more faint. Having been hardened by our experiences and knowing that our lives hung by a thread, we can accept more easily than you the misfortunes that befell our family and we want you, who have your whole future in front of you, also learn to accept your pain. There is not one single family in Europe that does not have voids to deplore; parents without children; children who lost their parents; wives who lost their husbands, etc. without even counting among the survivors those who lost everything that they owned. Really dear Susi despite all of our sadness, let us consider ourselves happy to have come out of this torment safe and sound; in London you too were menaced and think of the happiness that you have dear Joe, your dear little Helen and your parents-in-law.

Parents' great hope is always to know that their children are happy and it certainly was your parents desire to know that you were sheltered and happy; if your happiness is temporarily shaken up, take hold of yourself anyway and don't get sick in thinking too much of that which is irreparable. I don't know anything else regarding your parents that I haven't written to you already and so won't offer you condolences, but with the known immense loss of Jews, tell yourself that your parents are in a better world, and leave behind them unanimous regrets, and we can honor their memory best by bringing to our children, the love which they surrounded us with, and I think now of my mother who will also probably not return and whose memory will be perpetuated by your dear child who bears her name.

Be courageous dear Susi, and uphold yourself with dignity as we are forced to uphold ours.

In your letter you said that you did not receive an answer from Alice. But she wrote us two letters and the last one took only 5 days to get here. She is well as is her husband who is a physical trainer in the Jewish army of Palestine; his headquarters is nearby in Rehovot so that Alice and her husband Myron see each other every day; their son Dan who is 6 years old has started to go to school. Our Philippe starts his school studies tomorrow.

We send you dear Susi and all the others many kisses.
Affectionately
Jos Miryam and Philippe

5, rue Waldeck Rousseau
Asnieres (Seine)
January 29, 1946

Dear Susi,

You deserve a big thank you for the package that you sent us and we received approximately two weeks ago. It contained a sweater, gloves, a skirt and a box full of surprises, very agreeable for the big smoker that I am. The sweater is very useful, especially at my place of work at night. For about 15 days I have been working three days per week from 7PM to 7AM (the rest of the week I am free). Since I have been there and my work is strictly cerebral, it is very nice to have a good sweater for the body, and not to suffer from the cold, in a room with barely any heat. Your gloves are also excellent. Again I thank you Susi for these very useful things. The skirt you sent to Miryam is also as useful.

So you are coming to the continent at Easter time. That is only two months away and that time will pass quickly. We will be very happy to be able to see you, Joe, and your treasure, Helen, and to be able to talk together for the first time after 6 ½ years of awful events. It is especially now that you should rejoice in the joy of having your good little Helene, since at the age of 2 years and until 4, children are the most interesting to observe and are the cutest.

You ask if we still do not plan on returning to Belgium. I have not changed my opinion. For Miryam and Philippe it will probably be more agreeable to be in Brussels or Antwerp than for me; besides my in-laws, there is really nothing that attracts me to Belgium. And from the point of view of my professional work, I think that France would be more interesting, but for the time being I will not budge. Not that the situation in France is so good, on the contrary, everything is lacking and it will take a long and hard time before the situation in this country becomes easier. But we must hope that before long things will stabilize and finally be improved. For the time being food is very bad and we have no electricity three days per week, and the situation in general, as far as commerce and industry, as well as the press which I am especially interested in now, is characterized as apathetic. Perhaps the new government will succeed in reorganizing; but it will be a hard task, as all the regions seem to bungle things, as "a poilishe wirtshaft". (I think this quote is Polish and says "like a Polish worker").

How is it with Joe since he left his outfit? Has he easily resumed civilian life and how goes work? I hope that you are all in good health and ask you to transmit to everyone our good wishes, and I send you dear Susi, Joe and Helen, many kisses.

Jos. Mir. Philippe

5, rue Waldeck-Rousseau
Asnieres (Seine)
March 29, 1946

Dear Susi,

We received your long letter of March 8 with the ravishing photo of the three of you, and we thank you. We are happy that we will soon see you in person.

I also requested a passport for the three of us; there are different formalities to accomplish, but I hope that all will be in order so that we can leave in two weeks.

We were greatly pained to learn that your Uncle David died suddenly. I knew your Uncle David for many years and I will always have good memories of him. I suppose that you got this sad news from his children in Eretz. How are they? Please convey to them our sincere condolences.

It certainly is an uninterrupted list of cruel losses that have befallen you, and there are plenty to be sad about. Nevertheless dear Susi, do not lose your nerve and accept what cannot be changed. Time will heal all of our wounds.

How many of you will come to Antwerp? I suppose that there will be five of you/ that is with your sister-in-law and Jefke?

Perhaps you will be surprised to learn that I have applied for a job with the United Nations Secretariat (in English ONU). I knew that this organization was looking for personnel and so I sent an application because, whatever happens, I do not think that I will continue to work in the company where I am have been since last July, due to the fact that they have serious financial difficulties and are operating at a loss for the last few months.

If among your acquaintances or Joe's relatives or friends there is someone who knows anyone working for the UN in London could he make inquiries to find out "if my application has been taken into consideration" and do you know anyone who could recommend me? I gave them some very good references but it is sometimes not enough. If I am hired it would probably be to work in either the London, Paris, or Geneva office.

Here is the UN's address: United Nations Organization, Church House, Dean's Yard, London, S,W.1. My application was sent in on March 14, 1946 to the "Personnel Officer," Major P.T.V.Leith.

For the last few days the weather has been splendid; one would think it was summer. Let's hope that we will have just as good weather in Belgium. Don't forget to take your raincoats, because you must remember, that it rains approximately five days out of six over there.

Everything is well with us. Miryam and Philippe are impatient to go traveling. Philippe likes Antwerp very much, because he has had fun on each trip and a little because there are so many good things there that are practically non-existent in Paris. You too will be shocked when you compare the abundance of things in Belgium to that in England. It is really a land of plenty compared to France.

The trip for your dear Helen will evidently also be a big event; hours of train travel, crossing the sea on a big boat, etc. Are you going by way of Harwich-Antwerp or by Dover-Ostende (I suppose that this last route must be running by now), or are you coming by plane??

I hope to receive a note from you soon telling us the date you are leaving and I hope you will forgive me for not writing for two or three weeks.

We wish you many good things for the whole family, and many kisses for the three of you.

Affectionately,
Jos Miryam, Philippe

(This is a letter from my mother's parents to me for my birthday)

Antwerp
June 19, 1946

My dear little Philippe!

Soon it will be the day of your ninth birthday and I send you my sincere congratulations. Continue to learn as you have been and always obey your dear parents, and we will all get much joy from you. Now that you are nine years old it is time for you to start to learn about religion, as I know that you do not want to fall behind in your studies.

Soon you will be on vacation and we wait for you and we already rejoice in seeing you. Again I wish you a happy celebration and hug you very hard and a thousand times.

Your grandmother

My dear Philippe,

I congratulate you for your birthday and I wish you good health as you become a big and wise boy.

Aunt Ella should have told you that you are getting a suit from us as a gift. I think that it will be better to buy it here when you are on vacation.

I also have the same desires as grandmother as religion is very necessary.

Many kisses for you and for your dear parents
from your grandfather.

5 rue Waldeck-Rousseau
Asnieres (Seine)
July 12, 1946

Dear Susi,

Thank you for your letters of June 17 and July 7. The first one had a whole series of photos taken in Antwerp in April. Some of them are very good and are nice souvenirs. Please give our thanks to Jefke who went to the trouble and who succeeded in taking several good poses, especially those taken indoors with little lighting, where little Helene, next to Philippe, are in front of a large portion of ice cream.

I was happy to learn that all of the little packages have arrived. Today I gave Ella two flasks of Eupnine and as you request, at the end of the month she will give them to Jefke. It is with pleasure that I do this for your sick person; when passing pharmacies in Paris, I always go in and sometimes by chance I can find some. As far as settling up I think I wrote to you that for the first five flasks Ella reimbursed me; the expenses were 520 French francs. For the two flasks that I sent on June 26 and the two sent today to Ella, the expenses were 252 French francs total.

There is evidently absolutely no need to reimburse for the little things that we sent you. On the other hand you can help us occasionally by sending us cacao if possible. Thanks in advance.

Uncle Jules was in Antwerp for several days but it was impossible for him to come to Paris to spend several days with us as I had asked him to. We got a letter from him from Matadi (Congo); as soon as he arrived he wrote to us and to you. On July 2 he wrote to us from Southampton. He was counting on taking a short hop to see you in London but his boat was delayed by fog, and since the stopover in Southampton was shortened, he had to give up his trip to London. They had to board troops for Africa and at that time Uncle Jules did not know if that trip would be for several weeks, several months or even a year. He will write to me during his trip.

I wish you luck in finding an apartment where you will be on your own; the question of apartments is difficult in all cities but with a bit of luck, recommendations, and sometimes with a tip, one still finds one. I hope that you will soon be able to tell us of your new address.

Ella spent several days with us; she just left for Antwerp this afternoon and she took Philippe with her; schools are finished tomorrow and Philippe will first spend about ten days in Antwerp and then we expect to spend fifteen days of vacation somewhere in France, perhaps with my parents-in-law, who will spend a week with us anyway.

It is very hot right now; let's hope that the weather will still be nice when you are in Bournemouth and for us when we are probably somewhere in the Vosges.

You ask if I am still working for the same company. No, they had to suspend their activities as was predicted. I found similar work which pays me more and for some time I have been working at home. (That is why I write to you on the machine since I have one for use). I have other work possibilities, also with press agencies that are being formed.

It pleased us greatly what you wrote to us about your lovely Helen. It is good that you have this agreeable task of taking care of her and thus to find a diversion from the sadness of the last few years.

What you write to me about the situation of Jews in England only confirms what I learned from other sources. The anti-Semitic wave and pest that spread from the Nazi land throughout Europe did not disappear with the defeat of Germany. In England there are now certainly people who are interested in using the Palestinian question to provoke sentiments hostile to Jews. But the world is not taking precaution. The whole world knows that Great Britain did not honor the agreements that it made and there is little expectation that it will sustain its responsibilities in Palestine. As soon as England stops considering Palestine as one of its colonies, Jewish-Anglo relations will change. Besides the Zionist question, there are the relationships between Jews and non-Jews that in all nations have provoked animosity against us; we don't ask anyone to love us, and as far as enemies we have to fight them everywhere. It is what English Jews have also seemed to understand. I also think that besides the stupidity and lack of understanding by people, there must always be professional agitators in the world, including in Great Britain, who are paid to instigate the population against us. In France that is much less prevalent; people of all classes saw the Nazis at work and personally felt the effects of their abominable deeds; and here anti-Semitism is considered the Siamese twin of Fascism and Nazism and as such is condemned by the vast majority of people. There are certainly anti-Semites here but in general they do not dare show themselves for fear of being stomped on. Those who were in the Resistance, who were in the Maquis, who were in the war or who were prisoners in Germany are not afraid to go out their way to put anti-Semites on trial.

In England if there are any people who swallowed the nonsense that came from Berlin, Erfurth, etc, they will end up being sobered up and I suppose many British Jews will help with that. English prestige will tumble low if those who have political responsibilities allow anti-Semitic criminals and murderers to develop there in the same manner as it did in Germany. It seems to me that since England still wants to hold on to its prestige, it will overcome this shameful sickness.

Don't go crazy dear Susi; many people who we think are anti-Semitic are only people who minds were stuffed and each of us, in his own environment, needs to make them understand reason. But for those who are mean spirited it is impossible to discuss it and they deserve the same treatment as criminals.

I have spent much more time with these comments than they are worth.

With us all is ok. The house has become much quieter now that we are alone without our son.

I have nothing more to write for the moment.


Many kisses for you all and a big kiss for Helen,
From your Uncle and Aunt,
Jos – Miryam

(This was written in English.)

5 rue Waldeck-Rousseau
Asnieres (Seine)
August 12, 1946

My dear Susi, Joe and Helene,

We were very glad to receive your letter of the 21$^{st}$ July. I would have written before to your vacation residence at Bournemouth, but since I don't know your address over there, I delayed my writing. I hope you all made safely the travel to Bournemouth and enjoyed your first week of holidays very well. I suppose you will stay about a fortnight, so perhaps I'll still have an opportunity to write to Bournemouth if I get your address in time.

Meanwhile we received the visit of my parents-in-law, who arrived here last Wednesday evening together with Philippe who stayed in Antwerp about 3 weeks. My parents-in-law talked to your dear father-in-law whilst he was in Antwerp together with Jeff, and are full of praise for Mr. Pantzer. Philippe was given a fine pullover that is intended as a present from your patient, but really this was quite unnecessary, since I was only too happy to be of some assistance in procuring the medicine, and did by no means expect the least reward. Nevertheless please transmit our best thanks for the nice gift. Also be thanked yourselves for the cocoa and the sweets! And for the pajama that suits Philippe marvelously well.

Our parents are very pleased to have come over to Paris and are filled with wonder by what they have seen up to now; it is beyond all that they had expected. We are doing our best to have them spend some agreeable holidays and hope that they will stay with us at least two weeks. Philippe enjoyed his vacation in Antwerp and grew a few inches higher during his stay in Belgium; he learnt a little Flemish, but pronounces all the words "a la francaise", French having become his "mamme-loshun".

As I told you before, we intended to spend our holidays somewhere in France, but in the meantime something arose which upset our plans. You will remember that I made an application, some four or five months ago, for an employment with the Secretariat of UNO. There was a commission of the UNO in Paris to recruit personnel; I had some interviews with them, passed an examination and was engaged for work at the Secretariat at New York. Meanwhile time lapsed and I now have to accomplish some formalities with the consulates in order to have my passport and visas in order. I presume this will take me another ten days. My departure from Le Havre is booked in principle for August 30th. According to the engagement, Miryam and Philippe are entitled to accompany me to the States, but at our own expenses, since the present engagement is only provisional or temporary. (My own traveling expenses are paid, of course, by the UNO). After a few months, if the contract is turned into a definite one, Miryam and Philippe will be paid to travel to New York too, and according to the rules, we shall have the possibility, every two years, to spend some weeks' holidays on the continent, the expenses being paid by the Organization. But if I leave now, it is only for a temporary contract, as I told before, and the definite contract will be signed if they are satisfied of my work and if *I am satisfied with them and with the conditions of work, of living and prospects over there.* It is just a trial which I am prepared to make since it costs nothing and because, in the long run, the UNO may perhaps appreciate my services and offer me an interesting situation.

This will, of course, make a big change in our life, and I am sorry that the Channel, which only separated you and us up to now may be converted into an ocean if we all establish ourselves somewhere in the USA. In any case, if I am over there and I can be useful to you in whatever way, I'll always be anxious to satisfy you if there is anything with which you may be served in or from the States.

You probably already heard from your father or from Jeff about this prospective voyage, so it does not come quite unexpectedly to you.

From your Uncle Jules I received a letter, a fortnight ago, from Takoradi (West Africa). He is o.k. and arrived there "in winter" that is to say it is now wintertime over there and temperatures therefore are bearable. He writes that he does not know for how long he will be under way since he had to "play ferry-boat; -as he turns it- they go from Takoradi (in the Guinean Gulf) to Lagos and finally Victoria near the French Cameroon colony and afterwards back towards Freetown, Bathurst and Dakar. All these places seem to be familiar to him, as he has been there already several times during the war. He asks me about you and adds that he was sorry not to have been able even to phone you from Southampton due to lack of time: the arrival of their boat was delayed through the fog and whilst the boat was in the port, a strike broke out among the dockers so that the soldiers had to load the necessary things aboard and speed up the departure. Uncle Jules left an address where to send him a word by air-mail and perhaps if you write him, it will still be delivered to him: Pressel Jules, Infirmier, s/s Elisabethville, c/o Elder Dempster Ltd, FREETOWN-Sierra Leone.

I am now going to end this letter. It is Sunday (I put tomorrows date on this letter as I am waiting till tomorrow morning before posting it; perhaps we will receive by then, a card from you from Bournemouth, so I'll know whether this letter should be sent to London or Bournemonth). We are preparing to go with our parents on a tour of Versailles and spend our afternoon there amidst the park, the Chateau and all the splendors of France's one-time glory.

I hope you are all doing well, that the weather is warm if not hot, so that you may enjoy swimming or bathing which must give a lot of pleasure to your dear Helen. To play in the sand and work with a pail and shovel is quite a passionate entertainment for little children and I hope Helen is having a good time – and a good appetite – like all of you.

With good love and kisses from us all,
Your Uncle and Aunt,

Jos, Miryam

Monday morning,

We just received your card from Bournemouth.
Thanks,
J.

(Here are excepts from a 37-page letter that my father wrote to my mother during his trip to the US in 1946; he wrote every day and mailed it after his arrival in New York.)

Aboard the SS Washington
Sunday September 8, 1946

My dear Miryam and Philippe,

It is three o'clock in the after noon; today, Sunday, while I am on the ship, you are no doubt on a train heading for Antwerp. I suppose that tomorrow you will receive my first letter that I sent Saturday from Southampton and the second letter sent this morning from Ireland.

Now I start giving you an overall perspective of the trip day by day and I will send it all when we arrive at our destination, that is to say New York or in whatever port we arrive. According to the news that I read this morning on the newspaper that is on board, the American dockworkers strike is being extended and there is a question whether any transatlantic ship can dock and discharge passengers as long as a raise for the dockworkers is not approved. At the present there is a rumor aboard the ship that our ship will go to Canada to avoid being stuck offshore the American coast. We will see what happens in several days. At the moment the coast of Ireland is still in sight and according to my calculations we are headed in the Northwest direction, as the direction to New York is Southwest. Are we therefore effectively sailing towards Canada?

At 2:30 there was an alert on the ship. All passengers had to put on their lifejackets and go to their lifeboat station number corresponding to the one in their cabin. Ten minutes later men, women, children with their white jackets arrived at their posts. The officers asked that everyone line up properly next to their lifeboats.

As you have guessed it was just a false alarm. It had been previously announced at 1:30 on the loud speakers that are scattered all over the ship, that it was a general exercise. Most of the ship's staff did not participate in this exercise. At the same time they gave the passengers some recommendations to avoid the risks of fire. Everything was in English. At 4 o'clock there was milk and cakes.

Starting tonight our days will have 25 hours instead of 24. At midnight the clocks are turned back one hour each day in order to gradually make up the difference in time between Paris and New York.

At dinner there are several absentees at the table; these are several people who are starting to feel ill at ease with a slight case of seasickness.

I ate well again and then passed an hour at the movies playing in one of the dining rooms. It was an American comedy. At 10:30 I was in bed.

Monday, September 9

There was a lot of wind on deck in the morning. The sky and the ocean were like an ink spot. Now at 9:30 the sky is lightening up; perhaps it will be nice and I can be out in the air and sun outside. I am sitting in a large lounge where thee are long tables and many easy chairs; there are also two ping pong tables which are always occupied, and in the evening people play chess and cards; There is also a library here. Yesterday out of curiosity I registered for a short lecture soon. At 11:00 I will go see the news; they are published once a day and are posted at various places on the ship. Yesterday in Paris the "big five" were to decide on when to eventually convene the General Assembly of the UN that had been set for September 23.

Today four years ago, to the day, when we were separated from Philippe who went on vacation to Aunt Jeanne in Argenton on September 9, 1942, then in order to protect ourselves we were sheltered very close to the Marseille Police station.

Ten o'clock in the evening and again I am in the lounge which was used as the officer's mess during the war. Today I just smoked my second pipe; this morning I got a pack of American tobacco in a metal box for 15 cents, a real bargain, and of a real good quality.

Many people are laying down on deck chairs with blankets covering their legs (of course blankets are available on board). I keep busy part of the time with my steno. In the morning I had submitted my method to Mr. Pesch. In the afternoon he read several texts to me in the Groote steno system, without any difficulty. He is a real ace. I chatted with several occupants of my cabin.

Tuesday September 10

It is 9:00 and I am back in the lounge; the shaking has diminished I had a good breakfast. The ship's baker is certainly not American, because he has different shaped rolls every day. I had fried eggs with two slices of bacon; cheese and crackers; prune juice and oatmeal cakes, etc. I took another walk on deck. The sun reappeared but not for long; the Black Sea is certainly not as rough as the ocean we are on now; there are smaller waves than yesterday; the vibrations are just as much as before; certainly the engines are working hard. You can feel the noise and vibration in you bed, but you get used to it quickly and as soon as you get used to the steady and regular motion, you only should think of the ocean as swaying your cradle. This morning I am using a pen from the ship because my pen is empty. Yesterday evening I designed a new meal announcement text for the headwaiter and it will be printed today; it is an announcement in French with all of the meal schedules and food items; the previous announcement was in Americanized French; it was really funny but full of errors. Pesch and I went about correcting the text and the only word that did not need to be modified and that stayed intact was the name of the ship: Washington.

Now we are sailing to the South West in the direction of America. Philippe, earlier when I was on deck the sun was just over the horizon; it was therefore easy to determine the East direction and to find the other major directions and thus the ship's direction; Philippe, you do understand what I am talking about?

I constantly asked myself where you are and what you are doing. Perhaps the weather is better with you than it is here? I hope dear Mir that you won't forget to get four copies of Philippe's birth certificate. Philippe, did Uncle Maurice tell you about his two boys Willy and Rene? It may be hard for you to read this letter, but it is also hard to write it; it is like writing on a moving train; here you do not feel going forward but the motion makes the tables and chairs shake. I stop now; I am going to see if they have posted the news.

This morning on the information news bulletin board I saw that the General Assembly of the 57 countries of the UN will be held on October 23; if that is the case then it will probably be in New York, and there is little chance that we will be turned around when we arrive in New York.

All day long the bar is the rendezvous place for the "chics" people and for young people to go dancing (but no one dances). There is one piano and sometimes a radio station that plays jazz, thus everything I need to attract me and keep me in the most advanced of the four lounges on A deck. This evening I arrived late to hear a French choir singing popular and patriotic French songs (Madelon, good-bye song, song of the wooden shoes, etc). It is weird to be at sea so far away from our home on rue Waldeck-Rousseau and hear songs that we often hear on French radio.

Wednesday September 11
At 1:00 I returned to the deck after having as much food as one has on the eve of Yom Kippur; at every meal it is a gargantuan meal (that applies not only to me but nearly to all the passengers at my table and who have a well working stomach); the only thing missing is wine and an aperitif, but the water is good and pure, and the coffee (and cream) and tea is good. After a quarter of an hour walking on deck, I lay down

and I slept (I decided to get plenty of rest and even though resting under the present conditions that we would have on firm ground in the countryside, in the woods, on a mountain, I am doing everything I can to not get tired and especially to sleep enough; until now it has succeeded well).

If you are going to make the trip I recommend that you also choose the first service for the three meals; it is much more pleasant. However you are not there yet . Have a little patience. Everyone on board to whom I have spoken is unanimous in saying that I will not regret coming to the USA. Let's hope so.

The fact that I am without news from you for five days bothers me a lot. I hope to get your first letter Saturday or Sunday. Let's return to where I interrupted this letter. Everyday there are sweets from 3:45 till 4:30. There is a line where you hold a cup in one hand while the steward pours the hot tea; then each person takes as much sugar or milk  as you want as well as any number of little dry pastries (today it was some kind of ? biscuits).

I have not had the occasion to wear my light beige suit because the weather was not appropriate. Once I wore the good suit made in Asnieres. Other than that, everyday I wear the gray suit made by the same tailor. However today I did not wear my woolen sweater. My beret is very practical and I almost always have it on my head when I am on deck. Most of the Englishmen wear a cap. Many of the women and young girls wear pants. I have had very few expenses until now and I think that I will have about $35 out of the 50, when I leave the ship. I have not needed to use my own towels and soap. The two towels given to me on board are replaced everyday and I received two nice pieces of soap. During normal times one would not notice that, but we have not yet forgotten the time when suffered from not having any soap to wash ourselves. I stop now. I will write more tomorrow morning.

Thursday September 12, 1946
This morning in my bed I was sweating and I was very hot on deck at 7:30. I thought I had a fever but other people were in exactly the same state. It was a sudden change in temperature. It is very hot on board on deck even though it is always windy but it refreshes you nicely. After breakfast I lay on my deck chair for an hour with the sun in my face; at that time the sun in not too bright and it was very pleasant. This morning I took off my sweater and my suspenders, but I kept my vest on. In the morning at the table in the dining room there is always the menu for the three meals of the day, but today's menu, Thursday, only had the menu

for breakfast and lunch. Nothing for the evening diner; one must think that all the passengers have eaten everything and that there is nothing left to offer them for tonight. We are offered the captain's banquet tonight for which there will be a special menu printed. We are approaching the end of our journey; in 48 hours we should be in New York.

How are you, and what are you doing? I constantly ask myself that. I am happy to have your pictures near me; it gives me pleasure to look at them and one feels less lonely. No doubt dear Mir that you have gotten from Maurice and Uncle Elie indications of lifestyle in New York. But it is necessary for me to see for myself because that can differ from person to person. I was told that there is a great demand everywhere for workers and if I didn't have work for the UN, I could easily get work elsewhere. But let us put first things first since without the UN I would not presently be en route to America.

There were two interesting surprises this afternoon. You should have seen it dear Philippe. First around 2:00 I was sitting talking to my friend Mr. Pesch, when I heard people yelling (there were yells in all the languages and therefore it was impossible to understand) and everyone stood up to look at the ocean. I thought a man had fallen overboard. It was not as serious as that, rather not serious at all. In front of us about 20 meters away from the ship were a group of pointed heads poking out of the water; it was apparently a group of fish having fun near the surface of the water and you would first wee their heads then their tails; there was a group of at least twenty fish. Since they were staying in place and our ship was traveling at about 20 meters per second, the sight did not last long. I immediately thought of my American man that I spoke about yesterday or the day before yesterday; I looked along the side and I saw him in a very excited state with his photographic equipment pointed at the ocean, his cheek against the camera like a hunter aiming his rifle. "Have you finally taken pictures of fish?" I asked him. Yes, he answered, I got them several times. He said that they were dolphins (that is the name of those large fish). He also told me that last night he photographed two whales that were very visible, and that you can easily recognize from the spray of water that they throw up in the air like a fountain when their heads break out of the water.

The second surprise was an equipment drill that had been announced on all of the loud speakers. At 3:00 was the alert: repeating sounds of a siren. The captain commands: the rescue team and the fire squad go to your designated place on C deck. Immediately we saw groups of sailors exited onto the deck, all wearing their lifejackets, and heading for the locations of two fire extinguishers. They release the hoses that are full of water and one of them aims the nozzle at the ocean so that the water runs into it; however since there was a strong wind, some of the water sprayed curious onlookers who were close by. No doubt that the exercise was held as if the fire could not be controlled. There was a new alarm signal followed by the captain saying, "all crew members with your life jackets go on deck." Then we saw arriving on deck: Negroes, Chinamen, whites, cooks, nurses, all the chambermaids, and many of the ship's officers, all wearing their life jackets. Another command from the captain: all members of the crew report to your assigned lifeboat. At that moment the ships siren sounded 7 dismal whistles (that is probably the signal for "everybody to be saved") followed right away by the captain saying: "release the life boats!" This was done in the blink of the eye. Those boats are high up above the decks and must be lowered. The captain says: "lower the life boats slowly." Then on both sides of the ship you could see about 20 lifeboats descending slowly together on rails to a level of the ship where they were suspended above the water. They all stopped where there were ramps to allow the crew to go in them, but the captain does not ask the crew to enter them but for the 10 or 12 crewmembers, including an officer with each group, to remain lined up next to each lifeboat. In case of a real alert each boat can carry 70 to 80 people. The exercise is terminated. The captain and three senior officers stay at their command post high up on the ship. There was a last announcement to "put everything back in place" and the sailors spent the next half hour putting the lifeboats back and securing them. There my Philippe is the whole story that I had to tell you as I saw it happen today. If it doesn't interest mother, she would probably have entertained you and I assure you that it was interesting to see; I also did not tell you some of the minor details or little importance.

Friday September 13

My dears, here I am on the eve of arrival, Friday at 9:30. It was just announced on the loud speakers that the ship will be at the dock at 7:30 tomorrow morning, and that passport control will be right after docking. I think that I will be up earlier to see the approach to land and the ship's entry into New York. This is supposed to be very impressive. It was announced that we will be able to carry hand luggage from the ship onto the dock(apparently this has to do with the strike); the captain has not been advised yet of the possibility of placing our suitcases and large baggage on the dock. Therefore I am at ease with what concerns me. This afternoon I will put back everything that I removed from my suitcases and tomorrow morning I will only have to pack my pajamas and toiletries to be ready at any moment to put my feet on land.

After lunch 2:00. It is now eight days since we separated at the St. Lazare railroad station. Here I am for away from you, but you are near me in my thoughts and in my heart. I hope that you had a good first week in Antwerp; Philippe, in three weeks it will be time to go back to school and you will have to go back to studying because you may have forgotten some things, especially to make calculations. As a distraction spend a little time varying additions, subtractions, multiplications and divisions. If you arrive in America it will be necessary for you to take tests, certainly as far as arithmetic so that it can be determined which class you should be in.

In a little while one of the men from the UN will take my picture with a little group of French personnel and I hope to send you this photo from New York as soon as I get it.

On the ocean, near our ship and in the distance there are many fishing boats; from time to time birds fly nearby to greet us on behalf of America, which is now not far away.

(Author's note: at the top of the page there is a sketch of the Eiffel tower on the left, a ship amid waves in the middle and having the name Washington written on the bow, and on the right side some land labeled with a question mark and a star and the letters USA.)

Saturday September 14, '46

It is 6:00 in the morning. I just glimpsed outside. What animation! More and more boats following each other endlessly on both sides of our ship, which is stopped in the Hudson river I think, that leads to New York. On both sides of the ship several hundreds of meters away is a fairy tale of lights. There are thousands and thousands of lights glowing brilliantly on both sides of the river without lighting up anything. It is the movement of the ships that creates the animation, but you don't hear anything. Everything is silent and it is still dark. The Washington is probably waiting for the pilot ship to get back under way.

I had wanted to go to bed early last night but I wound up staying on deck until 11:30. At nine o'clock you could start to see the lighthouses and at ten o'clock it was Long Island (where I will work) whose coastline was one uninterrupted line of lights for a length of at least several kilometers. The ship stopped for a while and I went to bed for the last time. I was up at 5:00. In 20 minutes it will be time for the last breakfast on board. Right now it must be the start of daylight and I am going to go see the sunrise (if it is visible?) as a great panorama such as I imagine you observe from the Eiffel tower. So I will write later.

I felt like an "owl." In the semi light of dawn there appears before me a short distance away enormous silhouettes in which there are voids that are lit up. One can see enormous sky scrappers along the whole river and on the Hudson in front, behind and to the side of our ship, are many little boats that one would call pleasure boats, and they are all lit up. It is a beautiful effect. The sky is a dark gray and little by little the big buildings become clearer. It is very impressive.

It is 7:30 right now and it is clear; this morning we traveled 1000 to 1200 meters and the ship anchored opposite dock No.61 where it will dock later. Opposite us but in the distance is the tallest skyscraper "The Empire State Building." Closer to us not far away in the interior of the city emerge what looked like giant sculptured rocks in the earlier fog, but what are actually other sky scrappers of the city. Thus strangers are struck, before even setting foot on the ground, by the colossal dimensions of what is America. All along the docks there are giant letters painted by the various navigation companies wishing you, WELCOME, written in different places. The words hospitality and publicity are also written together as one word followed by the name of the navigation company.

It is 9:30 and the ship is at the dock for the last three quarters of an hour. The American citizens are all lined up for verification of passports. We come next. I think that it will be a long time before we disembark. At this moment the luggage is being transferred from the ship on a rolling ramp on the dock where they will be placed in the custom's hangar and identified by the initial of each family's last name (there are special tags that we got yesterday, each having the letter, that are on all the pieces of luggage). I am sitting now in a café, in the old Belgian style, on the promenade deck. There will be an announcement when the foreigners should go to passport control, and I was also informed by another source that there was a message for all the UN personnel saying that there was a representative waiting for us on the dock.

The public is not allowed to come near the ship, which is surrounded by hangars. We cannot see anyone and I hope that nobody is waiting for me outside, because it may take hours.

It is Saturday afternoon at 4:30, and I am writing to you from my hotel room. I emptied my suitcases of all the things that I will need and arranged them nicely. I will now tell you the last details of the arrival in New York. All of the UN employees obtained priority and at around 11:00 passed through the passport controllers who were installed on board. There were about twenty of us. At 11:50 I walked on the ramp and set foot on land. From there we went to the baggage hangar; some of the suitcases were not there yet. A summary of my costs is: I had to pay $7.50 for the 4 flasks that I declared at 2500 Francs. It was a long wait. When you get off the ship make sure that you have some food to eat. Several UN representatives eased our way. At around 3:00 I got into an American Navy car that brought me to the hotel. During the exit from the ship and from the dock I watched carefully but I did not see anyone from the family among the many people who were waiting near the street. The UN reserved a room for two people, including Mr. Pesch. It was impossible to get private rooms. It was a nice large room with two beds, bathroom, two dressers etc. It cost $5 per day to be split between the two of us, which will therefore cost me @2.50, and the UN will play me $7 per day. It is a magnificent and grand hotel, just around the corner from the celebrated 5th avenue.

Undoubtedly you received my cable sent around 1:30 of the afternoon during the time that I was waiting for passport control. Here I am at the end of the 36th page of my little description of my trip. Attached is the name and address of my hotel where you can write to me. I am on the 3rd floor in room 314, but you should not mention that on the envelope. Write my name clearly. Dear Mir add my room number (room 314) anyway.

Next Monday I must go to the Transport Service of the UN in New York at 9:00 from where I will be drive by car to Lake Success where the UN offices are.

I am going to mail this letter and then I shall take a stroll; we had breakfast at 6:00 in the morning and here I just ate a good part of the biscuits that you had put in my suitcase; on the ship this morning I ate the last of the fruit that I had brought from Paris, and so I am not starving. I think that I have gained weight, and that is not at all astonishing.

I am also going to see how to get in touch with Ruth; I hope to see her tonight or tomorrow Sunday.

So there you are my dears, the end of this voyage that all in all went well. I will give you my first impressions of work etc in several days.

The only thing left is for me to send you dear Mir and Philippe many kisses and to express the hope that we will see each other very soon.

I send you many good wishes to your dear parents, Ella, Maurice, Uncle Elie, and all other members of the family.

Have a good vacation and again many kisses
From your husband and from your father
Jos

(Letter from my mother and me to my father in New York)

Monday September 9, 1946

My Dear Jos,

When I got up this morning I received your first letter and we were very happy, especially since I did not expect a letter before tomorrow. I am happy that you are being well cared for on the ship.

After your departure, since I was crying, Philippe consoled me; he said to me that there was no reason to cry such as if you had gone off to war. I will tell you everything that I have done till now. Friday after you left we got our tickets for the trip to Antwerp and I did several errands for Ella, and in the afternoon I did an errand for Gunther that did not result in anything. Saturday I had a lot of arranging and wash to do and on Sunday morning we left the house at 10:00 to take the 11:05 train. Luckily I took food and drink with us because there was no restaurant car on this train. The trip went well; we had to get off the train at the two frontiers which made us lose one hour each time, but otherwise the trip was not tiring. At a quarter to nine we were at my parents house.

Maurice is still the same and has not changed. Uncle Elie is in Italy and returns in ten days. Mother and father are well.

I purchased a nice woolen scarf for Susi and have already sent it (Saturday at St. Lazare) and for myself I purchased a pair of black leather gloves, not too expensive. The coat that Ella picked for me and that I am getting as an anniversary gift is very beautiful and there is only a little to alter; it is just what is necessary for traveling.

This morning I went to the city hall of Berchem for Philippe's birth certificate and I will get several copies on Thursday; it will cost 46 Belgian Francs.

There is no other news for now. I will probably write again on Friday.
According to Maurice and also Uncle Elie, our future is in America.

Our Soto (?), we find it well.

Thank you again for your nice letter. Take good care of yourself.

I hug you very hard.
Your Mir

Dear Papa,

We received your letter. You forgot to tell me which bunk you slept in, the bottom one, or the middle one, or the top one? Are there several flags on the ship and tell me which ones? You will tell me what Sylvain, Willy, Rene tell you. In Brussels Aunt Ella was waiting for our train; she gave me 3 bananas. I have already played with Robby and Dani. You will write to me how you arrived in New York? You will also tell me if your hotel apartment is nice?

I hug you very hard.
Philippe

(This is a letter from my mother and me in Antwerp to my father in New York)
Friday September 20, 1946

My very dear Jos,

This morning we received your letter of Monday evening and it was also the first letter because the 37-page letter that you talk about has not arrived; I hope it is not lost because it must be very interesting. According to your letter your first impression is not bad, especially concerning your work where it appears that they appreciate your real value. I am very happy and proud of you. It is very nice and even astonishing that the family and friends made such a fuss about your arrival there. Maurice and I mutually console each other by teasing. Here in the house it is always the unknown, the telephone does not ring, father almost doesn't have enough time to eat he is so busy; the community does not lack for any work. Mother has a lot to do; for the time being a friend of Maurice from London is here, Mr. Schwab, who naturally eats with us. I am also busy all day long. I went with Maria to visit several people who had some things from Helen. One of those people wants to give us some things but they are in an attic and difficult to get things out of. We will have to wait until we have the time to do it. Another lady who has two fur coats is pretty tough but I hope that with a letter from the committee she will return them. The other people were not home. When there are some results I will write to you.

My dear it is amazing if you will get paid as of August 15. Do not be too generous and don't send us too much. According to your letter you were going to buy a gabardine coat; that is very nice but it is not indispensable especially since the new sport coat is very nice and practical. According to what Maurice told me, American prices in general are not too cheap, therefore don't buy me, or Philippe anything that I don't ask for. I suppose that you gave Ruth the $100. I will get the money next week. As far as I am concerned I will not need any money for the time being; it will only be necessary to pay for my passage in this manner and that will be much cheaper. Maurice told me to take linens, drapes, napkins and towels with me. All of these things we are missing and I will buy them in Belgium where they are cheap. I will leave everything here until my departure and then according to Maurice it is possible to send them right away to the departure port in transit.

I have two envelopes with mail from Miss Louise (Poupard); there is one letter from Sala telling me that Sally Beck will be in Paris at one of her sisters; there is also a letter from a Miss Klein for me asking if I can work for her; I answered that I will be back in October. Miss Poupard wrote to say that she is lost in her place and this bothers her. She will be happy when she sees us again.

Uncle Elie is still not back from Italy where he is with Uncle Jacque.

If things go well with you I should not delay in joining you soon, I would like it if you could forewarn me, and in that case I would perhaps stay in Antwerp longer for all my purchases and Philippe would not go to school but would get lessons, but I wait for your advice.

The engagement party was very nice with the whole family there. The pastries looked good. The fiancée is still very young; his father got married last Thursday to Miss Gross of KKL; he is the vice president of KKL. Papa made a very moving little speech.    I think I will finish now. I hope that your long letter will arrive tomorrow. I will write to you again on Sunday. Take good care of yourself and write to us when you have time.

A big pack of kisses
from your Mir

Dear Papa,

I received your letter but I do not understand that the 37-page letter has not arrived. I would have never thought that the building that you work in was so ornate and that there are so many cars and that it was so big. Since I have been in Antwerp I have read three books lent me by Mrs. Hershkowitz. Yesterday I went to the movies with Maman; it was very funny. Sunday afternoon I went to the engagement party for Mimi and Isi; I ate so many pastries that I had to go to the bathroom to empty and to make room for candy and ice cream; there were many people and many presents.

> Many kisses
> Philippe

52 Colgate Road
Great Neck,
Long Island, USA
Monday September 23, 1946

My dear Susi,

I am sending you belated congratulations on your anniversary that is due tomorrow. I lost sight of it during this first hectic week that I have passed in New York and Long Island. Forgive me and anyhow I send you my heartiest wishes for your anniversary for which I trust you have had a nice celebration. Miryam sent you a little present from Antwerp, which probably arrived early. Since we are far apart, dates only have a relative value, and the essential thing is that we can once again correspond and exchange good wishes. Good health and much happiness with your dear Joe and Helen, good luck in the future with whatever you undertake, including of course your moving into your own house.

On the occasion of Rosh Hashana, I send my best wishes to the three of you and for your whole family. I assume that by now it has already grown by one?

I only sent you a few words as I had just arrived and will now give you some more details. Since the UN's offices are far from New York I moved a few days ago to the address above and therefore if you write to me send it to that address and not to the hotel.

The trip on the SS Washington went well. As far as food is concerned, every meal was a feast (with the wine and spirits being the exception as they were non-existent on board). For the last week I have been at the UN; it is in an immense building where at the beginning one can get lost in all of the long hallways. It is a very interesting place and the majority of the personnel (other than several Englishmen, and this I tell you in confidence) are very nice. I passed a test that they would not let me take in Paris because one needed a university degree for that position, and which I don't have. I therefore was promoted to a higher category with a salary increase, and the Director of the Linguistic Division gave me excellent hope for the future. Thus I have no regrets about making the trip and I asked Miryam to make reservations as soon as possible; I hope that she will be able to come to New York with the least delay.

I have been to Miryam's two sisters several times. Ruth and Sonia and their children are well. As you can imagine we had a lot to talk about. Ruth's husband is in Antwerp at the present time. I also saw several old friends, but I do not have much time to spend visiting.

I hope that you are all well. Again my best wishes dear Susi, and many kisses for the three of you.

Your Uncle Jos

(This letter is from my mother)
Antwerp
Wednesday
September 25, 1946

Dear Suzi,

I hope that you will forgive me for making you wait so long to answer you. I have so many things to do before my departure, because I will not be coming back to Belgium, unless something unexpected happens before my departure for New York.

Uncle Jos telegraphed us to make our reservations as soon as possible. I cannot make my reservations from here, so I have written to Paris and hope to finalize Tuesday upon returning to Paris.

He has a better position than the one he was to have, and everything seems to please him pretty well. He had a good crossing; one is well cared for on the SS Washington; I hope that I can also go on that boat. If there is room it is possible that we could leave on October 24. That is fast isn't it? Until then you can imagine that I will be terribly busy.

Here in my parent's house everything is unpredictable; people come and go; there are always visitors. My brother-in-law, Ruth's husband, is here for several months, as is one of my father's brothers also from New York. All of that creates quite a bit of work; I help mother as much as I can because Ella is always traveling for her work.

The days of Yontef will do us good; it will be a forced rest. I am glad that you like the scarf; it is for your anniversary, a little early but better than being late.

I wish you and the whole family a good and happy year, good luck for you and Joe in your new house and "naches" from you Helene. I embrace you.

Your
Mir

Good luck to your sister-in-law for her upcoming delivery.
Mir

(From my mother)
Saturday evening
October 26, 1946

My dear Susi,

You must think that I forgot you, but that is not the case; I just didn't have the time until now. Jos wrote to me that he received a very nice letter from you, and that it gave him a lot of pleasure.

My dear Susi, my departure approaches, barring something unforeseen, Philippe and I leave November 12. Jos is very happy with his job and his bosses and now has a contract for one year. He wants us to join him as quickly as possible. We leave on the French boat, the Ile de France. I would have preferred an American ship but they are all on strike. Since there is nothing here to detain me and that everything calls me to go there, I took the quickest way to get there.

My dear Jos has already found a furnished room in a nice house. It is only temporary until we get our own apartment and furnish it to our taste. I rejoice at soon having my own place. You too must have the same feeling since you are probably in your new home by now. I hope that you are happy with everything and that Helen is pleased with her new room.

As for your hope that we can pass through London, that is not too easy. Getting a visa is almost impossible, and I must be here for all the luggage because this is a total move and I am the only one to manage everything.

If there are no obstacles I will telephone you on the eve of our departure. I have your number as Gladstone 4274, which I think is at your in-laws; if you have a phone at your house let me know as it will be easier for you.

Good bye, be well, and many kisses
from your,
Mir

1 Baker Avenue
Great Neck
February 7, 1947

My dear Susi, Joe and Helen,
I have really waited a long time to answer your letter of December 21. We are very happy to learn that you are settled in your new home and that you like it. At least now you know that you are a real "ballebuste" (housekeeper) and can arrange everything to your liking. I hope you do not suffer too much from the cold and that you can easily heat the house. Here as far as temperature is concerned we have been fortunate. It froze a little one day and the next it was like springtime. Here the cold is forecast and you are well protected and heat is available as the season advances. As far as winter sports, since there is no natural ice (it is too warm), Miryam, Philippe and I sometimes go skating together in a skating rink with artificial ice. I don't know if I already told you this. At the risk of repeating myself, Miryam was a beginner skater and from the start did well, and now she is making rapid progress. Philippe could skate well on roller skates and so he had no trouble ice-skating. As for myself I skated a little in Scheveningen in 1916. After a thirty years interval I put skates back on and I am doing better than in my childhood. It is a pleasant diversion and a little physical exercise at our age makes us younger.

You ask if Philippe likes school here. Very much so. Especially since the children don't learn much and there is hardly any homework. He has private lessons in English at home and already understands quite a bit of

English. At school (a good and attractive public school in Great Neck) the kids take history, singing, drawing, a little bit of arithmetic and gym. (Enclosed is a page from the N.Y. Herald Tribune that will surprise you as much as it did for us.)

I suppose that you had news of Uncle Jules. He wrote to me two/three weeks ago from Edinburgh (Scotland) telling me that he was going to make several trips from Scotland to Poland and back. I get the impression that after that he will go on vacation or retire from the merchant marines.

You ask for news about Miryam's sisters. As we wrote to you, the sisters, Ruth and Sonja live in New York, the first for slightly over a year, and Sonja since May 1946. Ruth (Schild) has two boys, one 7 and the other 8 ½ years old. Her husband is in Antwerp for several months to establish his pre-war metal export business. Sonja (Susskind) has a 10 year-old boy; her husband is in the diamond business. We get together almost every weekend in New York and spend agreeable times together; for the four boys together it is a real carnival. Tomorrow we go to New York for the weekend. Saturday evenings the family gets together at one or another's place and tomorrow several old friends from Antwerp are invited (Balken and Showerman).

As far as the United Nations it was decided to establish it's permanent headquarters in New York but for the moment we continue to work in Lake Success and it will probably be so for several years. There have been many personnel changes; a large number returned to Europe after having been discharged mainly because of economic reasons. I have not been touched by these measures and a promotion has been promised to me, but one must wait to hear about decisions from higher up, and decisions take a long time. I am still working as a translator and at this time I am translating French for the Weekly Bulletin of the United Nations (has a white cover) that is also for sale in London.

Listen Susi, if there are things that would please you and that we can send you from here please let us know. For example dried fruits, canned fruit, coffee, rice, canned fish, sausages, salami, soap, milk, etc. They have everything here in abundance of things that are restricted in England.

I hope that you are all in good health, also your sister-in-law and her children. Joe, how does your work go?

Helen must be surprised to see snow and ice! Please send us news of yourselves soon.

All the best to you and many kisses.

Jos Mir and Philippe

(This letter is on United Nations stationery)
Tuesday March 4, 1947

Dear Susi, Joe and Helen,

We received your two cards from February 12 and they gave us much pleasure. So you had a surprise visit from Uncle Jules. How much time did he stay? We just learned that he is in Antwerp now. His boat should be in England and he is therefore probably on paid vacation.

On your card dear Susi you wrote "letter follows" but we never got that letter. Therefore we prepared a package with different things that we think will please you now that you seem to suffer post war restrictions. I sent the package today. As soon as we know that they are things that you want we will send a new package. We remember the services you performed for us when we were in France and we are happy that we can help you in turn. Here everything is available except for sugar, and you can find anything you want without difficulty. So do not hesitate to tell us what you need.

We have had a lot of snow here but winter appears to end but that will not be of much comfort for you. All is well here. Next month (April) we hope to move into a new apartment house in Great Neck, especially built for United Nations personnel.

We hope that the three of you are in good health as well as the whole family there. How does Joe's work go? Many kisses

Uncle Jos, Aunt Miriam and Philippe

Great Neck
March 21, 1947

Dear Susi,

We were very happy to receive your letter of March 2, which got here March 8. Thank you very much for your portrait picture. It will find a place in our "art gallery" as soon as we are installed in our new apartment that is presently under construction. According to the picture Helen is gained weight as she has a beautiful round face; she must certainly weigh several kilos more than when you were in Antwerp almost a year ago. Have her digestion problems gone away after her treatment? Let's hope that she is cured of her cold and doesn't cough anymore. We have noted the things that you are lacking there, and you must have noticed them in the package that you must have by now. We guessed what you needed. A second package was sent yesterday and we hope that it will please you and be of service. We can appreciate the misery that you suffer now in England because we had them for years and we know what it is like. Susi, you should tell us if the butter and cheeses that we sent you are according to your taste and if we should continue to send them. Tell us also if you are interested in receiving: tea, coffee, cacao, and dried vegetables such as peas, beans, lentils, and white flower and egg powder.

Naturally we have noted the other products that you indicated to us that you need. Do not hesitate to tell us what other articles, no matter what they are, that we could send you from here.

I was happy to hear that Uncle Jules took the effort to travel from Liverpool or Southampton to London to visit you. Are you staying in London this year for Passover, or are you making plans? Last year you were in Antwerp and in 1945 you were at the beach if I recall?

Susi, are you happy in your new house? How are your sister-in-law and her baby?

Recently, Alice, my wife's youngest sister who is in Palestine, gave birth to a second boy and he is doing well. My in-laws wanted to go visit them but the consulate would only give one visa to my mother-in-law alone. They could certainly obtain a tourist visa for any country in the world but to go to Palestine, no!

You ask how life is here and if it is different from that in Europe. Here Americans "take it easy" as they say, and in the future perhaps we will do the same; but for the moment Philippe "takes it easy" while his parents have their hands full of work. Miryam just started to do dressmaking work in the house because household tasks are so simple here that it does not fill the day of an active woman. As a "dependent" of a UN official, she has the right to work even though we did not get an immigration visa. In the United Nations Secretariat, expenses are being restricted; some employees are still being sent back. I still have not received the raise that was promised me in January. I stop writing for today. I hope this letter finds you in good health. My best wishes to the whole family and acquaintances, and many kisses for the three of you.

Jos Miryam Philippe

Great Neck
January 31, 1948

Dear Susi,

We were very agreeably surprised to receive your nice letter of
January 25 so fast and are happy that one can say that all went well.
Mazeltov dear Susi, for you and your dear Joe, for your dear in-laws, and
for your adorable Helen. I hope that all will continue well with you, and
that little Carol will progress well. Good care will certainly not be
lacking with such an attentive mother and a father who must be in
seventh heaven. At least this time we received a message from Joe right
away to hear of your newborn daughter Carol. I hope that we will see
you this year and I accept your invitation to celebrate together the growth
of your family.

I am sending this letter to Cricklewood where you will probably get
it upon your return because if everything goes well you will no doubt be
back before the 12 days maternity stay at Queen Mary's Hopsital.

It is good to have hired a maid to help you because at the beginning
you will have your hands full with the two children and the household.
We hope you will manage everything well and as you have experience
with Helen, everything will seem easier with little Carol to whom we
send our best wishes.

Philippe was happy to learn the good news and asked me to convey
to you all his best wishes.

Last Friday my sisters-in-law Ruth and Ella arrived in New York.
They saw Jules in Antwerp before their departure. Ella is staying with us.
We hope to make her stay here as pleasant as possible. During Passover
my father-in-law may also come to visit and also perhaps my youngest
sister-in-law, Alice (who lives in Palestine) with her two children (two
boys).

With us all is well. It is pretty cold but there is enough heat and we
have nothing to complain about. Included in this letter are two photos of
Philippe taken two weeks ago in Great Neck in the snow.

I don't know if I will have the occasion to go to New York to see
your Aunt Rosa and Uncle Henry, because I am very busy at my work. If
I do not see them, give them my best wishes when you see them again in
London.

We think of you a lot and are waiting for other good news of your
dear newborn.

Many kisses for the four of your, and best wishes for the whole family there.

Uncle Jos, Aunt Miriam and Philippe

Congratulations and kisses from Philippe

Dear Susi,

I am happy that you had an easy delivery with the little girl since that is always a disagreeable prospect. I am looking forward to seeing you in the summer. We will send you a package soon with practical things for the baby. I wish you a prompt recovery and good luck with little Carole. Affectionate kisses.

Mir